Henrik Ibsen
Plays: Six

Peer Gynt, The Pretenders

This sixth volume, completing the Ibsen collection in the World Classics series, contains *Peer Gynt* and *The Pretenders*. These two plays, along with the equally ambitious *Brand* and *Emperor and Galilean* (published in *Ibsen Plays: Five*), complete the great epic quartet that stands at the fulcrum of Ibsen's career.

Ibsen wrote that 'of all my books I regard *Peer Gynt* as the least likely to be understood outside Scandinavia', but it has become one of his best known plays. It was praised by George Bernard Shaw for the power of Ibsen's 'grip on humanity . . . The universality of Ibsen makes his plays come home to all nations.' *The Pretenders*, though described by Kenneth Tynan as Ibsen's 'first great play', is less often seen in English despite being 'a historical drama of considerable sweep and force' (*Guardian*).

Michael Meyer's translations have won praise for their accuracy and liveliness on both stage and page. They have been performed extensively in the theatre and on radio and television. 'Where previous translators have adopted either a stiffly Victorian style, or one so modern as to destroy the illusion that we were seeing a period play, Mr Meyer has found a form of speech common both to the period in which the plays were written and to the present.' (*The Times*) 'Meyer's translations of Ibsen are a major fact in one's general sense of post-war drama. Their vital pace, their unforced insistence on the poetic centre of Ibsen's genius, have beaten academic versions from the field.' (George Steiner, *New Statesman*)

Michael Meyer is also Ibsen's biographer and a leading authority on his work. This edition includes Meyer's illuminating introductions to each play, as well as a chronology of Ibsen's life and writings.

HENRIK IBSEN

Plays: Six

Peer Gynt
The Pretenders

*Translated from the Norwegian
and introduced by
Michael Meyer*

METHUEN DRAMA

METHUEN WORLD CLASSICS

5 7 9 10 8 6 4

This collection first published in Great Britain in paperback in 1987
by Methuen London Ltd
Reissued with a new cover design 1994, 2000

Methuen Publishing Ltd
215 Vauxhall Bridge Road, London sw1v 1ej

Distributed in Australia and New Zealand by
Peribo Pty Ltd, 58 Beaumont Road, Mount Kuring-Gai
NSW 2080, Australia, ACN 002 273 761

Peer Gynt was first published in this translation in 1963
by Rupert Hart-Davis Ltd and subsequently by Eyre Methuen Ltd in 1973
Copyright © Michael Meyer 1963
Introduction copyright © Michael Meyer 1963
Corrected for this edition 1987

The Pretenders was first published in this translation by Rupert Hart-Davis Ltd
Copyright © Michael Meyer 1964
Introduction copyright © Michael Meyer 1964
Corrected for this edition 1987

Chronology copyright © Michael Meyer 1987

This collection copyright © Michael Meyer 1987

The right of Michael Meyer to be identified as the translator of these works
has been asserted by him in accordance with the Copyright, Designs and
Patents Act, 1988

Methuen Publishing Limited Reg. No. 3543167

A CIP catalogue record for this book
is available from the British Library

ISBN 0 413 15300-2

Printed and bound in Great Britain by
Cox and Wyman Ltd, Reading, Berkshire

Caution

Contents

Henrik Johan Ibsen: A Chronology

1828   Born at Skien in south-east Norway on 20th March, the second child of Knud Ibsen, a merchant, and his wife Marichen, *née* Altenburg.

1834-5   Father becomes ruined. The family moves to Venstœp, a few miles outside Skien.

1844   Ibsen (aged fifteen) becomes assistant to an apothecary at Grimstad, a tiny seaport farther down the coast. Stays there for six years in great poverty.

1846   Has an illegitimate son with a servant-girl, Else Sofie Jensdatter.

1849   Writes his first play, *Catiline* (in verse).

1850   Leaves Grimstad to become a student in Christiania (now Oslo). Writes second play, *The Warrior's Barrow*.

1851   Is invited to join Ole Bull's newly formed National Theatre at Bergen. Does so, and stays six years, writing, directing, designing costumes and keeping the accounts.

1852   Visits Copenhagen and Dresden to learn about the theatre. Writes *St John's Eve*, a romantic comedy in verse and prose.

1853   *St John's Eve* acted at Bergen. Failure.

1854   Writes *Lady Inger of Oestraat*, an historical tragedy in prose.

1855   *Lady Inger of Oestraat* acted at Bergen. Failure. Writes *The Feast at Solhaug*, another romantic verse-and-prose comedy.

1856   *The Feast at Solhaug* acted at Bergen. A small success. Meets Suzannah Thoresen. Writes *Olaf Liljekrans*, a third verse-and-prose comedy.

1857   *Olaf Liljekrans* acted at Bergen. Failure. Leaves Bergen to become artistic manager of the Christiania Norwegian Theatre. Writes *The Vikings at Helgeland*, an historical prose tragedy.

1858   Marries Suzannah Thoresen. *The Vikings at Helgeland* staged. Small success.

1859   His only child, Sigurd, born.

1860-1   Years of poverty and despair. Unable to write.

1862 Writes *Love's Comedy*, a modern verse satire, his first play for five years. It is rejected by his own theatre, which goes bankrupt.

1863 Ibsen gets part-time job as literary adviser to the Danish-controlled Christiania Theatre. Extremely poor. Applies unsuccessfully to Government for financial support. Resorts to moneylenders. Writes *The Pretenders*, another historical prose tragedy. Is granted a travel stipend by the Government; this is augmented by a collection raised by Bjœrnson and other friends.

1864 *The Pretenders* staged in Christiania. A success. He leaves Norway and settles in Rome. Remains resident abroad for the next twenty-seven years. Begins *Emperor and Galilean*.

1865 Writes *Brand*, in verse (as a play for reading, not acting), in Rome and Ariccia.

1866 *Brand* published. Immense success; Ibsen becomes famous throughout Scandinavia (but it is not acted for nineteen years).

1867 Writes *Peer Gynt*, in verse (also to be read, not acted), in Rome, Ischia and Sorrento. It, too, is a great success; but is not staged for seven years.

1868 Moves from Rome and settles in Dresden.

1869 Attends opening of Suez Canal as Norwegian delegate. Completes *The League of Youth*, a modern prose comedy.

1871 Revises his shorter poems and issues them in a volume. His farewell to verse; for the rest of his life he publishes exclusively in prose.

1873 Completes (after nine years) *Emperor and Galilean*, his last historical play. Begins to be known in Germany and England.

1874 Returns briefly to Norway for first time in ten years. The students hold a torchlight procession in his honour.

1875 Leaves Dresden after seven years and settles in Munich. Begins *The Pillars of Society*, the first of his twelve great modern prose dramas.

1876 *Peer Gynt* staged for first time. *The Vikings at Helgeland* is performed in Munich, the first of his plays to be staged outside Scandinavia.

8 **HENRIK JOHAN IBSEN**

1877 Completes *The Pillars of Society*. This makes him famous in Germany, where it is widely acted.

1878 Returns for one year to Italy.

1879 Writes *A Doll's House* in Rome and Amalfi. It causes an immediate sensation, though a decade elapses before it makes Ibsen internationally famous. Returns to Munich for a year.

1880 Resettles in Italy for a further five years. First performance of an Ibsen play in England (*The Pillars of Society* for a single matinée in London).

1881 Writes *Ghosts* in Rome and Sorrento. Violently attacked; all theatres reject it, and bookshops return it to the publisher.

1882 Writes *An Enemy of the People* in Rome. Cordially received. *Ghosts* receives its first performance (in Chicago).

1884 Writes *The Wild Duck* in Rome and Gossensass. It, and all his subsequent plays, were regarded as obscure and were greeted with varying degrees of bewilderment.

1885 Revisits Norway again, for the first time since 1874. Leaves Rome and resettles in Munich.

1886 Writes *Rosmersholm* in Munich.

1888 Writes *The Lady from the Sea* in Munich.

1889 Meets and becomes infatuated with the eighteen-year-old Emilie Bardach in Gossensass. Does not see her again, but the experience shadows the remainder of his writing. Janet Achurch acts Nora in London, the first major English-speaking production of Ibsen.

1890 Writes *Hedda Gabler* in Munich.

1891 Returns to settle permanently in Norway.

1892 Writes *The Master Builder* in Christiania.

1894 Writes *Little Eyolf* in Christiania.

1896 Writes *John Gabriel Borkman* in Christiania.

1899 Writes *When We Dead Awaken* in Christiania.

1901 First stroke. Partly paralysed.

1903 Second stroke. Left largely helpless.

1906 Dies in Christiania on 23rd May, aged seventy-eight.

Acknowledgements

I gladly express my thanks to Michael Elliott for many valuable suggestions concerning the translation; also to the Old Vic Theatre Company for commissioning it, and to everyone concerned with that memorable production.

I also gratefully acknowledge my debt to the writings of Professor Francis Bull, the greatest of Ibsen scholars, particularly to his monograph on the play (Oslo, 1956) and his introduction in the centenary edition of Ibsen's works (Volume VI, Oslo, 1931). I have incorporated in my notes on pp. 179–184 several of William Archer's perceptive comments.

M. M.

Peer Gynt

Introduction

Ibsen wrote *Peer Gynt* in 1867 at the age of thirty-nine, partly in
Rome, partly on the island of Ischia, and partly in Sorrento. Three
years earlier, embittered by poverty and failure, he had left Norway
to settle in Italy; but in the spring of 1866, the publication of *Brand*
had at last brought him fame and financial security. A short while
previously he had been voted the worst-clothed member of the
Scandinavian community in Rome; now he began to dress with a
touch of dandiness, sporting among other luxuries a velvet jacket.
A new tone appears in his letters; suspicion and resentment are
replaced by a buoyant confidence. Even his handwriting acquired a
new assurance. For the first time in his life, he felt economically
secure; more important, perhaps, he felt that his reputation was
established. This mood was enhanced by the news, in May 1866,
that the Norwegian Government had granted him an annual
pension of 400 specie-dollars (£100); to which was added 100
specie-dollars from the Society of Knowledge at Trondheim, plus,
later in the summer, a further grant of 350 specie-dollars from a
scholarship travel fund. 'I have such a longing for work, such
strength,' he wrote to Michael Birkeland on 4 May 1866, 'that I
could kill bears!' That autumn he actually asked his publisher,
Frederik Hegel of Gyldendal, not to send him certain royalties
before the following summer, since he did not want to have a
superfluity of cash in Italy.

For a while, however, he remained uncertain in which direction
to apply his energies. Shortly after completing *Brand* he had
struggled for some weeks with an historical drama about Magnus
Heineson which he had planned before leaving Norway. But this
came to nothing, and on 21 May 1866 he wrote to his publisher,
Hegel, that he felt more inclined to settle down to the actual
writing of *Emperor and Galilean*, the play about the Roman
Emperor Julian the Apostate which he had been researching
for two years. On 22 July he wrote to Paul Botten-Hansen: 'Now
I shall soon start to write in earnest; I am still wrestling with the
material, but soon, I know, I shall have the beast under me, and
then the rest will glide forward of its own volition.' But *Emperor
and Galilean* still resisted him, and towards the end of August he

laid it aside and set to work revising *Love's Comedy* for a new, Danish edition, removing some of the specifically Norwegian words so as to make the play more palatable to Danish readers. It is possible to discern in this deliberate deletion of Norwegian words the resentment which Ibsen still felt towards his native country, and his contempt for the campaign to purge the Norwegian language of its foreign influences – a campaign which he was shortly to castigate in a more direct and vehement fashion.

Once this work on *Love's Comedy* was finished, Ibsen thought of travelling to Greece (presumably to furnish himself with more material for *Emperor and Galilean*, which partly takes place there), and also to Paris; but both these projects fell through. On 2 November 1866, he wrote to Hegel that he was still uncertain to which of several subjects he would next turn: 'this very division of interest is proof that none of these themes has as yet sufficiently matured in my mind; but I feel confident that this will soon happen, and hope to be able to let you have the completed manuscript during the spring.'

It was around Christmas 1866, or the New Year of 1867, that his plans for *Peer Gynt* began to clarify. On 5 January 1867, he wrote to Hegel: 'At last I am able to tell you that my new work is well under way and will, if nothing untoward happens, be ready early in the summer. It will be a long dramatic poem, having as its principal character a part-legendary, part-fictional character from Norwegian folk lore during *recent* times. It will bear no resemblance to *Brand*, and will contain no direct polemics nor anything of that kind. I have long been pondering the material for this; now the whole plan is worked out and on paper, and I have begun the first act. It grows as I work on it, and I am confident that you will be satisfied with the result.'

In point of fact, the dates inscribed by him on his manuscript show that Ibsen did not begin writing the play until nine days after this letter, on 14 January 1867; he had a tendency, not unique among authors, to tell white lies to his publisher. He completed Act One six weeks later, on 25 February. Six days later, on 3 March, he started on Act Two, which, if we are to believe a further letter to Hegel (27 March 1867), he finished in three weeks. In mid-May he moved from the heat of Rome to the island of Ischia, where he lived for three months in the little town of Casamicciola on the northern side of the island, near the extinct volcano of

Epomeo. The weather was exceptionally hot, even for the natives, but Ibsen seemed to revel in it and worked throughout the day; according to Vilhelm Bergsœ, who was with him at this time, he took no siesta but spent the afternoons correcting what he had written in the mornings. He completed Act Three in as little as two and a half weeks, on 2 July. During this month the sirocco arrived and raised the temperature to above 100 °F, but Ibsen continued to work both afternoon and evening, revising and fair-copying. On 8 August he was able to write to Hegel, still from Ischia:

'I have today sent you, via Consul-General Danchertsen in Naples, the manuscript of the first three acts of my new work, entitled *Peer Gynt*, a dramatic poem. This section will come to around 120 printed pages, and the remainder will add up to about the same. I hope to be able to send you Act Four towards the end of the month, and the rest not long after that. In case it should interest you, Peer Gynt was a real person who lived in Gudbrands-dal, probably around the end of the last century or the beginning of this. His name is still famous among the people up there, but not much more is known about his life than what is to be found in Asbjœrnsen's *Norwegian Fairy Tales* (in the section entitled *Stories from the Mountains*). So I haven't had much on which to base my poem, but that has meant that I have had all the more freedom with which to work on it.'

One night in mid-August there was a slight earthquake on Ischia, and although the natives treated it lightly Ibsen left the island the next day and settled in Sorrento. Here he remained for two months, writing the last two acts; there was no earthquake to trouble him, but in near-by Naples there was an outbreak of cholera, and at one time he thought his wife had caught it; but this fear proved to be unfounded.

We do not know when he began Act Four, but he completed it on 15 September, and posted the fair copy to Hegel three days later, adding: 'If the printing of the list of characters could be delayed until I have sent you the remainder of the play, I should be grateful, since I might possibly wish to add a few minor charac-ters; but this isn't important.' The next day, 19 September, he began the final act, and completed it in twenty-five days on 14 October. Four days later he posted the fair copy of this to Hegel: 'and may luck attend it!'

Hegel was very quick to publish *Peer Gynt* after the success that had attended *Brand*, and it reached the Scandinavian bookshops on 14 November 1867, less than four weeks after he had received the final section of the manuscript. Ibsen was delighted at the book appearing in time to catch the Christmas sales. 'Let us hope the critics will be kind to us,' he wrote to Hegel on 23 November. 'I think the book will be much read in Norway.'

Peer Gynt, however, gained a mixed reception in Scandinavia. The first omens were good; Hegel sent word that the first edition of 1,250 copies had sold out almost at once, and that a second edition of 2,000 copies was in the press. Bjœrnson, that most patriotic of poets, who more than most might have been expected to take offence at the fun poked at Norwegian nationalism, wrote Ibsen a letter full of admiration: 'I love your spleen, I love the courage with which it has armed you. I love your strength, I love your recklessness – oh, it turned all my thoughts to laughter, like the smell of the sea after the closed air of a sick-room.' He also published a review in *Norsk Folkeblad* shortly after the book appeared, praising it hugely.

Ibsen penned a letter of thanks, but before he had posted it he read an attack on the play by Clemens Petersen in the Danish magazine *Fædrelandet*. This was the leading intellectual paper in Scandinavia, having a wide circulation in Norway and Sweden as well as in Denmark, and Petersen had a considerable reputation as a literary pundit; he had written generously, though not uncritically, of *Brand*, and Ibsen had sent him a rather fulsome letter while he was preparing *Peer Gynt*, expressing the hope that Petersen would recognize that in his new work he had 'taken a marked step forward.' Petersen had some good things to say of *Peer Gynt*, but complained of 'a lack of clarity in the conception and of absolute integrity in the execution'; he also declared, somewhat obscurely, that neither *Brand* nor *Peer Gynt* was real poetry because they 'lacked idealism,' objected that the characters in *Peer Gynt* were not fully rounded or alive, and summed the play up as 'an unsuccessful allegory' which frequently degenerated into 'an intellectual swindle.'

This review so enraged Ibsen that he tore up the letter he had written to Bjœrnson and composed another. This second letter reveals an emotional, even hysterical side to Ibsen's character such as he rarely allowed to emerge in his letters or conversation. 'Dear

Bjœrnson,' he wrote on 9 December 1867, 'What is this curse that at every juncture interposes itself between us? It is as though the Devil came in person to cast his shadow over us ... An hour ago, I read Hr. Clemens Petersen's review in *Fædrelandet* ... If I were in Copenhagen and anyone stood as near to me as Clemens Petersen does to you, I would have struck him senseless before allowing him to commit so calculated an offence against Truth and Justice ... My book *is* poetry; and if it isn't, it will *become* such. The conception of poetry in our country, in Norway, shall shape itself according to this book ... He says that the Strange Passenger represents the idea of *Angst*. Were I standing on the gallows and able to save myself by confessing to such an interpretation, the thought would never have occurred to me; I never dreamed of any such thing; I merely slipped the scene in as a caprice. And is not Peer Gynt a character rounded and individual? And the Mother? ... However, I am glad that this injustice has been flung at me; it is a sign of divine aid and dispensation; anger increases my strength. If there is to be war, then let there be war! If I am not a poet, what have I to lose? I shall try my hand as a photographer. I shall deal with my contemporaries up there, each and all of them, one by one, as I have dealt with these language reformers; I shall not spare the child in its mother's womb, nor any thought nor feeling that may have motivated the actions of any man who shall merit the honour of being my victim ... Do you know that all my life I have turned my back on my parents, on my whole family, because I could not bear to continue a relationship based on imperfect understanding?'

He did not post the letter at once, but added a postscript the following day: 'I have slept on these words and read them through in cold blood. The mood they express is that of yesterday; I shall send them, nevertheless.' After another and equally hysterical outburst ('Do not underrate my friends and supporters in Norway; the party whose paper has allowed its pages to carry an injustice against me shall realize that I do not stand alone ... My enemies shall learn that if I cannot build I have at least strength enough to destroy') he ended on a scarcely appeasing note: 'I reproach you merely with inactivity. It was not good of you to permit, by doing nothing, such an attempt to be made in my absence to put my literary reputation under the auctioneer's hammer.'

Bjœrnson accepted this abuse calmly, and wrote Ibsen a letter of splendid generosity and exhortation, begging him to 'be just towards us and have faith in yourself.' This reached Ibsen on Christmas Day, and so mollified him that in his next letter, on 28 December, he actually asked Bjœrnson to give Petersen* his regards. But his old feeling of resentment soon returned, and it was to be ten years before he wrote to Bjœrnson again.

Another Dane to find fault with *Peer Gynt*, and one whose condemnation must particularly have saddened Ibsen, was his old friend and admirer Georg Brandes. Writing in *Dagbladet*, he admitted that it contained great beauties and certain noble truths, but concluded: 'Beauties and Truths are far less important than Beauty and Truth in the singular, and Ibsen's poem is neither beautiful nor true; the misanthropy and self-hatred on which it is based are a poor foundation on which to build a work of art . . . What wormwood-tainted joy can he find in thus belittling human nature? It is time this campaign came to an end. We have had enough and the thing must stop.' Hans Andersen, too, disliked the play. 'Ibsen is repellent to him,' wrote Edvard Grieg to Bjœrnson, 'and *Peer Gynt* the worst that he has read.'

In Norway the book was better received than in Denmark, though there, too, the reception was mixed. *Morgenbladet* and *Aftenbladet* published long reviews which were on the whole laudatory; but the greatness of the play was not generally appreciated, at any rate by the critics. Apart from the anti-Norwegianism, some people were bothered by the ending, which they thought facile, and others by what seemed to them an incongruity between the young, the middle-aged and the elderly Peer. Camilla Collett, the pioneer of women's independence in Norway, was offended by the passivity of Solveig's character, declaring that a more forceful female would have shown Peer the error of his ways much earlier. And Kristofer Janson, the novelist, denounced the attack on the language reformers, of whom he was one. Ibsen, who had a long memory, used him seventeen years later as part-model for the self-pitying Hjalmar Ekdal in *The Wild Duck*.

After his first outburst of fury, Ibsen accepted these criticisms calmly. 'How goes it with *Peer Gynt*?' he wrote to Hegel on

* Petersen suffered swift retribution. Barely a year later, he became involved in a homosexual scandal in a school in which he had been lecturing, and was forced to leave for the United States, where he devoted himself to religious journalism among the Scandinavian-Americans—a fate which even Ibsen might have hesitated to wish on a leading literary critic.

24 February 1868. 'In Sweden, as far as I can tell from the newspaper reviews, it has been very well received; but has it sold accordingly? In Norway I gather the book has caused a great rumpus; which bothers me not in the least; but both there and in Denmark, people have discovered much more satire than I intended. Why can't people read the thing as a poem? That was what I wrote it as. The satirical sections are pretty isolated. But if, as seems to be the case, the Modern Norwegian recognizes himself in Peer Gynt, that is those good gentlemen's own funeral.'

Ibsen had no thought, when he was writing *Peer Gynt*, that it should ever be staged; he had too great a contempt for the limitations of the Norwegian theatre and of the men in charge of it. He wrote it, as he had written *Brand*, merely to be read. Five years later, however, the directorship of the Christiania Theatre passed into the hands of an enlightened Swede named Ludvig Josephson. In 1873 Josephson staged both *The Pretenders* and *Love's Comedy* in an imaginative fashion, and it occurred to Ibsen that, if suitably adapted, *Peer Gynt* might receive at the same hands a not unworthy presentation. Before approaching Josephson, however, Ibsen wrote (23 January 1874) to Edvard Grieg to ask if the latter would consider providing a musical accompaniment and to inform him of his plans regarding suitable cuts, which are sometimes surprising. 'Act 1 will be retained in its entirety,' he wrote, 'apart from some thinning out of the dialogue ... The wedding scene on p. 28 can be made much more of, with the help of ballet, than appears in the text ... In Act 2, the incident with the three peasant girls on pp. 57–60 should receive whatever musical treatment you feel appropriate; but there must be devilry in it! ... There will have to be some kind of musical accompaniment to the scene in the troll palace, though here too the dialogue will be considerably thinned out. The scene with the Boyg, also, which will remain uncut, must have music; the Bird Voices to be sung; the church bells and psalm singing to be heard in the distance ... Pretty well the whole of Act 4 will be omitted in performance. In its place, I thought we might have a great musical tone-picture to suggest Peer Gynt's wanderings in the wide world, with American, English and French melodies interwoven as changing and disappearing *motifs* ... Act 5 must be shortened considerably ... The scenes on the upturned boat and in the churchyard will have to go ... The scenes with the Button Moulder and the Old Man of the Mountains will be trimmed down. On p. 254 the churchgoers sing on the forest path; church bells and distant psalm singing should be indicated in the music during the dialogue which follows until Solveig's song concludes the play, at which point the curtain will descend while the psalm singing is heard again clearer and louder. This is roughly how I have imagined it ... If you agree to come in with me on this, I shall immediately approach the management of the Christiania Theatre, send them an acting script and ensure that the play is guaranteed a production. As a fee, I propose to ask 400 specie-dollars, to be shared equally between the two of us.'

Grieg did not receive this invitation with unmixed delight. 'I can't but admire,' he wrote to Bjœrnson (12 September 1874) 'the way from start to finish it splutters with wit and venom. But it will never win my sympathy. Though I think it the best thing Ibsen has written. Am I not right? But you don't imagine I had a free choice in the matter! I received the offer from Ibsen last year, and naturally baulked at the prospect of putting music to this most unmusical of subjects. But I thought of the 200 [specie-dollars] and of the voyage, and made the sacrifice. The whole thing sits on me like a nightmare.' The previous month, he had written to his friend Frantz Beyer: 'It is a dreadfully intractable subject, certain passages excepted – e.g., the part where Solveig sings – I've done that all right. And I've made something of the Old Man's palace in the mountains, which I literally can't bear to listen to, it stinks so of cow-dung and Norwegian insularity and self-sufficiency! But I think people will sense the irony behind it; especially where Peer says: "Both the dance and the music were really splendid. May the cat claw me if I lie!"'

Ludvig Josephson reacted enthusiastically to Ibsen's proposal, though he begged him not to omit the whole of Act Four, suggesting instead certain cuts to which Ibsen agreed. Grieg continued to grouse privately about his 'nightmare,' and it was not until eighteen months after he had accepted the commission, in August 1875, that he finished the music.

Peer Gynt received its first performance at the Christiania Theatre on 24 February 1876. It was the most expensive production that had yet been attempted in Norway, and was a great success; it was performed thirty-seven times, and would have continued even longer had a fire not destroyed the scenery. Despite the cuts, the play lasted for four and three-quarter hours (from 7 to 11.45 p.m.), and seems to have been produced with the accent on the lyrical rather than the satirical aspects. Ibsen did not attend the production, being still reluctant to revisit Norway; but, writing to Josephson from Munich on 5 March 1876, he declared: 'The outcome of this bold enterprise on the part of your theatre has exceeded all my expectations.'

Ibsen was still, at this time, little known outside Scandinavia, and it was not until 1880, thirteen years after the play had been published, that he received a request, from Germany, for permission to translate it. He replied to the inquirer, Ludwig Passarge (19 May 1880): 'It was a surprise to me to learn that you regard this work as suitable to be translated into German for publication there. I must confess that I at least entertain grave doubts on this score. Of all my books I regard *Peer Gynt* as the least likely to be understood outside Scandinavia. I beg you to reflect that few of your German readers will share your own capacity for understanding the poem. You yourself doubtless possess a close knowledge of the Norwegian character and the way the people live; you are acquainted with our literature and our way of speech; you know the people and the personalities one finds up there. But is not all this necessary if one is to find any real flavour in the poem? ... I hope you will not misconstrue my voicing thus openly the considerations which would, to my mind, operate against your project. I felt it my duty not to conceal them; should they prove unfounded, I shall of course be most gratified.'

Ibsen's doubts did indeed prove unfounded, for *Peer Gynt* has become the best known of all his works outside, as inside, Scandinavia. So far from being regarded as exclusively Norwegian, Peer himself seems to have been accepted everywhere as a national prototype; a Japanese critic has described him as 'typically Japanese.' Subsequent to its première in Christiania, *Peer Gynt* was staged before the end of the century in Copenhagen (1886), Gothenburg (1892), Stockholm (1895) and Paris (1896). This last production was by Lugné-Poe, and was the subject of a perceptive notice by Bernard Shaw in the *Saturday Review*. 'Ibsen's grip of humanity,' he wrote, 'is so powerful that almost any presentable performer can count on a degree of illusion in his parts which Duse herself failed to produce when she tried Shakespeare ... The universality of Ibsen makes his plays come home to all nations, and Peer Gynt is as good a Frenchman as a Norwegian, just as Dr Stockmann is as intelligible in Bermondsey or Bournemouth as he is in his native town.'

The first performance of the play in England* took place on 26 February 1911 at the Rehearsal Theatre in London with, improbably, an actress, Pax Robertson, in the part of Peer. (Her mother, Catherine Lewis, ran the Ibsen Studio, which presented the production). Among the many notable interpretations of the role in this century have been those of Werner Krauss in Berlin and L. M. Leonidov in Móscow, both in 1928, Gösta Ekman in Stockholm in 1934, Ralph Richardson in London in 1944 (with Laurence Olivier as the Button Moulder), Max von Sydow in Malmö in 1957 (in a production by Ingmar Bergman), Leo McKern in London in 1962, Brian Cox at Birmingham in 1967 and Tom Courtenay at Manchester in 1970. *Peer Gynt* has also been filmed on no less than three occasions: in America in 1915 (directed by Oscar C. Apfel, with Cyril Maude); in Germany in 1934 (directed by Fritz Wendhausen, with Hans Albers); and again in America in 1941 (directed by David Bradley, with Charlton Heston).

Apart from what Ibsen had read in Asbjœrnsen's collection of fairy tales, the historical-legendary Peer Gynt of Gudbrandsdal may well have come to his notice five years before he wrote the play, when, having been refused a poet's stipend, he received a kind of consolatory grant to travel around the Norwegian country-side collecting folk lore. Some doubt exists as to who exactly was the original of the legend; possibly a Peder Olsen Hage who died in 1785, possibly one Peder Laurissen who lived a century earlier. William Archer noted the debts Ibsen's play owes to Asbjœrnsen: the adventure of Gudbrand Glesne on the Gjendin Edge, the encounter with the three peasant girls, the meeting with the Boyg, the devil in the nutshell, the Greenclad One and the Ugly Brat, the proposed correction of Peer's eyesight to measure up to troll standard, Soria-Moria Castle, and the threadballs (though these last recur frequently in Norwegian folk lore). The character of Peer as conceived by Ibsen, however, has little in common with that of the legendary Peer, and for this Ibsen seems to have drawn on certain of his contemporaries, including himself. Georg Brandes

---

* But there had been an amateur performance in Édinburgh in 1908, by the local lodge of the Theosophical Society.

speaks of 'a young Dane whom Ibsen often saw on Ischia, a notably affected and pompous daydreamer and braggart. He told the young girls on Ischia and Capri that his father (a schoolmaster) was a close friend of the King of Denmark, and that he himself was a person of great distinction, who sometimes wore a suit of white satin. He called himself a poet, but had to visit wild regions in order to find inspiration ... He died not far from Ibsen in Rome. Some traits of his character have survived in Peer Gynt.' Ibsen's old chief at Bergen, Ole Bull, is also believed to have served as part-model for Peer; soon after he had established his Norwegian Theatre there, he left it (in the spring of 1852) to go to America and found an ideal community on the model approved by the French Socialists. This was to be called Oleana, and Ibsen doubtless had this in mind when he made Peer dream of his ideal community, Gyntiana, in Act Four.

Another who lent something to Peer's character was the poet A. O. Vinje, whom Ibsen had known in his Christiania days, an incurable optimist who was always quoting his own verses and aphorisms. Vinje had written a sequence of attacks on *Brand*, and Ibsen's friends in Norway at once assumed him to have been the model for Peer. And there were several lively young Scandinavian poets in Rome during 1866–1867 who may have contributed something.

Ibsen also confessed, in a letter to Peter Hansen (28 October 1870) that he had, when creating Peer, drawn on certain traits of his own character. 'After *Brand*,' he wrote, '*Peer Gynt* followed, as it were, of its own volition. I wrote it in Southern Italy, on Ischia and in Sorrento. Thus far removed from one's readers, one loses one's inhibitions. This poem contains much that has its roots in my own childhood; my mother, with necessary exaggerations, served as the model for Aase.' Later he told Georg Brandes that he had used his contrasting memories of life in Skien before his father's bankruptcy and in Venstœp afterwards as 'a kind of model for my picture of life in "the house of rich John Gynt."'

Peer Gynt is unusual among Ibsen's plays in betraying an apparent debt to certain literary influences. Ibsen owed less to other authors than almost any other writer of comparable stature; he was an unwilling reader, at any rate of books (though he read newspapers most minutely, including the advertisements). Four works, however, all of them Danish, would seem to have left their mark on *Peer Gynt*. One was Frederik Paludan-Müller's epic poem *Adam Homo*, published some twenty years previously, which had already had its effect upon *Brand*. Adam, like Peer, is a weak character who deserts his true love, loses his grip on life, gains riches and worldly success at the cost of his soul, and finally, in the presence of death, senses the possibility of salvation through the love of the woman he had deserted. Another influence, noted by Brandes, appears to have been Oehlenschlæger's *Aladdin*, Aladdin, like Peer, is a dreamer; when contemplating suicide he says, in a phrase which has its echo in the last act of *Peer Gynt*:

> Receive this wretched, failed experiment
> Into your crucible. Melt me down again.

The phrase *at være sig selv*, to be oneself, appears in *Aladdin*; and Aladdin's mother, Morgiane, alternates like Aase between admiration and despair at her son's unpredictability. Aladdin, however, is presented as a heroic character, the apotheosis of the dreamer, where Peer is a *reductio ad absurdum* of the type. Œhlenschlæger regarded the life of the imagination as the highest form of existence; Ibsen knew its dangers.

Two other works that need to be studied by anyone interested in the origins of *Peer Gynt* are J. L. Heiberg's poem *A Soul after Death* (1840) and Hans Egede Schack's novel *The Fantasts* (1858). John Paulsen, who knew Ibsen intimately, has recorded that these were two of the few books that he ever heard Ibsen praise; and that Ibsen once told a young poet that he ought to read everything that Heiberg had written. In *A Soul after Death*, the soul, like Peer, is condemned, not for great sins, but for common bourgeois pettiness; it had lived only for material comfort, and had never tried to be itself. And there are two meetings in Heiberg's poem, one between the Actor and Death, and one between the Soul and Mephistopheles, which carry strong echoes of Peer's encounters with the Button Moulder and the Thin Person. *The Fantasts*, a remarkable psychological analysis of the danger of daydreaming, would seem to have exerted a general rather than a particular influence. It is also perhaps worth noting that Hans Andersen's story *Elverhøj*, itself an earlier satire on Norwegian nationalism, also contained a character named The Old Man of the Mountains. A sixth Dane, Sœren Kierkegaard, is supposed by some to have influenced *Peer Gynt*; but the exact measure of Ibsen's debt to Kierkegaard, if any such debt existed, must remain in doubt. Ibsen once stated that he had 'read little of Kierkegaard, and understood less'; but many writers have been unconsciously influenced by authors whom they only partly understood.

Some of Ibsen's rough notes for *Peer Gynt* have survived, plus one draft and the fair copy. The notes were long assumed to have been lost, but as late as 1932 fragments of them were discovered among papers in the possession of his daughter-in-law, Bergliot Ibsen. The first 'ark' of four pages is unfortunately missing, and the manuscript begins in the middle of Act Two, where Solveig asks Aase to tell her more about Peer, and ends in the middle of Act Four. Since nearly three sides of this last four-page sheet are left blank, it would seem that Ibsen had made no further notes before beginning to write his first draft. Neither the notes nor the draft contain any very significant differences from the play as we know it. The state of the draft suggests that it was a first one; some sections were originally written in prose, others in regular trochaic and iambic metres which he later worked into a looser rhythm.

The main differences from the final version occur in the first two acts. Originally, Peer's father was not a wastrel but a 'man of honour' whom 'Our Lord cut off in his prime,' and Peer was not an only son but had an elder brother, a very different character, who was killed in war. The troll scene as at first conceived contained a good deal of satirical matter which Ibsen later deleted; for example, it opened with the trolls irreverently singing 'For Norway, the birthplace of heroes,' presenting the anthem as a symbol of chauvinism. And there was a scene in Act Two on the mountain (after Peer's renunciation of Ingrid) between Peer and Solveig, who are later joined by Aase and Solveig's parents; her father tells Peer that he can marry her if he is prepared to go to prison as a penance for his crime, an offer which Peer refuses. Most interesting from a psychological viewpoint is the fact that as originally conceived the Boyg stands outside Aase's house and prevents Peer from returning home to his mother after he has left the troll palace. The notes for this scene read: 'He stands in pitch darkness outside Aase's house and finds his way blocked by the Great Boyg. Fights with the Great Invisible One. He wins his way in. It is empty. Fights his way out again. The Boyg is everywhere. Despair seizes him. Alone, alone! Everyone has abandoned him.'

A curious fact about these notes is that they give the lie to Ibsen's account of how he wrote the play, as described in his letter to Peter Hansen and also as reported by William Archer. On Ibsen's death in 1906, Archer wrote an article in the *Monthly Review* entitled *Ibsen as I knew him*, in which he stated: 'He wrote *Brand* and *Peer Gynt* at very high pressure, amounting to nervous overstrain. He would go on writing verses all the time, even when asleep or half awake. He thought them capital for the moment; but they were the veriest nonsense. Once or twice he was so impressed with their merit that he rose in his nightshirt to write them down; but they were never of the slightest use ... He began *Peer Gynt* at Ischia and finished it at Sorrento. He set to work on it with no definite plan, foreseeing the end, indeed, but not the intermediate details. For instance, he did not know that Peer was to go to Africa. "It is much easier," he said, "to write a piece like *Brand* or *Peer Gynt*, in which you can bring in a little of everything, than to carry through a severely logical scheme, like that of *John Gabriel Borkman*, for example."'

In fact, we know from Ibsen's letters and from the dates on his manuscript that he began the play not in Ischia but in Rome, and that he had a detailed synopsis worked out well past the opening of the African sequence. The conversations reported by Archer, however, took place long after Ibsen had written *Peer Gynt*, and it is not surprising that the old man's memory should have played him false.

As stated, Ibsen wrote *Peer Gynt* to be read, not staged; and the consequent rejection of the accepted limitations of stagecraft proved, as with *Brand*, tremendously liberating. It was not merely that he felt free to move uninhibitedly in time and space (*Peer Gynt* contains forty scenes). He had done that in *Brand*. More importantly, he felt free to ignore other frontiers, the frontiers between reality and fantasy, between (as we should now say) the conscious and the unconscious. Nobody, one hopes, any longer takes the last act of *Peer Gynt* at its face value, as the return of an old man to his youthful love; such an ending would have been, for Ibsen, most untypically banal and sentimental, two adjectives which recur frequently in contemporary criticisms of it. Whether one regards Peer as having died in the madhouse at the end of Act

Four, or in the shipwreck at the beginning of Act Five, we must surely take that fifth Act as representing either the unreeling of his past life in his mind at the moment of death or (which is perhaps the same thing) as the wandering of his soul in purgatory, '*limbo patrum*, nigh to hell'. Viewed thus, the last hour of the play is Peer's life seen in a distorting mirror, just as the troll scene in Act Three is the wedding party and Peer's hopes and fears concerning it, dreamed by a drunken and confused man: the desirable yet (once he has got her) repulsive girl, the wrathful vengeance-seeking father, the conflict between lust and conscience. To present *Peer Gynt* on a purely realistic level, as still, alas, occasionally happens, is to reduce it to an amiable and confused pantomime with a facile ending, an interpretation to which Grieg's music, for all its intrinsic merits, has lent authority. Ibsen was not Freud's favourite playwright, and Joyce's, for nothing; he understood, as few of their predecessors did, the power of the unconscious, the truth behind dreams and nightmares, the higher reality of what most of his contemporaries dismissed as unreality; and *Peer Gynt* may be regarded as the first prolonged exploration, whether deliberate or unconscious, of this field, to which, nearly twenty years later, he was to return with such effect in *Rosmersholm*, *The Lady from the Sea* and the powerful and, to his contemporaries, scarcely intelligible plays which followed. *Peer Gynt* is the direct ancestor of Strindberg's *A Dream Play*. But at the time of its appearance, as Ibsen complained, it was regarded mainly as a satire.

Yet in one sense, at least, Ibsen's critics came nearer the truth than some of the play's later admirers. They were right to find it disturbing, discordant and offensive. It is one of the most upsetting and uncomfortable plays ever written. Trolls, properly understood, are not mere goblins but, as Professor Francis Bull has written: 'the evil forces of Nature ... embodying and symbolizing those powers of evil, hidden in the soul of man, which may at times suppress his conscious will and dominate his actions ... By ever pandering to his evil instincts and desires they have come to be really his rulers – mysterious powers that make him afraid of himself.' This is what *Peer Gynt* is really about – the struggle between the divine purpose and our undermining passions and egocentricities, between man's deeper self and his animal, or troll, self; in Stekel's phrase: 'how the soul, oppressed by the primal passions, struggles to escape the hell of the instincts.' The Boyg, the Greenclad One and the Strange Passenger are, like the Thin Person, lackeys of the Enemy; as is Peer himself, apart from the image of him which Solveig keeps

With the mark of destiny on his brow
As he sprang forth in the mind of God.

Peer Gynt is an Emperor *manqué*, searching to discover what he is Emperor of – to find at the end that the one thing of which he was meant to be, and was not, Emperor, was himself. The turning-point in his quest for salvation is that moment of despair when he sees the star fall, because the moment of despair is the moment of hope.

Twenty years after he had completed *Peer Gynt*, Ibsen wrote a letter to its first German translator, Ludwig Passarge, in which he seems to endorse this view that the play is about the struggle between the troll in man and the divine purpose. Referring speci-fically to *Peer Gynt*, he stated (16 June 1890): 'Everything that I have written is most minutely connected with what I have lived through, if not personally experienced; every new work has had for me the object of serving as a process of spiritual liberation and catharsis; for every man shares the responsibility and the guilt of the society to which he belongs. That was why I once inscribed in a copy of one of my books the following dedicatory lines:

To live is to war with trolls in heart and soul.
To write is to sit in judgement on oneself.

MICHAEL MEYER

This translation of Peer Gynt *was commissioned by the Old Vic Theatre Trust, and was first performed at the Old Vic Theatre, London, on 26 September 1962. The cast was:*

AASE, *a farmer's widow*	Catherine Lacey
PEER GYNT, *her son*	Leo McKern
TWO OLD WOMEN, *with sacks of corn*	Ida Goldapple
	Brenda McGuinne
ASLAK, *a smith*	Brian Coburn
MASTER COOK	Endré Muller
SOLVEIG'S MOTHER, *immigrant*	Phillada Sewell
SOLVEIG'S FATHER, *immigrant*	Fulton Mackay
SOLVEIG	Dilys Hamlett
HELGA, *her sister*	June Dartnall
INGRID'S FATHER, *the farmer at Heggstad*	Esmond Knight
BRIDEGROOM	Trevor Peacock
BRIDEGROOM'S FATHER	Anthony Morton
BRIDEGROOM'S MOTHER	Stella Lewis
INGRID	Adrienne Corri
SÆTER GIRLS	Irene Hamilton
	Judi Bloom
	Anna Middleton
THE GREENCLAD ONE	Adrienne Corri
OLD MAN OF THE MOUNTAINS	Esmond Knight
OLDEST TROLL COURTIER	Russell Hunter
UGLY CHILD	Francis Attard
THE BOYG	Leo McKern
KARI, *a cottar's wife*	Ida Goldapple
MR COTTON, *a traveller*	Anthony Morton
M. BALLON, *a traveller*	Vernon Dobtcheff
HERR VON EBERKOPF, *a traveller*	Esmond Knight
HERR TRUMPETERSTRAALE, *a traveller*	James Maxwell
OVERSEER	Jeffry Wickham
THIEF	Endré Muller
RECEIVER	Patrick Kavanagh
ANITRA, *daughter of a Bedouin chieftain*	Adrienne Corri

BEGRIFFENFELDT, *D.Phil., director of the asylum in Cairo*	James Maxwell
HUHU, *a language reformer from the Malabar coast*	James Kerry
FELLAH, *carrying a royal mummy*	Fulton Mackay
HUSSEIN, *an Oriental Minister*	Russell Hunter
SHIP'S CAPTAIN	Eric Thompson
BOATSWAIN	James Kerry
STEERSMAN	Eric Flynn
WATCH	Jeffry Wickham
COOK	Anthony Morton
STRANGE PASSENGER	Vernon Dobtcheff
PRIEST	Fulton Mackay
PARISH OFFICER	Russell Hunter
BUTTON MOULDER	Wilfrid Lawson
THIN PERSON	David William

Designed by Richard Negri.
Directed by Michael Elliott.

Also in the cast were Peter Brookes, Roger Clissold, Robert Hewitt, Ian Hughes, Rosalind Knight, Barbara Latham, Fletcher Lightfoot, Barry Usher, Michael Wells, Fiona Walker and Rosalind Whitman.

The action, which opens in the early years of the last century and closes about fifty years later, takes place partly in the Gudbrand Valley in Norway and on the mountains around it, partly on the Moroccan coast, partly in the Sahara Desert, the asylum in Cairo, at sea, etc.

Act One

SCENE ONE

A wooded hillside near AASE's *farm. A stream is rushing down it. On the far side is an old millhouse. It is a hot summer's day.*

PEER GYNT, *a strongly built youth of twenty, comes down the path.* AASE, *his mother, small and frail, follows him. She is angry and is scolding him.*

AASE. Peer, you're lying!

PEER (*without stopping*). I am not!

AASE. Well, then, swear it's true!

PEER. Why swear?

AASE. Ah, you daren't! It's all rubbish.

PEER (*stops*). It's true, every word.

AASE (*squares up in front of him*).

> Aren't you ashamed?
> First you sneak off into the mountains
> For weeks on end in the busy season
> To stalk reindeer in the snow –
> Come home with your coat torn,
> Without the gun, without the meat.
> And then you look me straight in the face
> And try to fool me with your hunter's lies!
> Well, where did you meet the buck?

PEER. West near Gjendin.

AASE (*laughs scornfully*). Did you, now?

PEER. I suddenly smelt him on the wind.

> Hidden behind an elder-bush
> He was scratching in the snow for lichen –

AASE (*still scornfully*). Oh, yes!

PEER. I held my breath

> And stood listening. I heard his hoof
> Crunch, and saw one branching antler.
> I wormed on my belly through the stones towards him.

Still hidden, I peered out.
Oh, mother, you never saw such a buck!
So sleek and fat –!

AASE. No, I'm sure!

PEER. I fired. Down he dropped, smack on the hill!
But the moment he fell, I straddled his back,
Seized his left ear, and was about
To plunge my knife into his neck –
Aah! The brute let out a scream,
Suddenly stood on all fours,
Hit the knife and sheath from my hand,
Forced its horns against my thigh,
Pinned me tight like a pair of tongs,
And shot right on to the Gjendin Edge!

AASE (*involuntarily*). In the name of Christ!

PEER. Have you seen the Gjendin Edge?
Three miles long and sharp as a scythe.
Down over glacier, slide and cliff,
[Straight down over sheer grey scree],*
You can see, on either side,
Straight into the lakes that sleep
Black and heavy, more than four thousand
Feet below. The length of the Edge
He and I cut our way through the air.
I never rode such a steed!
Before us as we thundered
It was as though there glittered suns.
Brown backs of eagles swam
In the huge and dizzy void halfway between us
And the lakes below – they fell behind
Like motes of dust. Ice-floes broke
And crashed on the shore, but we couldn't hear their
     thunder.
Only the spirits of dizziness leaped
As in dance. They sang, they swung in a ring
In my eyes and ears.

* Square brackets indicate cuts made for the 1962 Old Vic production.

AASE (*dazed*). Ah, God preserve me!

PEER. Suddenly, on a sheer impossible spot
   A great cock-ptarmigan flew into the air
   Flapping, cackling, terrified,
   From the crevice where it lurked
   Hidden at the buck's foot on the Edge.
   He swung half round, gave a high leap to heaven,
   And down we both plunged into the abyss!
   AASE *totters and gropes at the trunk of a tree.* PEER *continues:*
   Behind us the black walls of the mountain,
   Beneath a bottomless void!
   First we clove sheets of mist, then a flock of gulls,
   Which turned in the air and fled to every side,
   Screeching. Still we fell.
   But in the abyss something gleamed
   Whitish, like a reindeer's belly.
   Mother, it was our own reflection
   In the calm water of the mountain lake,
   Darting up towards the surface
   With the same wild speed with which we fell.

AASE (*gasps for breath*). Peer! God help me! Tell me quickly –!

PEER. Buck from air and buck from deep
   In a moment smashed together,
   So that the foam rose high about us.
   We plunged, we gasped and choked.
   At long last, mother, I don't know how,
   We reached the northern shore.
   The buck swam, and I hung behind him.
   I ran home –

AASE. But the buck, Peer?

PEER. Oh, still there, I expect.
   Snaps his fingers, turns on his heel, and adds:
   If you find him, you can have him.

AASE. And you haven't broken your neck? Or both
   Your legs? Not fractured your spine? Oh, Lord,
   Praise and thanks be to Thee, who saved my son!
   Your breeches are torn, but what's that

When one thinks what you might have suffered in such
   a fall –?
Stops suddenly, stares at him open-mouthed, wide-eyed, and
speechless. At length she explodes:
Oh, you bloody story-teller! How you can lie!
I remember now, I heard all this rubbish
Before, when I was a girl of twenty.
It happened to Gudbrand Glesne, not to you,
You –!

PEER. To both of us.
   Such a thing can happen twice.

AASE (*hotly*).
   Yes, a lie can be stood on its head,
   Smartened up and put in new clothes,
   So its own mother wouldn't know its skinny carcase.
   [That's what you've done, letting on wild and great,
   Tricking it out with eagles' backs
   And all that humbug, lying right and left,
   Yarning away and scaring me dumb
   So I couldn't recognize a story
   I'd heard in my mother's lap.]

PEER. If anyone else spoke to me like that
   I'd bash him senseless.

AASE (*weeps*).
   Oh God, I wish I was dead.
   I wish I was asleep in the black ground.
   Prayers and tears don't touch him. Peer, you're lost,
   And always will be.

PEER. Dear, beautiful, little mother,
   Every word you say is the truth.
   Calm yourself. Be happy –

AASE. Shut up!
   How can I be happy with such a pig for a son?
   Isn't it bitter for a poor, helpless
   Widow like me to be always put to shame?
   Weeps again.
   What has the family left now from the days

When your grandfather was a wealthy man?
Where are the sacks of silver
Left by old Rasmus Gynt? Your father
Gave them feet, wasted them like sand,
Bought land in every parish, drove
In gilded carriages! Where's what he wasted
At the great winter feast, when every guest
Threw glass and bottle over his shoulder
To splinter against the wall?

PEER. Where are the snows of yesteryear?

AASE. Shut up while your mother's speaking!
Look at the house!
Half the window-panes stuffed with rags,
Hedge and fence fallen down,
Cows and chickens exposed to wind and weather,
Fields and meadows lying fallow,
Never a month but I have the bailiffs in –

PEER. Stop that old wives' tattle!
Many's the time our luck has failed –
[And sprung again to its feet as tall as ever.]

AASE. [There's salt strewn where that grew.] Lord, you're a fine
one!
[As proud and uppish as ever, just as bold
As when the priest that came from Copenhagen,
Asked you your name, and swore it was one
That many a prince where he came from would envy you,
So that your father gave him a horse and bridle
In gratitude for his civil talk.
Oh, things were fine then. The Bishop and the Captain
And all the rest of them turning up every day,
Guzzling and boozing and stuffing themselves
Till they were nearly bursting. But
It's when times are hard that a man knows his neighbour.
Empty and silent it was here the day
John Moneybags set off to tramp the roads
With a pedlar's pack on his shoulder.
Dries her eyes with her handkerchief.

You're a fine, strong lad.] You ought to be a rod
And staff for your frail old mother, work the farm,
And guard the little you've left of your inheritance.
Weeps again.
God help me, it's little use I've had of you!
Lounging all day by the hearth, poking the embers,
Frightening the girls out of the barn on dance-nights,
Making me the game of the whole county
And swapping blows with every ruffian in the parish –

PEER (*walks away from her*). Oh, let me be!

AASE (*follows him*).
Can you deny you were the ringleader
In that shindy at Lunde, when you fought
Like mad dogs? Wasn't it you who broke
The arm of Aslak the smith? Or at least
Put one of his fingers out of joint?

PEER. Who's been filling your ears with such rubbish?

AASE (*heatedly*). The crofter's wife heard him hollering.

PEER (*rubs his elbow*). No, that was me.

AASE. You?

PEER. Yes, mother. I was the one that took the beating.

AASE. What!

PEER. He's a nimble man.

AASE. Who's nimble?

PEER. Aslak the smith. I'm telling you, I know.

AASE. Shame upon you, shame! Now I must spit!
That loafing sot, that swaggerer,
That boozing sponge! Did you let him beat you?
Weeps again.
Many's the shame I've suffered, but this is the worst.
Nimble, is he? Need you be weak?

PEER. Whether I bash a man or get bashed,
You start moaning. (*Laughs.*) Now cheer up, mother –

AASE. What! Have you been lying again?

PEER. Yes, just this once. So dry your tears.
Clenches his left fist.

This was my tongs. With this I held the smith
Bent double; my right fist was my hammer –

AASE. Oh, you ruffian! You'll send me to my grave!

PEER. No, you're worth better. Twenty thousand times better.
Sweet, ugly little mother, you take my word.
The whole parish shall honour you. Just wait
Till I do something, something really big!

AASE (*snorts*). You!

PEER. Who knows what will happen?

AASE. You'll learn to mend your breeches first!

PEER (*hotly*). I'll be King! Emperor!

AASE. God help me!
Now he's losing the little wit he's got.

PEER. Yes, I will! Just give me time!

AASE. Oh, yes! I've heard that one before.

PEER. You'll see, mother!

AASE. Shut your gullet. You're out of your mind.
Oh, it's true enough something might have come of you
If you hadn't got lost in lies and twaddle.
The Heggstad girl fancied you.
You could have won her easily if you'd wanted –

PEER. Do you think so?

AASE. Her dad's a ninny, he'd not have argued with her.
He's a stubborn old fool, but she gets her way in the end,
And where she leads he'll follow, grumbling.
Begins to weep again.
Ah, Peer, my son, she's rich. The land's all hers.
Just think. If you'd only put your mind to it
You'd be wearing the bridegroom's coat,
Not standing here black and tattered.

PEER (*briskly*). Come on, let's go a-wooing!

AASE. Where?

PEER. At Heggstad.

AASE. My poor boy, you'll find no bride there.

PEER. Why?

AASE. [Wait while I dry my eyes.]
You've lost your chance, your luck's ended –

PEER. How?

AASE (*gulps*).

> While you were away
> In the western mountains, riding stags through the air,
> Mads Moen's got the girl.

PEER. What! That scarecrow?

AASE. Yes, now she's taking him to her bridal bed.

PEER. Wait here while I harness a horse to the cart –

> *Turns to go.*

AASE. Save your pains. The wedding's tomorrow.

PEER. Good. I'll be there tonight.

AASE. Shame on you! Haven't I grief enough?

> [Without your bringing a general scorn on our heads.]

PEER. Don't worry, it'll be all right.

> *Shouts and laughs at the same time.*
> Yippee, mother! We'll do without the cart.
> I can't waste time running after the mare –
> *Lifts her high into the air.*

AASE. Put me down!

PEER. No! I'm carrying you to my wedding in my arms!

> *Wades out into the stream.*

AASE. Help! Lord save us! We'll be drowned!

PEER. I was born for a nobler death –

AASE. Yes! You'll end by being hanged!

> *Seizes him by the hair.*
> Oh, you brute!

PEER. Keep still. The bottom's slippery here.

AASE. Donkey!

PEER. That's right; carry on. [Talk never hurt a man.]

> Look, now it's getting shallow again –

AASE. Don't drop me!

PEER. Get up there now, hup! Let's play Peer and the stag.

> *Gallops.*
> You're Peer and I'm the stag.

AASE. I'm out of my wits!

PEER. There, we've made it.

> *Wades ashore.*

Give your stag a nice kiss.

Let the driver have his fare.

AASE (*boxes his ears*). That's your fare!

PEER. Ow! That's a fine reward! Mother!

AASE. Put me down!

PEER. First to the wedding. You must speak for me.

You're clever. Talk to the old fool.

Say Mads Moen's a good-for-nothing –

AASE. Down!

PEER. And tell him what a fine fellow is Peer Gynt.

AASE. Never you fear! A grand character I'll give you!

I'll tell them all about you, I'll tell them

All your devilries –

PEER. Oh?

AASE (*kicks him angrily*).

I won't stop

Till the old man sets his dog on you like a tramp.

PEER. Hm. Then I'll have to go alone.

AASE. Yes, but I'll follow.

PEER. Dear mother, you haven't the strength –

AASE. Haven't I? The way I feel

I could crumble rocks in my bare fingers.

Ugh, I could eat flints! Put me down!

PEER. All right, if you promise –

AASE. Promise nothing! I'm coming there with you.

I'll let them know you for what you are.

PEER. You'd better stay here.

AASE. No. I want to go with you.

PEER. Sorry.

AASE. What are you going to do?

PEER. Put you on the millhouse roof.

He puts her up there. AASE *screams.*

AASE. Take me down!

PEER. Yes, if you'll listen –

AASE. Don't be a fool –

PEER. Mother dear, I beg you –

AASE (*throws a turf at him*). Peer, take me down this instant!

PEER. I would if I dared. (*Comes closer.*)
    Remember, sit still now. Don't kick
    Or start pulling down the tiles, or you'll hurt yourself.
    [And maybe fall down.]

AASE. You brute!

PEER. Don't kick!

[AASE. Oh, why weren't you blown up the chimney like a
    changeling![1]

PEER. Mother, for shame!]

AASE. Grr!

PEER. Give me your blessing on my journey. Will you? What?

AASE. I'll thrash you, you hulking lump!

PEER. Well, goodbye then, mother dear.
    Be patient. I shan't be long.
    Moves away, but turns and raises his finger warningly.
    Remember now. No kicking. (*Goes.*)

AASE. Peer! God help me, he's going! Liar!
    You with your tales of riding on stags!
    Hi! Will you listen to me? No, he's gone. (*Screams.*)
    Help! I'm getting giddy!
    TWO OLD WOMEN *with sacks of corn on their backs*
    come down towards the mill.

FIRST OLD WOMAN. God a'mercy, who's that screaming?

AASE. It's me!

SECOND OLD WOMAN. Aase! Look! Well, you've gone up in the
    world!

AASE. Not far enough. Please God I'll soon be in heaven.

FIRST OLD WOMAN. Have a nice trip.

AASE. Get a ladder! I must get down!
    That devil Peer –!

SECOND OLD WOMAN. Is it your son –?

AASE. Now you can say you've seen with your own eyes
    What he gets up to.

FIRST OLD WOMAN. We will.

AASE. Help me down! I've got to get to Heggstad –

[1]For notes on the text, see pp. 181 ff.

SECOND OLD WOMAN. Is he there?

FIRST OLD WOMAN. Then you'll be revenged. The blacksmith's coming too.

AASE (*wrings her hands*). Oh, God protect the boy!
They'll kill him before he's through.

FIRST OLD WOMAN. Well, it's happened before.
Comfort yourself. [It's the ways of Providence.]

SECOND OLD WOMAN. She's out of her mind. (*Shouts up the hill.*) Eyvind! Anders! Come down here!

MAN'S VOICE. What's the matter?

SECOND OLD WOMAN. Peer Gynt's put his mother on the mill-house roof!

SCENE TWO

A small hill with bushes and heather. The high road crosses behind it, with a fence running alongside. PEER GYNT *comes along the footpath, walks briskly up to the fence, stops, and looks out across the landscape.*

PEER. There lies Heggstad. I'll soon be there.
Climbs half over the fence, then stops and thinks.
Is Ingrid sitting there alone, I wonder?
Shades his eyes and peers.
No, the guests are swarming in like mosquitoes.
Hm. Perhaps I'd better turn back.
Swings back his leg.
People always snigger behind your back,
And whisper so that it burns right through you.
Walks a few paces from the fence and absently plucks a few leaves.
If only I had a dram of something strong.
Or could go unnoticed. [If only they didn't know me.]
A drink'd be best. Then the laughter doesn't bite.
Suddenly he looks round as though frightened, then hides among the bushes. Some GUESTS *carrying gifts of food for the wedding walk down past him in the direction of the farm.*

A MAN (*in conversation*). His dad was a boozer and his ma's a
    ninny.
A WOMAN. It's no wonder the lad's a good-for-nothing.
They pass on. A few moments later PEER GYNT *reappears. He looks
after them, his face red with shame.*
PEER. Were they talking about me?
    With a forced toss of the head.
    Well, let them talk. That won't kill me.
*Throws himself down in the heather, lies full length on his back with
his hands beneath his head and stares at the sky.*
    What a strange cloud! It's like a horse.
    There's a man on it too, with saddle and bridle.
    And behind him's an old woman riding a broomstick.
    Chuckles to himself.
    It's mother.
    She's scolding and screaming: 'You brute! Stop, Peer!'
    Gradually closes his eyes.
    Yes, now she's afraid. Peer Gynt rides at the head
    Of a mighty army. His horse has a crest
    Of shining silver and four shoes of gold.
    He has gloves on his hands and a sword and a scabbard,
    And a trailing cloak lined with scarlet silk.
    It's a fine bold body of men he has with him,
    But none sits his horse as proudly as he,
    Or glitters as he does against the sun.
    Crowds throng below as he passes by them.
    They take off their hats and their eyes gape up at him.
    The women curtsey, for everyone knows
    Emperor Peer Gynt and his thousand warriors.
    He scatters sovereigns and shining shillings
    On the roadside like pebbles. Every man
    In the parish he'll make as rich as a lord.
    Peer Gynt rides high over the white sea. The Prince
    Of England stands on the shore and waits for him.
    And all the maidens of England are with him,
    The great men of England and the mighty King
    Of England himself rise in homage

From their high table as Peer Gynt comes riding.
King raises his crown from his head and says –
ASLAK THE SMITH (*to several others as they walk past on the far
        side of the fence*). If it isn't that boozing pig Peer Gynt!
PEER (*half-raises himself*). What's that, Your Majesty?
ASLAK (*leans on the fence and grins*). Time to get up, me lad.
PEER. What the devil –?
        Is it Aslak the Smith? What the hell do you want?
ASLAK (*to the others*). He's still dopey from our last encounter.
PEER (*jumps up*). Clear off!
ASLAK. Man, where have you been?
        Six weeks away! Did the mountain trolls get you?
PEER. I've been doing strange deeds, Aslak smith.
ASLAK (*winks at the others*). Tell us, Peer.
PEER. It's my business.
ASLAK (*after a moment*). You'll be coming to Heggstad?
PEER. No.
ASLAK. They used to say the girl was keen on you.
PEER. Why, you black crow –!
ASLAK (*takes a step back*). Don't get angry, Peer. If Ingrid's jilted
        you
        There are others. Think! John Gynt's son!
        Come with us to the feast. There'll be juicy young lambs,
        And widows too –
PEER. Go to hell!
ASLAK. You'll find someone who'll have you.
        Good night. I'll give your love to the bride!
        They go, laughing and whispering.
PEER (*looks after them a moment, tosses his head and half turns*).
        Let her marry whom she pleases!
        It's nothing to me.
        Looks himself up and down.
        Breeches torn. Tattered and filthy.
        If only I had something new to wear –
        Stamps his foot.
        I'd tear the laughter out of them
        Like a butcher pulling the guts from a rabbit.

Looks round suddenly.
What's that? Who was that sniggering?
I could have sworn –! I suppose it was no-one.
I'll go home to mother.
Starts up the hill again, but stops and cocks an ear towards the fence.
The dancing's begun!
*Stares and listens; walks back down the hill, step by step. His eyes
glitter. He rubs his thigh.*
What a fine swarm of lasses!
Seven or eight to every man!
Oh, flames, I must go and join in the fun!
But mother's up on the millhouse roof.
His eyes are drawn towards the feast again. He jumps and laughs.
Hey, how the dancers fly over the grass!
By God, he's a boy on the fiddle! It laughs
And splutters just like a waterfall.
And oh, what a covey of glittering girls!
Yes, flames, I must go and join in the fun!
Leaps over the fence and goes down the road.

SCENE THREE

*The farm at Heggstad. In the background is the farmhouse itself.
Many* GUESTS. *A dance is in lively progress on the green. The*
FIDDLER *is seated on a table. The* MASTER COOK[2] *stands in the
doorway.* KITCHEN WOMEN *carrying food and drink go back and
forth between the various buildings.* OLDER PEOPLE *sit here and
there chatting.*

A WOMAN (*joins a group sitting on some logs*). The bride? Oh yes,
    she's crying a little,
    But that's always the way.
MASTER COOK (*in another group*). Come on, good people, empty
    your glasses.
A MAN. Thank you. But you never stop filling them.
A LAD (*to the* FIDDLER, *as he runs past clutching a* GIRL *by the
    hand*). Play up, man! Don't spare the strings!

GIRL. Scrape till it echoes out over the meadows.

OTHER GIRLS (*in a circle around a* LAD *who is dancing*). That's a
    fine leap!

A GIRL. He's a nimble leg.

THE LAD (*dancing*). It's a high roof here, and the walls are wide!

BRIDEGROOM (*comes snivelling up to his* FATHER, *who is standing
    talking to two or three others, and pulls his coat*). She
    won't, father. She's so proud.

FATHER. What won't she?

BRIDEGROOM. She's shut herself in.

FATHER. Well, find the key.

BRIDEGROOM. I don't know where.

FATHER. You dumb halfwit!

He turns back to the others. The BRIDEGROOM *wanders away
    across the yard.*

A LAD (*comes from behind the house*). Hey, girls! Now things'll be
    livening up!

    Here comes Peer Gynt!

ASLAK (*who has just joined them*). Who asked him?

MASTER COOK. Nobody. (*Goes towards the house.*)

ASLAK (*to the* GIRLS). If he tries to speak to you, don't listen to
    him.

A GIRL (*to the* OTHERS). No, we'll pretend we never saw him.

PEER GYNT (*enters hot and excited, stops in the middle of the
    CROWD and claps his hands*). Now, which girl's got the
    nimblest pair of legs?

A GIRL (*as he approaches*). Not me.

ANOTHER (*similarly*). Nor me.

A THIRD GIRL. I'm sure I haven't.

PEER (*to a* FOURTH GIRL). Well, let's have you, if there's no one
    better.

FOURTH GIRL (*turns away*). Haven't time.

PEER (*to a* FIFTH). You, then.

FIFTH GIRL (*walks away*). I'm going home.

PEER. Tonight? Are you out of your wits?

ASLAK (*after a moment, in a low voice*). Look, Peer. She's dancing
    with somebody's granddad.

PEER (*turns sharply to an* OLDER MAN). Hey, you! Where are the
    free ones?

MAN. Find them for yourself. (*Walks away from him.*)

PEER GYNT *falls suddenly silent. He glances shyly and furtively at
the group. They all look at him but do not speak. He approaches
other groups. As he reaches them, they fall silent; as he walks away,
they smile and follow him with their eyes.*

[PEER (*quietly*). Their glances and smiles are needles in my back.
    My nerves grate like a sawblade under the file.]

He walks away along the fence. SOLVEIG, *holding little* HELGA *by
the hand, enters the yard with her* PARENTS.

A MAN (*to another standing near* PEER GYNT). Look. The strangers.

SECOND MAN. The strangers from the west?

FIRST MAN. Yes, from Heydal.

SECOND MAN. Ah, yes.

PEER (*walks in front of the newcomers, points at* SOLVEIG *and asks
her* FATHER). May I dance with your daughter?

SOLVEIG'S FATHER (*quietly*). You may; but first we must go
    inside and greet
    The people of the house.

MASTER COOK (*to* PEER, *offering him a drink*). Since you've come,
    you might as well have one.

PEER (*keeps his eyes fixed on them as they go*). Thanks, I'm going
    to dance. I'm not thirsty.

THE MASTER COOK *leaves him.* PEER *looks towards the house and
laughs.*

PEER. How fair she is!
    I never saw such a girl! She dropped
    Her eyes to her shoes and her white apron,
    And clutched tight to her mother's skirt,
    And carried a psalmbook wrapped in linen.
    I must look at that girl.
    Is about to enter the house.

A LAD (*comes out of the house with several others*). Why, Peer!
    Are you leaving the dance already?

PEER. No.

LAD. Then you're heading the wrong way.
Takes him by the shoulder to turn him round.

PEER. Let me past!

LAD. Are you scared of the smith?

PEER. *I* scared?

LAD. Yes, have you forgotten what happened at Lunde?
They all laugh and go down to the dancing-green.

SOLVEIG (*in the doorway*). Are you the boy that wanted to dance?

PEER. Of course I am. Don't you remember me?
Takes her by the hand.
Come along.

SOLVEIG. I mustn't go far, Mother said.

PEER. Mother said! Mother said! Were you born yesterday?

SOLVEIG. You're making fun –!

PEER. Well, you're almost a child. How old are you?

SOLVEIG. I was confirmed by the priest last year.

PEER. Tell me your name, girl, and we'll talk more easily.

SOLVEIG. My name's Solveig. What's yours?

PEER. Peer Gynt.

SOLVEIG (*draws her hand away*). Oh, heaven!

PEER. What is it now?

SOLVEIG. My garter's come loose. I must tie it tighter.
Leaves him.

BRIDEGROOM (*tugs at his* MOTHER'*s dress*). Mother, she won't.

BRIDEGROOM'S MOTHER. Won't? Won't what?

BRIDEGROOM. Won't, mother.

BRIDEGROOM'S MOTHER. What?

BRIDEGROOM. Unlock the door.

BRIDEGROOM'S FATHER (*quietly, angrily*). Oh, you're only fit to feed with the pigs.

BRIDEGROOM'S MOTHER. No, don't scold him. Poor lad, he'll be all right.
They walk away.

A LAD (*comes with a crowd from the dancing-green*). Have a real drink, Peer?

PEER. No.

LAD. Oh, come on, have a drop.

PEER (*scowls at him*). Have you got some?

LAD. Maybe.

> *Takes out a pocket flask and drinks.*
>
> Oh, how it burns! Well?

PEER. Let's have a sniff. (*Drinks.*)

SECOND LAD. Try mine too.

PEER. No.

SECOND LAD. Come on, now, don't be a fool. Drink up, Peer!

PEER. All right. (*Drinks again.*)

A GIRL (*whispers*). Come on, let's go.

PEER. Are you scared of me, lass?

A THIRD LAD. Who isn't scared of *you*?

FOURTH LAD. You showed us at Lunde what you could do.

PEER. I can do better than that, once I really cut loose.

FIRST LAD (*whispers*). Now he's off!

SEVERAL LADS (*form a circle round him*). Tell us, tell us! What can you do?

PEER. Tomorrow.

THE OTHER LADS. No, now, tonight!

A GIRL. Can you do black magic, Peer?

PEER. I can conjure up the Devil!

A MAN. My grandmother could do that before I was born.

PEER. Liar! There's no one else can do what I can.

> Once I conjured him into a nut.
>
> It was worm-eaten, you see.

LADS (*laugh*). Sure, it would be.

PEER. He swore and wept – said he'd give me whatever I wanted –

ONE OF THE CROWD. But he had to go in?

PEER. Of course! I plugged the hole with a peg.

> Oh, you should have heard him spluttering and skippering!

GIRL. Fancy that!

PEER. Just like a bumble-bee!

GIRL. Have you still got him there?

PEER. No, he's gone back to Hell.

> It's his fault the smith doesn't like me.

LAD. Really?

PEER. I went to Aslak and asked if he'd smash it for me.
    He swore he would; put it down on his anvil;
    But he's a clumsy lout – well, [it isn't surprising,]
    He spends all day swinging that sledgehammer –

A VOICE FROM THE CROWD. Did he kill the Devil, now?

PEER. He laid to like a man.
    But the Devil shot in a flame through the roof,
    Splitting the walls.

SEVERAL. And the smith –?

PEER.   Stood there
    With his hands fried black; since when we've not been
        friends.
    They all laugh.

SEVERAL. That's a good yarn.

OTHERS. It's near his best.

PEER. You think I'm making it up?

A MAN. Oh no, you're not!
    I've heard most of it from my granddad.

PEER. That's a lie! It happened to me!

MAN. Sure, what hasn't?

PEER (*with a gesture*). I can ride through the air on horseback!
    There's a lot I can do, I'm telling you!
    They shout with laughter again.

ONE OF THE CROWD. Peer, ride through the air for us!

SEVERAL. Yes, dear Peer Gynt!

PEER. Oh, there's no need to beg me!
    I'll ride over the lot of you like a storm.
    The whole parish shall fall at my feet!

AN OLDER MAN. He's out of his mind.

ANOTHER. He's daft.

A THIRD. You swaggering braggart!

A FOURTH. He's a bloody liar!

PEER (*threatens them*). Just you wait! You'll see!

A MAN (*half drunk*). Just you wait. You'll get your trousers
        dusted.

OTHERS. And a tender bottom. And a fine black eye.

The CROWD *disperses, the older ones in anger, the younger ones laughing scornfully.*

BRIDEGROOM (*in his ear*). Peer, is it true you can ride in the air?

PEER (*brusquely*). I can do anything, Mads. I'm a man, believe me.

BRIDEGROOM. Then you've the cloak of invisibility, too?

PEER. The hat, you mean? Of course I've got it.

Turns away from him. SOLVEIG *walks across the yard leading* HELGA *by the hand.*

PEER (*approaches them. His face lights up*). Solveig! Ah, it's good you've come!

Takes her by the wrist.

Now I'll swing you fast and free!

SOLVEIG. Let me go.

PEER. Why?

SOLVEIG. You're so wild.

PEER. So is a stag when spring is dawning.

Come on, girl, don't be stubborn!

SOLVEIG (*pulls away her arm*). I daren't.

PEER. Why?

SOLVEIG. No, you've been drinking.

Goes away with HELGA.

PEER. Oh, to stick a sharp knife through them, all of them!

BRIDEGROOM (*nudges him with his elbow*). Can't you help me to get at the bride?

PEER (*absently*). The bride? Where is she?

BRIDEGROOM. In the storehouse.

PEER. Mm.

BRIDEGROOM. Oh, come on, Peer Gynt. Please try.

PEER. No, you'll have to manage without my help.

A thought occurs to him. He says quietly but sharply.

Ingrid in the storehouse!

Goes across to SOLVEIG.

Have you changed your mind?

She turns to go. He steps in front of her.

You're ashamed because I look like a tramp.

SOLVEIG (*quickly*). You don't! It isn't true!

PEER. It is. And I *have* been drinking, too.

But that was to spite you for hurting me.
Come on, then!

SOLVEIG. I daren't now, even if I wanted to.

PEER. Who are you afraid of?

SOLVEIG. Father, mostly.

PEER. Father? Oh, yes. He's one of those quiet ones.
A godly soul, eh? What? Come on, answer!

SOLVEIG. What shall I answer?

PEER. Is your father a bible man?
And you and your mother, too? Will you answer me?

SOLVEIG. Let me go in peace.

PEER. No.
Softly but sharply and menacingly.
I can turn myself into a troll!
I'll come to your bedside tonight at midnight.
If you hear something hissing and spitting
Don't think it's the cat. It's me, my dear!
I'll be drawing your blood in a cup,
And your little sister, I'll gobble her up!
For at night I'm a werewolf. I'll bite you
All over your loins and your pretty back.
Changes his tone suddenly and begs as though in anguish.
Dance with me, Solveig!

SOLVEIG (*looks darkly at him*). Now you're ugly.
She goes into the house.

BRIDEGROOM (*wanders back*). I'll give you a cow, if you'll only
help me.

PEER. Come!

They go behind the house. As they do so, a large CROWD *comes
from the dancing-green, most of them drunk. Hubbub and confusion.*
SOLVEIG, HELGA *and their* PARENTS *appear in the doorway with
some of the* OLDER PEOPLE.

MASTER COOK (*to* ASLAK *the* SMITH, *who is at the head of the*
CROWD). Keep the peace now, will you?

ASLAK (*takes off his coat*). No. We'll settle it now.
Someone's nose must be rubbed in the dirt,
Peer Gynt's or mine.

SOME OF THE CROWD. Sure, let them fight.

OTHERS. No, let's have no violence.

ASLAK. It's fists or nothing.

[For we've come to the stage where words are useless.]

SOLVEIG'S FATHER. Control yourself, man.

HELGA. Are they going to beat him, mother?

A LAD. Let's stuff his lies down his throat.

ANOTHER. Kick him out of the feast!

A THIRD. Spit in his eye!

A FOURTH MAN (*to the* SMITH). Are you backing out?

ASLAK (*throws down his jacket*). I'll slaughter the pig!

SOLVEIG'S MOTHER (*to* SOLVEIG). You see what they think of
him?

AASE (*enters with a stick in her hand*). Is my son here?
Wait till I get his pants down!
I'll thrash the holy life out of him!

ASLAK (*rolls up his sleeves*). That stick's too puny for a fat lout
like him.

SOME OF THE CROWD. The smith'll thrash him.

OTHERS. Butcher him.

ASLAK (*spits on his hands and nods at* AASE). Hang him!

AASE. What! Hang my Peer? Just you try!
I've teeth and claws! Where is he?
Shouts across the yard.
Peer!

BRIDEGROOM (*enters running*). Oh, God have mercy on us all!
Mother and father, come quickly!

BRIDEGROOM'S FATHER. What's the matter?

BRIDEGROOM. Just fancy! Peer Gynt –!

AASE (*screams*). Have they killed him?

BRIDEGROOM. No, Peer Gynt –! Look up there, on the hillside –!

CROWD. He's got the bride!

AASE (*lowers her stick*). Monster!

ASLAK (*as if thunderstruck*). By God, he's climbing like a goat!

BRIDEGROOM (*weeps*). Oh, mother, he's carrying her like a
pig!

AASE (*shakes her fist up at him*). May God strike you down –!
   Shrieks in terror.
   Be careful!
BRIDE'S FATHER (*enters bareheaded and white with rage*). Bride-
   rape! I'll have his life for this!
AASE. I'll burn in Hell before you do!

Act Two

SCENE ONE

A narrow path high up in the mountains. It is early morning.
PEER GYNT *is hurrying ill-temperedly along the path.* INGRID,
still half-dressed in her bridal clothes, is trying to hold him back.

PEER. Get away from me!

INGRID (*weeps*). After this! Where can I go?

PEER. Anywhere you like.

INGRID (*wrings her hands*). You have betrayed me!

PEER. It's no good moaning. It's finished.

INGRID. Our crime binds us. Our double crime.

PEER. All memories belong to the Devil.
    All women belong to the Devil.
    Except one –

INGRID. Which one?

PEER. Not you.

INGRID. Who is it, then?

PEER. Go! Go back where you came from!
    Quick! To your father!

INGRID. Dear, kind –!

PEER. Oh, shut up.

INGRID. You can't mean what you say.

PEER. Can and do.

INGRID. To seduce me, and then leave me!

PEER. What wealth have you to offer me?

INGRID. Heggstad farm, and more besides.

PEER. Have you a psalmbook wrapped in linen?
    Golden hair about your shoulders?
    Do you drop your eyes to your apron?
    Do you cling to your mother's skirt?
    Tell me!

INGRID. No, but –?

EER. Did you read with the priest last spring?

NGRID. No, but Peer –?

EER. Is there modesty in your eyes?
When I ask, do you deny?

.NGRID. Oh God – I think he's mad –

PEER. When I see you, does the sun shine?
Well!

INGRID. No, but –

PEER. What's all the rest, then? (*Turns to go.*)

INGRID (*steps in front of him*). Don't you know they'll hang you
if you leave me?

PEER. All right!

INGRID. You can have wealth and honour if you take me –

PEER. Can't afford it.

INGRID (*bursts into tears*). You raped me –!

PEER. You were willing.

INGRID. I was desperate.

PEER. I was mad.

INGRID (*threateningly*). You'll pay dearly!

PEER. The dearest payment would be cheap.

INGRID. Your mind's made up, then?

PEER. Like stone.

INGRID. Very well. We'll see who wins.
Goes down the path.

PEER (*is silent for a moment, then suddenly cries*). All memories
belong to the Devil!
All women belong to the Devil!

INGRID (*turns her head and shouts scornfully up at him*). Except
one!

PEER. Yes. Except one.
They go opposite ways.

SCENE TWO

By a mountain lake. The ground is soft and boggy. A storm is
brewing. AASE, *in despair, is shouting and searching everywhere.*
SOLVEIG *has difficulty in keeping pace with her.* SOLVEIG'S
PARENTS *and* HELGA *follow a short way behind.*
AASE (*waves her arms and tears her hair*). Everything's against me.
     The world's angry!
   The sky, the water and the ugly mountains.
   The sky's sending down fogs to drive him crazy,
   The cunning water's waiting to rob him of his life,
   The mountains are throwing landslides and avalanches,
   And the whole parish is shouting for his blood.
   Which they shan't have, for I can't live without him.
   Oh, the fool, to let the foul fiend tempt him!
   Turns to SOLVEIG.
   Isn't it beyond belief?
   He that did nothing but lie and romance,
   That never exercised any limb but his tongue,
   That never did an honest day's work in his life –
   That –! Oh, should I laugh or cry?
   Mind, when times were tough we stuck together,
   For my man had a tongue red for drink.
   An idler he was with his bragging, wasting our wealth,
   While I and my baby sat at home
   Trying to forget. What else could we do?
   For I was never a one for arguing.
   [It's fearful to look into the eyes of Fate,
   And there isn't a woman but likes to bury her grief,
   And shove her cares out of sight if she can.]
   Some take to drink, others to lying,
   So we took to romancing of princes and trolls
   And all kinds of beasts. And stealing brides
   From their white wedding-beds. But who'd have thought
   Those daft ideas would have stuck in his head?
   Frightened again.

Ow, what a screech! It's a goblin, sure,

Or a flibbertigibbet! Peer, Peer!

Up there, on that hillock –!

She runs up a little hill, and looks out across the lake.

SOLVEIG'S PARENTS *come to her.*

Not a sign of him!

SOLVEIG'S FATHER (*quietly*). The worse for him.

AASE (*weeps*). Oh, my Peer! My lost lambkin!

SOLVEIG'S FATHER (*nods gently*). Yes, indeed. Lost!

AASE. No, don't speak like that!

He's a good lad. There's nobody like him.

SOLVEIG'S FATHER. Foolish woman!

AASE. Oh, yes, yes. I'm foolish. But the boy's all right.

SOLVEIG'S FATHER (*still quiet-voiced and mild-eyed*). His heart
    is hardened. His soul is lost.

AASE (*fearfully*). No, no! Our Lord is not so hard!

SOLVEIG'S FATHER. Do you think he can sigh away his debt of
    sin?

AASE (*eagerly*). No, but he can ride through the air on a stag!

SOLVEIG'S MOTHER. Merciful heaven, are you mad?

SOLVEIG'S FATHER (*to* AASE). What do you mean, woman?

AASE. No deed's too big for him. You'll see,

If only he lives long enough –

SOLVEIG'S FATHER. It would be best if you saw him hang on the
    gallows.

AASE (*screams*). Providence and Mercy, spare us all!

SOLVEIG'S FATHER. In the hangman's hands,

Please God, his heart will turn to repentance.

AASE (*dazed*). Oh, you'll soon be talking me out of my senses.

We must find him.

SOLVEIG'S FATHER. To save his soul.

AASE. And his body!

If he's sitting in the bog, we must haul him out.

If the trolls have got him, we must ring the church bells.

SOLVEIG'S FATHER. Hm. There's a sheep track here.

AASE. The Lord will repay you for your help.

SOLVEIG'S FATHER. It's my Christian duty.

AASE. Bah! Then the rest are heathen savages.
      There wasn't one who would come with me –
SOLVEIG'S FATHER. They know him too well.
AASE. He was too good for them. (*Wrings her hands.*)
      And to think – to think his life's at stake!
SOLVEIG'S FATHER. Here's a man's footprint.
AASE. Then it's here we must search.
SOLVEIG'S FATHER. We'll cover the ground up to our farm.
      He and SOLVEIG'S MOTHER *go ahead.*
SOLVEIG (*to* AASE). Tell me more.
AASE (*dries her eyes*). About my son?
SOLVEIG. Yes. Everything.
AASE (*smiles and tosses her head*). Everything? You'd soon be
      weary!
SOLVEIG. You'd weary quicker of telling than I of hearing.

SCENE THREE

*Low treeless heights at the foot of the mountain plain, with peaks
visible in the distance. Long shadows fall. It is late in the day.*
PEER (*runs in at full tilt and stops on the hillside*). The whole
      parish is after me in a mob!
      They've armed themselves with rifles and sticks.
      I can hear Ingrid's father hollering at their head.
      The news has spread quickly: Peer Gynt's on the loose!
      This is better sport than bashing a smith!
      This is life! I feel as strong as a bear!
      Punches around and jumps in the air.
      To smash and overturn! To dam the waterfall!
      To strike! To wrench the fir up by the root!
      This is life. It hardens and elevates.
      To hell with all bloody lies!
THREE SÆTER[3] GIRLS (*run across the hills screaming and singing*).
      Trond of the Valfjeld! Boord and Kaare!
      Troll-pack! Will you sleep in our arms?
PEER. Who are you calling?

GIRLS. Trolls! Trolls!

FIRST GIRL. Trond! Come gently!

SECOND GIRL. Boord! Come and rape me!

THIRD GIRL. All the beds in the hut stand empty!

FIRST GIRL. Gently means rape!

SECOND GIRL. And rape means gently!

THIRD GIRL. If there aren't any boys, we'll play with trolls!

PEER. Where are the boys, then?

ALL THREE GIRLS (*howl with laughter*). They can't come!

FIRST GIRL. Mine called me his love and called me his darling.
  Now he's married to an old grey widow.

SECOND GIRL. Mine met a gipsy-girl north on the moor.
  Now they're tramping the roads together.

THIRD GIRL. Mine got tired of our bastard's crying.
  Now his head grins high on a stake.

ALL THREE. Trond of the Valfjeld! Boord and Kaare!
  Troll-pack! Come and sleep in our arms!

PEER (*takes a sudden leap into their midst*). I'm a three-headed
      troll, and a boy for three girls!

GIRLS. Three? Could you, lad?

PEER. Try me and see!

FIRST GIRL. To the hut! To the hut!

SECOND GIRL. We've a barrel of mead!

PEER. Let it flow!

THIRD GIRL. There'll be no bed empty this Saturday night!

SECOND GIRL (*kisses him*). He sputters and sparks like white-hot
      iron!

THIRD GIRL (*kisses him*). Like a baby's eyes from the black
      bottom of the lake!

PEER (*dances among them*). The heart is heavy, the head plays
      wanton.
  In the eyes, laughter; in the throat, tears.

THE GIRLS (*make long noses towards the mountain tops, scream and
      sing*). Trond of the Valfjeld! Boord and Kaare!
  Troll-pack! Did you sleep in our arms?
  They dance away across the mountains with PEER GYNT
  among them.

SCENE FOUR

Among the Ronde mountains. Sunset. Snow-peaks glitter around.
PEER (*enters dazed and bleary*). Castle rises on castle!
          Hey, what a shining gate!
          Stop! Will you stop? It's shrinking
          Farther and farther away!
          [The weathercock on the steeple
          Is lifting its wings to fly.
          It's all getting blue and misty,
          And the mountain's shut and barred.
          What are these trunks and roots
          That grow from the clefts in the ridge?
          It's soldiers heron-footed;
          Now *they're* fading away!]
          It swims before me like rainbows;
          It hurts my eyes and brain.
          What's that that chimes in the distance?
          This weight pressing my eyes?
          Ugh, how it splits my forehead –
          This binding, white-hot ring!
          Oh, I cannot remember
          Who in Hell put that round my brain!
          Sinks down.
          The flight along Gjendin Edge –
          It was all a fake and a lie!
          Up the cliff with the bride –
          Then drunk for a night and a day.
          Hunted by hawks and kites,
          Threatened by trolls and the like,
          Sporting with crazy wenches –
          A bloody lie and a fake!
          Stares for a long time upwards.
          There sail two brown eagles.
          The wild geese fly to the south.

And I must trudge here and stumble
Knee deep in the mire and filth.
Jumps up.
I'll join them! I'll wash myself clean,
Scoured by the sharpest winds!
I shall soar! I'll wash myself pure in
The gleaming christening-font!
I'll fly high over the farmhouse,
I'll ride till my black soul shines,
Far over the salty sea
And high over England's prince!
Yes, you can stare, my pretties.
I haven't come here for you.
It's no use standing and waiting –
Well, I might take a minute or two –!
    What? Where have those eagles got to?
Oh, what the hell do I care?
There soars the crown of a gable.
It's rising up everywhere.
It's growing out of the ruins.
The gate stands open and fair.
    Ah, now I recognize it!
It's my granddad's fine new home!
The rags are gone from the windows.
The tumbledown fence is gone.
The light pours from every window.
They're feasting in the great room.
    Look, now the old Bishop's clinking
His knife on his silver cup.
The Captain has tossed back his bottle,
And broken the looking-glass up.
Let them squander away. What do we care?
Hush, mother! We don't have to stint.
The rich John Gynt gives a banquet.
Hurrah for the tree of Gynt!
But what's all this bustle and hubbub?
What can the shouting be?

The Captain's proposing the son's health!
The Bishop is calling for me!
Go in, Peer Gynt, to your judgment.
The welcoming cheers fill the room.
Peer Gynt, thou wast born to greatness,
And to greatness thou shalt come!

Takes a running jump forward, but strikes his nose against a rock, falls and remains lying on the ground.

SCENE FIVE

A hillside, with great rustling trees. Stars twinkle through the leaves. Birds sing in the treetops. A GREENCLAD WOMAN *is walking on the hillside.* PEER GYNT *follows her, indulging in various amorous antics.*

THE GREENCLAD ONE (*stops and turns*). Is it true?

PEER (*makes a cutting gesture with his finger across his throat*).
　　　As true as my name's Peer!
　　As true as you're a beautiful woman!
　　Will you have me? I'll be good to you.
　　You shall neither weave nor spin.
　　I'll fill you with food till you're ready to burst.
　　I'll never pull you by the hair –

GREENCLAD ONE. Nor beat me?

PEER. What an idea! We princes don't beat women.

GREENCLAD ONE. Are you a King's son?

PEER. Yes.

GREENCLAD ONE. My father's the King of the Ronde.

PEER. Is he? Well, that makes us two of a kind.

GREENCLAD ONE. My father's palace is inside the mountain.

PEER. My mother's is bigger, believe you me.

GREENCLAD ONE. Do you know my father? His name is King
　　　Brose.

PEER. Do you know my mother? Her name's Queen Aase.

GREENCLAD ONE. When my father's angry, the mountains crack.

PEER. They shake when my mother opens her mouth.

GREENCLAD ONE. When my father dances he kicks the stars.

PEER. My mother can ride through rivers in flood.

GREENCLAD ONE. Have you any other clothes beside those rags?

PEER. Oh, you should see me in my Sunday suit!

GREENCLAD ONE. I always wear gold and silks.

PEER. They look to me more like tow and straw.

GREENCLAD ONE. Well, there's one thing you must remember.
    That is the way of the mountain people.
    Everything there has another meaning.
    If you come to my father's house, you may easily think
    You're just in an ugly heap of stones.

PEER. Well now, it's exactly the same with us.
    Our gold may seem scrap to you.
    You may think each crystal window-pane
    Is just a fistful of socks and rags.

GREENCLAD ONE. Black seems white and ugly seems fair.

PEER. Great seems little and foul seems clean.

GREENCLAD ONE (*falls on his neck*). O, Peer! I see it! We were
    made for each other!

PEER. As the leg fits the breeches, the comb fits the hair.

GREENCLAD ONE (*calls across the hill*). Bridal steed! Bridal steed!
    Come, my bridal steed!

*A huge pig canters in with a rope's end round its neck as a bridle,
and an old sack as a saddle.* PEER GYNT *swings himself astride its
back and sets the* GREENCLAD ONE *in front of him.*

PEER. Hup, now! We'll ride in through the Ronde gate!
    Gee-up, gee-up, my beauty!

GREENCLAD ONE (*amorously*). Just now I was feeling so sad and
    lonely.
    Who can tell what life will bring in its course?

PEER (*slaps the pig and rides away*). You can tell a great man by
    the cut of his horse!

SCENE SIX

The palace hall of THE OLD MAN OF THE MOUNTAINS. *A great gathering of* TROLL COURTIERS, ELVES *and* GOBLINS. THE OLD MAN OF THE MOUNTAINS *is seated on his throne, sceptred and crowned. His* CHILDREN *and* NEAREST RELATIVES *surround him.* PEER GYNT *stands in front of him. There is a great hubbub in the hall.*

TROLL COURTIERS. Kill him! Kill him! The Christian dog
    Has bewitched the Troll King's fairest daughter!

TROLL CHILD. Can I cut off his fingers?

ANOTHER. Can I pull out his hair?

A TROLL MAIDEN. Huh, ha! Let me bite his bottom!

TROLL WITCH (*with a ladle*). Shall I boil him down into soup?

ANOTHER WITCH (*with a carving-knife*). Shall we roast him on
    the spit or brown him in the pot?

THE OLD MAN OF THE MOUNTAINS. Calm yourselves, my
    children!
    Beckons his COUNSELLORS *nearer.*
    We can't afford to be grand.
    We've been slipping backwards in recent years.
    Our position has become precarious,
    And we can't look down our noses at offers of help.
    Besides, the lad has no obvious defects,
    And seems well-built. True, he's only got one head,
    But my daughter is no better off in that respect.
    Three-headed trolls are going right out of fashion.
    Even two heads are rare nowadays,
    And they are not what they used to be.
    To PEER GYNT.
    So you want my daughter?

PEER. Your daughter, and your kingdom as her dowry.

OLD MAN. You shall have half my kingdom while I live,
    And the other half when, eventually, I die.

PEER. That suits me.

OLD MAN. Ah, but wait, my lad.

There are certain promises you, too, must make.
If you break one of them, the pact is broken,
And you shall not leave this place alive.
First, you must swear you'll never think
Of what lies outside the kingdom of the mountain.
Day you must shun, action, and anything touched by light.

PEER. Well, if I'm to be King, that's easy.

OLD MAN. Next – and this will test your wits –
Rises in his seat.

OLDEST TROLL COURTIER (*to* PEER). Let's see if you have a
    wisdom tooth
    To crack the nut of the Troll King's riddle.

OLD MAN. What is the difference between troll and man?

PEER. No difference, as far as I can see.
    Big trolls want to roast you, small trolls want to claw you.
    It's the same with us, if we dared.

OLD MAN. True. We're alike in that, and more.
    But morning is morning and night is night,
    And there is a difference nevertheless.
    I'll tell you what it is.
    Out there, under the shining vault of heaven,
    Men tell each other: 'Man, be thyself!'
    But in here, among us trolls, we say:
    'Man, be thyself – and to Hell with the rest of the world!'

OLDEST COURTIER (*to* PEER). You fathom it?

PEER. Not entirely.

OLD MAN. 'To Hell with the world!' Those sharp and fateful
    words
    Must be engraven on your crest, my son.

PEER (*scratches behind his ear*). Yes, but –

OLD MAN. They *must*, if you would be master here!

PEER. Oh, hell. All right. I really can't see –

OLD MAN. Next you must teach yourself to value
    Our simple and homely way of life.

He beckons. Two TROLLS *with pigs'-heads and white nightcaps
bring in food and drink.*
    Our cake flows from the cow, our mead from the bull.

Don't ask yourself if it tastes sour or sweet.
The main thing is, and this you mustn't forget,
It's all home-made.

PEER (*pushes the things away*). To hell with your home-made
        drink!

I'll never get used to this place.

OLD MAN. The bowl goes with it. It's gold. Who owns
The golden bowl has my daughter's love.

PEER (*thoughtfully*). [It is written: 'Thou shalt subdue thy
        nature.']

Well, I dare say in time it won't taste too bad.
All right! (*Tastes.*)

OLD MAN. That's a sensible lad. Did you spit?

PEER. Taste is a question of what you're used to.

OLD MAN. Next you must throw away
Your Christian clothes. For this you must know
To the greater glory of the mountain kingdom
Everything here is made within the mountain.
Nothing comes from the valley except
The silken bow at the tip of your tail.

PEER (*angrily*). I haven't got a tail!

OLD MAN. Well, then you must have one.
Prime Minister, tie my Sunday tail on him.

PEER. I'll be damned if you will!
Do you want to make a fool of me?

OLD MAN. You cannot court
My daughter with a bare backside.

PEER. Make a man into a beast?

OLD MAN. My son, you're wrong.
I'm only making you a respectable suitor.
You'll have a flame-yellow bow,
Which we count as the highest honour.

PEER (*thoughtfully*). Well, [they say: 'Man is but a speck of dust,'
And I suppose] one must toe the line of fashion.
Tie away!

OLD MAN. You're a co-operative boy.

OLDEST COURTIER. Now see how well you can flip and twitch it.

PEER (*angrily*). What, will you force me further yet?
    Must I give up my Christian faith?
OLD MAN. No, you're welcome to keep that.
    [Faith is free. We charge no tariff there.
    You can tell a troll by his outside.]
    As long as we agree on manners and dress
    You can go on calling your freakish fancies faith.
PEER. For all your conditions, you're
    A more reasonable chap than one might think.
OLD MAN. My son, we trolls are better than our reputation.
    That's another difference between you and us.
    But now we're through with the serious business
    So let's delight our eyes and ears.
    Music-girl, forth! Let the mountain-harp sound!
    Dancing-girl, forth! Tread our palace floor!
    Music and dance.
OLDEST COURTIER. How do you like it?
PEER. Like it? Hm –
OLD MAN. Don't be afraid to speak. What do you see?
PEER. Something horribly ugly.
    A cow with a harp and a dancing sow.
TROLL COURTIERS. Eat him!
OLD MAN. Remember, his eyes and ears are human.
TROLL MAIDENS. Oh, tear off his ears! Pull out his eyes!
GREENCLAD ONE (*weeps*). Must we hear and endure such insults
    While I and my sister play and dance?
PEER. Oh, is it you? Well, you know,
    A joke at a feast isn't meant unkindly.
GREENCLAD ONE. Do you swear to that?
PEER. Both the dance and the music were really splendid.
    May the cat claw me if I lie!
OLD MAN. That's a funny thing about human nature.
    It hangs on to people a remarkable time.
    [If it gets a gash in the fight with us,
    It leaves a scar, but that soon heals up.]
    My son-in-law was proving as pliant as any.
    Willingly he's thrown off his Christian clothes,

Willingly drunk from our cup of mead,
Willingly tied a tail to his backside.
So willing, in short, to do all that we bade him,
That I really began to think the old Adam
Had been hunted out of our gate for good and all.
But now he's suddenly popped up again.
Well, well, my son, we must give you some treatment
To cure this human nature of yours.

PEER. What will you do?

OLD MAN. In your left eye
I'll make a little cut, so that you'll see awry.
But all you see will seem bright and fair.
Then I'll nip out your right window-pane –

PEER. Are you drunk?

OLD MAN (*lays several sharp instruments on the table*).
        Here you see the glazier's tools.
We'll blinker you, like a surly bull.
Then you'll see that your bride is beautiful.
And there'll be an end to these illusions
Of dancing sows, and cows playing harps –

PEER. This is madman's talk!

OLDEST COURTIER. The Old Man of the Mountains speaks!
He is wise. It is you that's mad.

OLD MAN. Think how much pain and worry you'll save yourself.
Don't forget that sight is the source
Of the bitter and searing lye of tears.

PEER. That's true. It says in the holy book:
'If thine eye offend thee, pluck it out.'
Wait! Tell me, when will my sight be healed
So that I can see again as a man?

OLD MAN. Never, my friend.

PEER. Indeed! Well, thanks very much.

OLD MAN. Where are you going?

PEER. On my way.

OLD MAN. No, wait. It's easy to get in here,
But the mountain gate doesn't open outwards.

PEER. Surely you'll not keep me by force?

OLD MAN. Now listen, Prince Peer, and be sensible.
    You've a talent for trolldom. Isn't that true?
    You're already shaping quite like a troll.
    And you do want to become a troll?
PEER. Indeed I do.
    [For a bride with a well-lined kingdom thrown in
    I'd put up with losing a thing or two.]
    But there's a limit to everything.
    I've accepted a tail, that's true enough;
    But I can remove what your Minister tied on.
    I've thrown off my breeks. They were old and patched.
    But I can soon button them on again.
    [And I can just as quickly slip my moorings
    From all your mountain way of life.]
    I don't mind swearing a cow's a maiden.
    A man can always swallow an oath.
    But to know one can never free oneself,
    Nor be able to die like a Christian soul;
    To live like a mountain troll all one's days,
    And never go back – that's what you want.
    And that is something I'll never agree to.
OLD MAN. Now you're beginning to make me angry.
    I'm not to be trifled with. You pale-faced
    Pigmy! Do you know who I am?
    First you take liberties with my daughter –
PEER. That's a lie!
OLD MAN. You must marry her!
PEER. You dare to accuse –?
OLD MAN. What! Can you deny
    You desired and lusted after her?
PEER (snorts). Is that all? Who the hell cares about that?
OLD MAN. You human beings are always the same.
    You're always ready to admit an impulse,
    But won't accept the guilt for anything
    Unless you've actually done it in the flesh.
    So you think that lust doesn't count?
    Wait. You'll soon see with your own eyes –

PEER. You won't catch me with a bait of lies.

GREENCLAD ONE. My Peer, before the year's end you'll be a
     father.

PEER. Open the door! Let me out!

OLD MAN. We'll send the baby after you in a ram's skin.

PEER (*wipes the sweat from his brow*). I wish to God I could wake!

OLD MAN. Shall we send him to the palace?

PEER. Send him to the parish!

OLD MAN. Very well, Prince Peer. It's your affair.
     But one thing's certain. What's done is done.
     Your child will grow. And these mongrels shoot up
     Indecently fast –

PEER. Old man, now don't be a stubborn ox.
     Be reasonable, madam. Let's come to terms.
     [Whether you measure me or weigh me]
     You'll profit little by keeping me.
     The truth is I'm neither a prince nor rich.

The GREENCLAD ONE *collapses and is carried out by* TROLL
MAIDENS.

OLD MAN (*looks at him with deep disdain for a moment, then says*).
          Bash him to bits on the rocks, my children.

TROLL CHILDREN. Oh father, can't we play owl and eagle first?
     The wolf game? Grey mouse and fire-eyed cat?

OLD MAN. All right, but hurry. I'm out of temper
     And sleepy. Good night. (*Goes.*)

PEER (*as the* TROLL CHILDREN *chase him*). Let me go, you little
          beasts!
     (*Tries to climb up the chimney.*)

TROLL CHILDREN. Goblins! Elves! Bite him in the bottom!

PEER. Yow! (*Tries to get down through the cellar-flap.*)

TROLL CHILDREN. Close every crack!

OLDEST COURTIER. What fun they're having, the little dears!

PEER (*fighting with a* TROLL CHILD *which has fastened its teeth
          in his ear*). Get away, you little wretch!

OLDEST COURTIER (*strikes him across the fingers*). Brute! Learn
          to respect a royal child.

PEER. A rat-hole! (*Runs to it.*)

TROLL CHILDREN. Block it up, brother imp!

PEER. The old man was bad, but the young ones are worse!

TROLL CHILDREN. Tear him!

PEER. Oh, why aren't I the size of a mouse? (*Runs around.*)

TROLL CHILDREN (*milling around him*). Close the circle! Close
the circle!

PEER (*weeps*). Why aren't I a louse? (*Falls.*)

TROLL CHILDREN. Now for his eyes!

PEER (*buried beneath the heap of* TROLL CHILDREN). Help!
Mother! I'm dying!

Church bells are heard tolling distantly.

TROLL CHILDREN. Bells on the mountain! The Black-Frock's
cows!

The TROLLS *flee in turmoil, yelling and screaming. The hall
crashes in ruins. Everything disappears.*

SCENE SEVEN

Pitch darkness. PEER GYNT *is heard hewing and beating about
with a great branch.*

PEER. Answer me! Who are you?

A VOICE IN THE DARK. Myself.

PEER. Get out of my way!

VOICE. Go round, Peer. The moor is big enough.

PEER (*tries to go through at another point, but is blocked by something*). Who are *you*?

VOICE. Myself. Can you say the same?

PEER. I can say what I like; my sword is sharp.
Beware! Huh, hah, now it strikes and crushes!
King Saul slew hundreds, Peer Gynt slays thousands!
Strikes and hews.
Who *are* you?

VOICE. Myself.

PEER. You can keep that rubbish. It doesn't help. *What* are
you?

VOICE. The Great Boyg.

PEER. Ah! Now I begin to understand.
     Out of my way, Boyg!
VOICE. Go round, Peer.
PEER. No, through! (*Hews and slashes.*)
     He's fallen! (*Tries to advance but comes up against something.*)
     Oh-ho! Are there more?
VOICE. The Boyg, Peer Gynt! One, only one.
     The Boyg that's unharmed, and the Boyg that you wounded.
     The Boyg that's dead, and the Boyg that is alive.
PEER (*throws down his branch*). My sword is troll-smeared; but I
     have my fists!
     Fights his way forward.
VOICE. Yes, trust to your fists. .Trust to your strength.
     He-he, Peer Gynt. That's the way to the top.
PEER (*tries again*). Forward or back, it's equally far.
     Outside or in, I'm still confined.
     There he is! And *there*! And round that bend!
     As soon as I'm out I'm back in the middle,
     Encircled. Name yourself! Let me see you!
     What on earth are you?
VOICE. The Boyg.
PEER (*gropes around*). Not dead. Not alive. Slimy. Misty.
     And shapeless. [It's just like bumping around
     In a herd of growling, half-awake bears!]
     Shouts.
     Hit me back!
VOICE. The Boyg is no fool.
PEER. Strike!
VOICE. The Boyg does not strike.
PEER. Fight! You shall!
VOICE. The Great Boyg wins without fighting.
PEER. If only there were a goblin to prick me,
     Or even a baby troll!
     Something to fight! But there's nothing.
     Now he's snoring! Boyg!
VOICE. What do you want?
PEER. Use force!

VOICE. The Great Boyg wins by doing nothing.

PEER (*bites his own arms and hands*). Let me feel claws and teeth
     in my flesh!

    I must feel the drip of my own blood!

    The wing-beats of great birds are heard.

BIRD CRIES. Is he coming, Boyg?

VOICE IN THE DARK. Yes. Step by step.

BIRD CRIES. O Sisters, sisters far away!

    Fly hither! The time is come!

PEER. If you're going to save me, girl, do it quickly!

    Don't look at your lap, so humble and shy.

    Your prayer-book! Throw it in his eyes!

BIRD CRIES. He's swaying!

VOICE IN THE DARK. We have him.

BIRD CRIES. Sisters! Come quickly!

PEER. An hour of this consuming strife

    Is too dear a price to pay for life. (*Sinks to the ground.*)

BIRD CRIES. Boyg, he's fallen! Take him! Take him!

The tolling of church bells and psalm song are heard in the distance.

THE BOYG (*shrinks to nothing, and gasps*). He was too strong.

    There were women behind him.

SCENE EIGHT

Sunrise. On the mountain outside AASE's *sæter. The door is shut.
Everything is still and deserted.* PEER GYNT *is lying asleep outside
the sæter wall.*

PEER (*wakes and looks round dully and heavily. He spits*). Oh, for
     a salted herring!⁵

    Spits again. As he does so, he sees HELGA *coming with a hamper
     of food.*

    Hullo, child, are you here? What do you want?

HELGA. It's Solveig –

PEER (*jumps up*). Where is she?

HELGA. Behind the wall.

SOLVEIG (*hidden*). If you come near me, I'll run away!

PEER (*stops*). Are you afraid I'll kiss you?

SOLVEIG. For shame!

PEER. Do you know where I was last night?
   The Old Man of the Mountains' daughter
   Is after me everywhere like a gadfly.

SOLVEIG. Then it was lucky they rang the bells.

PEER. They can't fool Peer Gynt. Can they?

HELGA (*starts to cry*). Oh, she's running away!
   Runs after her.
   Wait!

PEER (*seizes her by the arm*). Look what I've got in my pocket!
   A silver button, child! You shall have it –
   Only say a good word for me.

HELGA. Let me go. Let me go!

PEER. Here it is.

HELGA. Let me go. There's the basket.

PEER. God have mercy on you if you don't –!

HELGA. Oh, you're frightening me!

PEER (*quietly, lets go of her*). No, I only meant – ask her not to
      forget me!

   HELGA *runs away.*

Act Three

SCENE ONE

Deep inside the pine forest. Grey autumn weather. Snow is falling.
PEER GYNT *is standing in his shirtsleeves, felling timber.*
PEER (*hacks at a large fir-tree with twisted boughs*).
    Oh yes, you're tough, old friend. But it's no use.
    You're coming down.
    Hacks at it again.
    You're wearing a chain shirt, are you?
    I'll cut through it. That's right,
    Yes, you can shake your twisted arm at me.
    I know you're angry.
    It can't be helped. I'll bring you to your knees –!
    Breaks off suddenly.
    Lies! It's only an old tree!
    Bloody lies! It was never an armoured knight!
    [It's only a fir with crevices in its bark.
    It's heavy enough hewing timber,
    But hewing *and* dreaming – it's bloody murder!]
    I'm done with it, this living in mists and dreaming.
    You're an outlaw, my lad. They've hunted you into the
        woods.
    Hacks vigorously for a while.
    Yes, an outlaw.
    You've no mother now to look after you.
    If you want to eat, you must help yourself,
    [Fetch it raw from the forest and river,
    Split your own wood and light your own fire.
    You'll have to start doing your own work now.]
    If you want a warm coat, you must shoot a deer.
    If you want a house you must break stones.
    If you want walls, you must fell your own wood,
    And carry it there upon your back.

His axe sinks to the ground. He stares unseeingly.
It'll be a grand sight! A tower with a weathercock
I'll have on the roof-beam! And I'll carve on the gable
A mermaid, shaped like a fish from her navel!
There'll be brass on the weathercock and all the locks.
And glass! I must try to have some of that!
Strangers will stare and wonder at it
Glittering there high on the hillside –
Laughs angrily.
Bloody lies! There they are again!
You're an outlaw, my lad.
Hacks fiercely.

A bark-thatched hut
Will keep out the worst of the rain and frost.
[*Looks up at the tree.*
Now he's trembling. There! Just a kick
And he totters and measures his length on the ground,
The undergrowth milling and shuddering about him.
Begins to lop the branches.] *Suddenly he listens and stands still with
his axe raised.*

Someone's after me! [Is it Ingrid's father?
Old Heggstad gaffer! Ah, you'd cheat me, would you?]
Ducks behind the tree and peeps round it.
[A boy. All alone. He seems to be frightened.
He glances around. What's he got hidden there
Under his jacket? A sickle. He stops and looks round.
Lays his hand flat on the rail of the fence.
What's this, now? Why is he suddenly swaying –?]
Oh, my God! Why, he's chopped his finger off![6]
A whole finger! Right off! [He's bleeding like an ox!
Now he's running away with his hand in a clout!]
Gets up.
What a fool! An irreplaceable finger!
Right off! And of his own free will!
Ah! I see! That's the only way
To free oneself from serving the King.
That's it. They wanted to send him to the war

And the boy didn't want to go.
But to chop –? To lose for ever –?
Yes, to think – wish – to *will* it even;
But to *do* it! No, that I don't understand.
Gives a little shake of his head, then returns to his work.

SCENE TWO

A room down at AASE'*s house. Everything is in disorder. Boxes lie open, clothes are everywhere, a cat is on the bed.* AASE *and* KARI, *a crofter's wife, are busy packing and putting things in order.*

AASE (*runs over to one side of the room*). Kari, come here!
KARI. What is it?
AASE (*on the other side of the room*). Come here –!
    Where is –? Where can I find –? Answer me! Where is
        the –?
    What am I looking for? I'm losing my wits.
    Where's the key to the chest?
KARI. In the keyhole.
AASE. What's that rumbling?
KARI. The last wagon-load going off to Heggstad.
AASE (*weeps*). I wish it was me they were taking away
    In a black box. Oh, the things a mortal
    Has to endure! God in His mercy help me!
    The whole house stripped!
    What the girl's father left, the bailiff has taken.
    They didn't spare the clothes on my back.
    Fie! The Devil rot them for being so hard!
    Sits on the edge of the bed.
    The land and the house are lost to our family.
    [The old man was harsh, but the law was harsher.]
    There was no help and no mercy.
    Peer was gone. I'd no one to save me.
KARI. At least you can stay in this room till you die.
AASE. Yes; my cat and I will be fed by the parish.
KARI. God pity you, mother. Your Peer's cost you dear.

AASE. Peer? You're out of your mind!
     Ingrid came safely home in the end.
     It's the Devil they ought to blame. He's the villain
     And no one else. He led my boy astray.
KARI. Don't you think I'd better send for the priest?
     [I'm fearing things may be worse than you know.]
AASE. The priest? Oh, yes, I almost think so.
     Starts up.
     But, oh God, no, I can't! I'm the lad's mother.
     I must help him. It's my duty
     To do what I can when the rest fail.
     They've left him this coat. I must patch it up.
     I wish I'd hidden the skin rug too.
     Where are his stockings?
KARI. There, with the other rubbish.
AASE (*roots around*). What's this?
     Oh, Kari, look! It's an old casting-ladle!
     With this he played at being a button-moulder;
     Melted and shaped and stamped.
     One day at a feast, the little lad came
     And asked his father for a lump of tin.
     'Tin!', said John. 'No! [Good King Christian's coin!]
     Silver! Let people know you're John Gynt's son!'
     God forgive the poor man, he was drunk,
     And then he cared neither for tin nor gold.
     Here are the stockings. Oh dear, they're all holes.
     We must darn them, Kari.
KARI. I'm afraid so.
AASE. When it's done, I must get to bed.
     I feel weak and wretched and frail.
     (*Joyfully.*) Look, Kari! Two woollen shirts! They've missed
          them!
KARI. Yes, so they have.
AASE. What a piece of luck! You'd better hide one.
     No, wait. I think we'll take both.
     The one he's wearing is worn and thin.

KARL. God forgive you, Mother Aase! It's a sin!
AASE. And if it is? What's the priest for?

He'll pardon this sin, as he pardons others.

SCENE THREE

Outside a newly built cabin in the forest. A reindeer's antlers over the door. The snow is piled high around. It is twilight. PEER GYNT *is standing outside the door making fast a large wooden bolt.*

PEER (*laughing now and then*). I must have bolts!

Bolts against trolls, and against men and women.
[I must have bolts.]
Bolts to lock out all nagging hobgoblins.
They come with the darkness. They knock and they tap.
'Let us in, Peer Gynt! We're as swift as thoughts!
We scratch under the bed, we hiss in the ashes,
We breathe down the chimney like white-hot dragons!
He-he, Peer Gynt! Do you think nails and planks
Can shut out nagging hobgoblin thoughts?'

SOLVEIG *comes over the heath on skis. She has a shawl over her head and a bundle in her hand.*

SOLVEIG. God speed your work. Don't turn me away.

You sent for me, and so you must take me.

PEER. Solveig! It can't be –! Yes, but it is!

Aren't you afraid to come so near me?

SOLVEIG. You sent me a message by little Helga.

Others followed, in storm and in calm.
All that your mother said carried a message
That bred each morning as I awoke.
The lonely nights and the empty days
Bore me the message that now I must come.
It became as though life down there had been quenched
I couldn't laugh or cry from my heart.
I didn't know how you felt about me.
I only knew what I had to do.

PEER. But your father?

SOLVEIG.   In all God's earth
    I have no one to call father or mother.
    I have made myself free.
PEER. Solveig, my fairest – to come to me?
SOLVEIG. Yes, to you alone. You must be
    All to me. My friend and comforter.
    [*Weeps.*
    The worst was to leave my little sister.
    But even worse to be parted from Father.
    But worst of all, to leave her who bore me at her breast.
    No, God forgive me, the worst was the grief
    At being parted from all of them – all of them.]
PEER. You know the judgment read in the spring?
    I have lost my home and my inheritance.
SOLVEIG. Do you think I left my dearest ones
    For the sake of an inheritance?
PEER. – that anyone who meets me
    Outside the forest may freely seize me?
SOLVEIG. I ran here on my skis. I asked my way.
    They said: 'Where are you going?' I answered: 'Home.'
PEER. Then to hell with nails and planks!
    Now I need no lock against hobgoblin thoughts!
    If you dare come in to live with the hunter
    I know that a blessing will fall on this house.
    Solveig! Let me look at you! Not too close!
    I just want to look at you. You're so bright and pure.
    Let me lift you. You're so delicate and light.
    Let me carry you, Solveig. I'll never get tired!
    I shall never soil you. I'll stretch out my arms
    And hold you from me, my fair, my warm one!
    Oh, who would have thought I could draw you to me?
    Oh, but I've longed for you night and day.
    Here you see I've been hewing and building.
    I must pull it down. It is mean and ugly –
SOLVEIG. Mean or fine, it is what I want.
    Here one can breathe against the wind.
    Down there it was airless. I felt shut in.

[It was partly that that frightened me away.]
But here where I hear the fir tree whisper –
In stillness and song! Here I am at home!

PEER. Are you sure you want this? For the rest of your life?

SOLVEIG. I have chosen my path. I shall never turn back.

PEER. Then I have you! Go in! Let me see you inside!
I'll bring pine logs to make you a fire.
It will shine brightly and make you warm.
You shall sit softly and never be cold.

He opens the door. SOLVEIG *goes in. He stands still for a moment,
then laughs aloud with joy and jumps in the air.*

PEER. My princess! Now at last I've found and won her!
Hey! Now I'll build my palace on firm, true ground!

He seizes the axe and walks away. As he does so, an OLD-LOOKING
WOMAN *dressed in green rags comes out of the trees. An* UGLY
CHILD *with an ale-flagon in its hand limps after her, clutching her
by the skirt.*

WOMAN. Good evening, Peer Lightfoot!

PEER. What? Who are you?

WOMAN. Old friends, Peer Gynt.
My cottage lies near by. We're neighbours.

PEER. Oh? That's news to me.

WOMAN. As you built your house, mine rose beside it.

PEER (*turns*). I'm in a hurry –

WOMAN. You always were, lad.
But I'll trudge behind, and one day I'll catch you.

PEER. You've made a mistake, grannie.

WOMAN. I did before.
I did when you made such promises to me.

PEER. *I* promised –? What damned nonsense is this?

WOMAN. Have you forgotten the night you drank
With my father? Have you forgotten –?

PEER. [I've only forgotten what I never knew.]
What are you talking about? When did we meet?

WOMAN. We last met when we first met.
To the CHILD.
Give your father a drink. I dare say he's thirsty.

PEER. Father –? Are you drunk? Are you suggesting that he –?
WOMAN. Can't you tell the pig by its skin?

Where are your eyes? Can't you see he's crippled
The way you're crippled, in your soul?

PEER. Are you trying to make me believe –?
WOMAN. Are you trying to deny it?
PEER. That long-legged brat –?
WOMAN. Yes, he's shot up quickly.
PEER. You damned troll-snout, do you dare to accuse me –?
WOMAN. Wait a minute, Peer Gynt! I want none of your insults.

Weeps.

Can I help it if I'm not beautiful
As I was when you seduced me on the hillside?
Last fall, when I bore him, the Fiend gripped my back,
So it's not surprising I've become ugly.
But if you want to see me as fair as before
Just take that girl and show her the door.
Turn her out of your mind and out of your heart –
Do that, my dear, and I'll lose my snout.

PEER. Get away, you witch!
WOMAN. Yes, see if I do!
PEER. I'll split your skull –!
WOMAN. Try if you dare! Oh no, Peer Gynt.

I'm not frightened of blows. I'll come back every day.
I'll pull the door open and peer at you both.
When you're snuggling up to your girl on the hearth,
When you kiss her, Peer Gynt, when you'd pet her and play
with her,
I'll sit down beside you and demand my share.
She and I will take you by turns.
Goodbye, my love. You can marry tomorrow.

PEER. You hell-born nightmare –!
WOMAN. Oh, I nearly forgot.

You must raise the brat, you lecherous devil.
Come on, baby devil, go to your father.

CHILD (*spits at him*). [You keep away from me!]

I'll hit you with my axe! Just you wait! Just you wait!

WOMAN (*kisses the* CHILD). [You've a wise head on those little
     shoulders.]
     You'll be the spit of your father when you grow up.
PEER (*stamps his foot*). Would God you were as far –!
WOMAN. As we are near?
PEER (*clenches his fists*). And all this –!
WOMAN. For nothing but *thinking*?
     It's bad luck on you, isn't it? Poor Peer!
PEER. It's worse for another.
     O Solveig, my taintless, my purest gold!
WOMAN. Ah, well. It's the innocent who have to suffer;
     As the Devil said when his mother hit him
     Because his father was drunk.
She trudges off into the wood with the CHILD, *who throws the
ale-flagon at* PEER.
PEER (*after a long silence*). Go round, said the Boyg. So I must
     here.
     There falls my palace in ruins about me.
     It has walled her round when I stood so near.
     Everything here is suddenly ugly.
     My joy has turned old. Go round, my lad.
     There's no way straight through to her.
     Straight? Hm, but there *should* be one.
     [There's a text, if I remember aright –]
     'If a man repent –'. How does it go?
     I've forgotten, and there's no one here to guide me.
     [Repent? It might take years to fight my way through.
     That would be a poor life;
     To smash what is pure, precious and beautiful,
     And piece it together from broken fragments.
     You can do that with a fiddle, but not with a bell.
     Where the grass would grow green, one mustn't tread.
     But anyway, the witch was lying.]
     They have gone. Gone, yes; but I can't forget them.
     Tiptoeing thoughts will follow me in.
     Ingrid! And those three that danced on the mountain!
     Will they join me too? With cruel laughter

Demanding like her to be clasped in my arms?
To be gently lifted and lovingly laid
At arm's length? Go round, lad.
If my arm were as long as a pine tree's trunk
I fear even then I'd hold her too near
To set her down white and unstained as before.
I must find some way round, so that if I gain nothing
At least I shan't lose. One must try to forget.
Goes a few steps towards the hut, but stops again.
To go in after this? So ugly and soiled?
To take in all those black trolls with me?
To speak, yet be silent? Confess, yet conceal –?
Throws away his axe.
[It's a Sabbath evening.]
To keep tryst as I am would be sacrilege.
SOLVEIG (*in the doorway*). Are you coming?
PEER (*half to himself*). Round!
SOLVEIG. What did you say?
PEER. You must wait.
   It's dark, and I've something heavy to carry.
SOLVEIG. Wait. I'll help you. We'll share the burden.
PEER. No. Stay where you are. I must bear it alone.
SOLVEIG. Don't go too far, Peer.
PEER. Be patient.
   I may be long, but wait for me. Wait for me!
SOLVEIG (*nods after him*). Yes, I'll wait.
PEER *goes away down the forest path.* SOLVEIG *remains standing in the open half-door.*

SCENE FOUR

AASE's *room. Evening. A log-fire is burning in the open hearth, and gives light to the room. The cat sits on a chair at the foot of the bed.* AASE *is lying in the bed, her hands moving restlessly on the coverlet.*
AASE. Oh, God! Won't he come? He's so long!

I've no one to send and so much to say.
There's no time to lose. It's so quick!
Who'd have thought –? Oh, if only I knew
I'd not been too strict with the lad –!

PEER (*enters*). Hullo!

AASE. Oh, God bless you! You've come at last, my son.
But how dare you come down here?
Don't you know they're after your life?

PEER. My life can look after itself. I had to come to you.

AASE. Well, Kari was wrong. Now I can go in peace.

PEER. Go? Now what are you saying?
Where do you think you're going?

AASE. Oh, Peer, I'm near the end. I haven't much time left.

PEER (*squirms and walks up the room*). Oh, God! [I can't escape
sorrow anywhere!]
I thought I'd be free from it here –! Are your feet and hands
cold?

AASE. Yes, Peer. It'll soon be over. When you see
My eyes glaze, you must close them carefully.
And then you must see to the coffin. Now, my dear,
Be sure it's a fine one. Oh no, I'd forgotten –

PEER. Be quiet. There's time enough to think of that.

AASE. Yes, yes. (*Looks restlessly round the room.*)
This is all they left me. Just like them.

PEER (*writhes*). Again! (*In a hard voice.*)
I know it's my fault. Why remind me of that?

AASE. You? No, it's that damned liquor. [That's the cause
Of all the trouble.] My darling boy, you were drunk.
Then a man doesn't know what he's doing. Besides,
You'd been riding the stag. It's no wonder your head was
turned.

PEER. [Yes, well, never mind that.]
Let's forget all that. Let's not be unhappy now.
Sits on the edge of the bed.
Now, mother, let's chat together,
But only of little things.
Let's forget what's ugly and crooked,

And all that's painful and sore.

Look! The old cat! So he's still alive!

AASE. He howls so at night. You know what that means.

PEER (*changes the subject*). What's the news around here?

AASE (*smiles*). They say there's a girl who keeps her eyes

    Turned to the mountains –

PEER (*quickly*). Mads Moen, is he happy?

AASE. [They say she won't listen to her parents' tears.]

    You ought to see them, Peer. [You might be able to help –]

PEER. Aslak the smith, what's happened to him?

AASE. Don't mention that rascal to me!

    I'd rather tell you *her* name –

PEER. [No, mother, let's chat together,

    But only of little things.

    We'll forget what's ugly and crooked.

    And all that's painful and sore.]

    Are you thirsty? Can I fetch you a drink?

    Can't you stretch your legs? This bed is short.

    Let me see! Why, isn't this the bed

    I slept in when I was a child?

    Do you remember how often of an evening

    You sat by my bedside and spread the fur rug over me

    And sang me songs?

AASE. Yes, do you remember? When your father

    Was away on a journey, we'd play sledges.

    The rug was a sledge and the floor was an icebound fjord.

PEER. Yes, but the best of all – oh, mother,

    Do you remember that too? – was the white horses!

AASE. [Of course I do!] Do you think I've forgotten that?

    We'd borrow Kari's cat and sit it down on a chair –

PEER. To the castle west of the moon

    And the castle east of the sun,

    To Soria-Moria Castle

    The road ran high and low!

    We found a stick in a closet

    And you used that as a whip –

AASE. I sat up here on the box-seat –
PEER. Yes, yes! You threw loose the reins
    And kept turning round as we rode
    To ask me if I was cold.
    God bless you, ugly old mother!
    You were always a loving soul!
    Why are you crying?
AASE. It's my back. The hard board hurts it.
PEER. Stretch out, now. Let me settle you.
    There, now you're lying softly.
AASE (*restlessly*). No, Peer. I want to go.
PEER. Go?
AASE. Yes, go. It's all I want.
PEER. What nonsense! Spread the rug over you.
    Let me sit on the edge of the bed.
    There! Now we'll shorten the evening with song.
AASE. No, get the prayer-book from the closet.
    My soul's restless.
PEER. In Soria-Moria Castle[7]
    The great King's giving a feast.
    Rest there on the sledge-cushion, mother.
    I'll drive you over the moor –
AASE. But Peer, have I been invited?
PEER. Yes, we both have been.
Throws a string round the chair on which the cat is sitting, takes a
stick in his hand and sits on the foot of the bed.
    Gee-up! Will you stir yourself, Grane![8]
    Now, mother, you're sure you're not cold?
    Oh, yes! You can feel you're speeding
    Once Grane begins to go!
AASE. Peer dear, what's that ringing?
PEER. It's the silver sleigh-bells, mother!
AASE. Oh dear, what's that hollow rumbling?
PEER. We're driving over a fjord.
AASE. I'm frightened! What's that wild sighing?
PEER. It's the pine trees, mother, whispering on the moor.
    Sit still, now –

AASE. There's something winking and sparkling in the distance.
    Where's that light coming from?
PEER. From the windows and doors of the Castle.
    Can you hear? They're dancing.
AASE. Yes.
PEER. St Peter's standing outside. He's asking you to step in.
AASE. Is he speaking to us?
PEER. Yes, and he's taking his hat off. He's offering his sweetest
    wine.
AASE. Wine? Are there cakes too?
PEER. Oh, yes! A tasty plateful!
    And the Bishop's wife is offering coffee and sweets.
AASE. Oh, Lord! Am I going to meet her?
PEER. As often as you wish, and as equals.
AASE. Oh Peer, what a spree you're taking my poor old bones on!
PEER (*cracks his whip*). Hey! Hup! Come on, rouse yourself,
    Grane!
AASE. Peer dear, are you driving carefully?
PEER (*cracks his whip again*). The road's broad here.
AASE. Don't drive so fast. I feel so old and tired.
PEER. I can see the Castle towering ahead of us.
    Our journey will soon be done.
AASE. I'll lie back and close my eyes,
    And trust in you, my son.
PEER. Gee-up now, Grane, my beauty!
    By God, the excitement is great!
    They've spotted Peer Gynt and his mother,
    And they're fighting to get to the gate!
    What's that you're saying, St Peter?
    You won't let her in? My good sir,
    You can sit on your backside till Doomsday
    And you'll find no one better than her.
    [I'm not going to boast of my virtues.
    I can turn and go back where I came.
    If you want me, I'll come in and thank you.
    If not, many thanks just the same.
    Sure, I've told as many lies as the Devil in any pulpit,

And sworn at my mother and called her a bloody old hen
Because she was always crowing and cackling at me.
But] You see she's received with respect, mind.
You make her feel really at home!
She's the best soul you'll get from this parish.
If you don't like her, go back to Rome!
Ho-ho! Here comes God the Father!
Now, St Peter, we'll soon see who's who.
In a deep voice.
None of your bloody butler's airs, now.
Just let Mother Aase come through.
Laughs aloud and turns to his mother.
There, isn't it just as I told you?
That's made the old so-and-so run!
Frightened.
Why are you so silent, mother?
Speak to me! It's Peer, your son!
Goes to the bed-head.
Don't lie there and stare at me, mother!
Don't open your eyes so wide!
*Feels her forehead and hands carefully. Then he throws the string
on to the chair and says softly.*
I see. You can rest now, Grane.
We've come to the end of our ride.
Thank you for all your days.
For your beatings and kisses, my dear.
But now you must thank me too.
Presses his cheek against her mouth.
So; the driver has had his fare.

KARI (*enters*). Peer! Are you here? Then the worst of our troubles
        are over.

Dear God, how soundly she's sleeping! Or – is she –?
PEER. Hush. She is dead.
KARI *weeps over the body.* PEER *walks round the room for a while.
At length he stops by the bed.*
PEER. See my mother is buried with honour.
        I must get away from here.

KARI. Where are you going?

PEER. Seawards.

KARI. So far?

PEER. And far beyond.

    He goes.

Act Four

SCENE ONE

On the southwest coast of Morocco. A palm grove. A table laid for dinner, with a sun awning and rush mats. Hammocks have been hung farther back in the grove. Offshore lies a steam yacht flying the Norwegian and American flags. On the beach is a dinghy. It is towards sundown.

PEER GYNT, a handsome middle-aged gentleman in elegant travelling clothes, with a gold lorgnette hanging from his waistcoat, is presiding as host at the dinner-table. MR COTTON, M. BALLON, HERR VON EBERKOPF *and* HERR TRUMPETERSTRAALE[9] *are finishing their meal.*

PEER. Drink, gentlemen! Man was made for pleasure.
      What's done is done; what's past is past concern.
      [What can I offer you?]

TRUMPETERSTRAALE. You're a superb host, Peer.

PEER. You must allow some credit to my wealth,
      My steward and my cook.

COTTON. Here's to the four of you!

BALLON. Monsieur, you have a *goût*, a *ton*,
      Such as one seldom finds today
      Among men living *en garçon*.
      A certain – *qu'est-ce qu'on dit* –?

VON EBERKOPF.[10]   A measure
      Of spiritual contemplation,
      [A marvellous lack of chauvinism,
      A vision that can pierce the fog
      Of prejudice,] the ability
      To grasp Truth in its higher aspects –
      [Added to which] an *Ur-Natur,*
      [An unspoilt nature, all this crowned]
      With a fine wealth of worldly knowledge –
      Mein herr, was that not what you meant?

BALLON. *C'est bien possible.* [It doesn't sound
  Quite so *magnifique* in French.]
VON EBERKOPF. [*Ei was!* Your language is so stiff.] But if
  We wish to find the cause of the phenomenon –
PEER. It's easy. I've never married.
  [Why, gentlemen, it is as clear as daylight.]
  What should a man be? Himself. [That's all.]
  He must live for himself and himself alone.
  How can he if he spends his life
  [Playing the pack-camel to a wife and children.]
  Carrying the woes of others?
VON EBERKOPF. But to achieve this independence
  You must have had to pay a price –
PEER. Oh, yes. Indeed – when I was young.
  [But I always emerged an honourable victor.]
  Once I was very nearly trapped.
  I was a gay and good-looking boy
  And the lady to whom I lost my heart
  Was of royal birth –
BALLON. Royal?
PEER (*nonchalantly*). One of those ancient mountain families –
  You know –
TRUMPETERSTRAALE (*thumps the table*). Aristocrats!
PEER (*shrugs his shoulders*). Degenerate idiots, who count it their
      chief pride
  To keep plebeian stains from the family escutcheon.
COTTON. The romance fell through?
BALLON. Her family opposed the match?
PEER. On the contrary.
BALLON. Ah!
PEER (*forbearingly*). Well, there were circumstances,
  You understand, that made it desirable
  That we should marry with all decent speed.
  But frankly, I found the whole business
  From first to last somewhat unappetizing.
  In certain respects I'm a fastidious man.
  [And I always like to stand on my own feet.]

So when her father started dropping hints
That I should change my name and my profession
And take out a licence of nobility,
With other suggestions that were equally
Distasteful, not to say unacceptable,
[I bowed my thanks, rejected his ultimatum
And renounced my youthful bride.]
Drums with his fingers on the table and looks pious.
Yes, yes; there's a destiny that shapes our ends.
[We mortals can safely put our trust in it.]
It's a great comfort to know it.

BALLON. That was the end of the affair?

PEER. Oh, no. Far from it. [Various outsiders
Poked in their noses and created mischief.
Her brothers and cousins were the worst.]
I had to fight duels with seven of them.
[It was a time I shall never forget.]
But I survived with honour. [It cost me blood.
However, that same blood attests my worth.
And is a further proof that our lives are ruled
By that wise fate of which I spoke just now.]

VON EBERKOPF. You have an outlook upon life
Which entitles you to be called a Philosopher.
[Where ordinary mortals guess,
Seeing each detail separately,
For ever groping, you are able
Fully to integrate your vision.
Measuring life by an unchanging norm
You gather scattered inspirations
So that they radiate like beams
Of one supreme philosophy.]
And you've never been to University?

PEER. [As I've told you before,] I am a self-taught man.
[I've studied nothing methodically.]
But I've thought and [speculated and] read a little
About most things. I started late in life.
[And, you know, it becomes a trifle wearisome

To plough through page after page, trying to absorb
What's dull with what is lively.]
I've learned my history by fits and starts.
It was all I had time for.
And since one must have some spiritual security
[To put one's trust in when times are hard]
I read religion – intermittently.
[That way it's easier to digest.
One shouldn't read to gulp down everything.]
One must select [what one will be able to use.]

COTTON. Very practical.

PEER (*lights a cigar*). My dear friends,
Consider my own career. What was I
When I came to the West? A penniless lad.
I had to sweat to earn my bread.
Believe me, things were very hard.
But life, my friends, is sweet; and death is bitter.
Fortune smiled upon me, as you see.
[And old man Fate was tolerant.] I prospered.
[And, since my own philosophy was elastic,
Things went from good to better.] Within ten years
The Charleston ship-owners were calling me Croesus.
My fame spread from port to port. Luck sat in my sails –

COTTON. What did you carry?

PEER. Mostly Negro slaves to Carolina,
And heathen images to China.

BALLON. *Fi donc!*

TRUMPETERSTRAALE. My dear sir –!

PEER. You think it was a trifle unethical?
I felt the same myself – oh, very keenly.
I may even say I hated it.
But believe me, once you've begun, it's hard to stop.
And I didn't want to create unemployment.
[In so gigantic an enterprise as this
Which keeps whole thousands in employment,
It's very hard to call things to a halt
For good. 'For good.' I can't abide those words.

On the other hand, I must confess
I've always had the healthiest respect
For what men call the consequences.
And the prospect of overstepping the mark
Has always induced a certain timidity in me.]
Well, I was beginning to grow old;
[Approaching fifty. My hair was turning grey.]
And though my health was excellent, one thought haunted
    me:
'Who knows how soon the hour of judgement will strike?
[And the great judgement separate sheep from goats.]'
What could I do?
To stop the China trade was impossible.
But I found a solution. [I quickly opened
Another trade with the same country.]
Each spring I sent them idols, and each autumn
Exported missionaries, generously equipped
With woollen stockings, Bibles, rice and rum –

COTTON. At a profit, I presume?

PEER. Of course. [This enterprise
    Also prospered. They worked indefatigably.]
    For every idol that I sold
    They got a coolie honestly baptized.
    Thus the effect was neutralized.
    [The field of holy work never lay fallow,
    The idols being countered by the missionaries.]

COTTON. But what about your African cargoes?

PEER. There too my sense of morality triumphed.
    [I realized it was a foolish traffic
    For one advanced in years. One never knows
    When the summons to judgement may come.
    Besides, there were the patrol boats
    Not to mention the philanthropists
    And the risks of wind and weather.
    All these considerations won the day.]
    'Peter,' I said, 'it's time to reef your sails.
    You must right your wrongs.'

I purchased a plot of land in the South,
And kept the last cargo [which happened
To be of the primest quality,] for myself.
They flourished, and grew [sleek and] fat,
Giving the highest satisfaction
Both to themselves and me. Indeed,
I think I can say without boasting, I was
A father to them. And reaped my just reward.
[I built schools, and kept the strictest watch
To ensure the maintenance of morality].
And now I have withdrawn from the whole concern.
I've sold the plantation, with all its stock
Of hide and hair. [The day I left
I gave to every man, woman and child
Grog, *ad lib* and *gratis*; so that they all got drunk,
And every widow had an ounce of snuff.]
So surely, [if] the old saying holds true:
'Who doeth not evil worketh good'
[The follies of my past are now forgotten,
And, more than most men, I can safely claim
That my good deeds are weightier than my sins].

VON EBERKOPF (*clinks glasses with him*). It is wonderful to meet
    a man
Who lives according to his principles.
[Uninhibited by foggy theories,
Immutable in the face of outward chaos.]

PEER (*who during the preceding dialogue has been helping himself
steadily from the various bottles*).
[We Northern warriors know how to carry a battle
Through to its harsh conclusion.] The key to life
Is simply this. Close your ear against
The infiltration of a dangerous serpent.

COTTON. What serpent, my good friend?

PEER. A little one that is most seductive.
The one that tempts you to commit yourself.
Drinks again.
The art of success is to stand free

And uncommitted amid the snares of life.
To know that the day of battle is not the day
Of judgement. There are other days to come.
To know that a bridge always remains open
Behind you. That theory has shaped my whole career.
[This theory is a national inheritance.
I entered into it in my parents' home.

BALLON. You're Norwegian, aren't you?

PEER. By birth. But cosmopolitan by temperament.
For my success I'm indebted to America
For my book-learning to the new German schools.
From France I have acquired my waistcoat here,
My manners, and the little wit I own.
From England I have learned industriousness
And a quick eye for opportunity.
The Jew has taught me patience, and Italy
Gave me a taste for *dolce far niente*.
And once, in an awkward situation,
I lengthened the measure of my days
With the help of Swedish steel.

TRUMPETERSTRAALE (*raises his glass*). Ah! Swedish steel!]

VON EBERKOPF. Let us raise our glasses to the free man!
They clink glasses with him and drink. He begins to grow a little tipsy.

COTTON. All this is fine. Fine.
But tell me, sir, I'm curious to know
What you propose to do with all your money.

PEER. Hm! Do with it? Eh?

ALL FOUR (*edge closer*). Yes! Tell us!

PEER. Well, first of all
I want to travel. That's why I took you aboard
As travelling companions in Gibraltar.
I needed a chorus of friends to dance
Around the altar of my golden calf.

[VON EBERKOPF. Very witty.]

COTTON. But no one sails merely for pleasure.
You must have a goal. What is it?

PEER. To become Emperor.

ALL FOUR. What?

PEER (*nods*). Emperor.

ALL FOUR. Of what? Where?

PEER. Of the whole world.

BALLON. But how, my friend –?

PEER. By the power of gold. It's not a new idea.
    The thought of it has been with me all my journey.
    When I was a child, I rode in my dreams
    Far over the ocean on a cloud.
    I soared with a host of men behind me.
    [And a golden scabbard]. But I fell
    Flat on my face. But that remained my goal.
    Someone – I forget who it was – once said
    That if you gain the whole wide world
    But lose yourself, your victory
    Is but a wreath about a cloven brow.
    [Those were the words, or something similar.]
    It's the truth.

VON EBERKOPF. But who *is* your self?

PEER. The world behind my forehead's vaulted arch,
    By cause of which I am myself alone,
    [And no one else, any more than God is Satan].

TRUMPETERSTRAALE. Now I get it!

BALLON. Sublime *penseur*!

VON EBERKOPF. Most mighty poet!

PEER (*with increasing passion*). My self – it is the army
    Of wishes, appetites, desires,
    [The sea of whims, pretensions and demands,]
    All that swells here within my breast
    And by which I, myself, exist.
    But, as Our Lord has need of common clay
    To make Him omnipotent, so I need gold
    To make me Emperor.

BALLON. But you have gold.

PEER. Not enough. [Yes, perhaps for a nine days' wonder;
    As Emperor *à la* Lippe-Detmold.[11]

But I must be myself entirely;
Every inch a Gyntish inch,
From top to toe, Sir Peter Gynt.

BALLON (*carried away*). Possess the loveliest woman on earth!

VON EBERKOPF. Your *Reich* last for a thousand years![12]

TRUMPETERSTRAALE. Stand in history with Charlemagne![13]

COTTON. Aye. But first may you find a profitable opening –

PEER. I have found it. Thanks to our anchoring here!]
    This evening we sail northward. [The newspapers
    I received on board brought tidings of importance.]
    Gets up and raises his glass.
    Dame Fortune ceaselessly assists the brave.

ALL FOUR. What? Tell us!

PEER. Greece is in revolt!

ALL FOUR (*jump up*). What? The Greeks!

PEER. They have risen against their masters.

ALL FOUR. Hurrah!

PEER. And the Turkish army is in confusion.
    Empties his glass.

BALLON. To Hellas! The gate of glory is thrown wide!
    [I'll help them with my Gallic rapier!

VON EBERKOPF. And I with fearful war-cries – from a distance.

COTTON. I, too, with arms. On pre-payment, of course.

TRUMPETERSTRAALE. Lead on! I'll find in Bender to assist
    them
    The famous buckles of King Charles's spurs!]][14]

BALLON (*falls on* PEER GYNT's *neck*). Forgive me, *mon ami*,
    that I misjudged you!

VON EBERKOPF (*presses his hand*). Stupid dog that I am, I took
    you for a scoundrel.

COTTON. Not as bad as that. A fool, perhaps –

TRUMPETERSTRAALE (*tries to kiss him*). [I took you, Uncle, for
    an example
    Of the worst kind of rotten Yankee brood.]
    Forgive me –

VON EBERKOPF. [We have all been groping in the dark.]

PEER. What's all this?

VON EBERKOPF. [Now we see the whole Gyntish host
    Of wishes, passions and desires
    Most gloriously assembled –]
BALLON (*admiringly*). So *this* is being Monsieur Gynt!
VON EBERKOPF (*similarly*). This is to be Peer Gynt with honour!
PEER. But please tell me –?
BALLON. You don't understand?
PEER. No, I'll be hanged if I do.
BALLON. What! But surely you are on your way
    To help the Greeks with ships and money?
PEER (*snorts*). No, thank you! I side with strength.
    I am lending money to the Turk.
BALLON. Impossible!
VON EBERKOPF. Very witty. You're joking.
PEER (*is silent for a moment, then leans against a chair and assumes
    a lofty mien*). Gentlemen, it is best we part [before
    The last shreds of friendship flicker away like smoke].
    The empty-fisted are always rash to gamble.
    [The man who scarcely owns the strip of earth
    His shadow covers, is natural cannon fodder.]
    But when a man is as rich as I am,
    He has much to lose.
    Go to Hellas. I will arm you *gratis*,
    And set you safe ashore. The more you fan
    The flames of patriotism, the more I have
    To gain. Stand up for freedom! Fight for justice!
    [Charge! Storm onwards! Stoke up hell for the Turk!]
    And gloriously end your days
    Upon the lances of the Janissaries!
    But please excuse me. (*Slaps his pocket.*) I have gold,
    And am myself, Sir Peter Gynt.
*Opens his sunshade and goes into the grove, where the hammocks
can be glimpsed.*
TRUMPETERSTRAALE. The darned swine!
BALLON. No sense of honour!
COTTON. To hell with honour!
    Think of the profit if the Greeks should win!

BALLON. [I saw myself wreathed with the victor's garland,
 Surrounded by beautiful Grecian maidens.

TRUMPETERSTRAALE. I saw the spurs of Charles the Twelfth
 Resting where they belong, in Swedish hands.

VON EBERKOPF. I saw my fatherland's prodigious Kultur
 Spreading itself over land and sea.

COTTON. It's the material loss that bothers me.
 Goddamit! I could weep real tears.
 I saw myself as the master of Olympus,
 And if that mountain's reputation is correct
 There are copper mines to be found there
 Which I could open up and work afresh.
 And that river Kastale they talk so much about –
 All those waterfalls must at the lowest calculation
 Be worth over a thousand horse-power –]

TRUMPETERSTRAALE. I shall go, nevertheless. [My Swedish
    sword
 Is worth twice as much as Yankee gold.

COTTON. Possibly. But if we merely join the ranks
 We'll be swallowed up with the rest. And where will our
    profit be then?

BALLON. *Mon Dieu!* To climb so near success –*!*
 And then to find oneself standing by its grave!]

COTTON (*shakes his fist towards the yacht*). And that black coffin
    holds all the gold
 That blasted Nabob sweated from his niggers.

VON EBERKOPF. An inspiration! What are we waiting for?
 His empire lies within our grasp. Hurrah!

BALLON. What are you going to do?

VON EBERKOPF. Perform a *coup!* We have only to bribe the
    crew,
 [Which won't be difficult] and the yacht is ours.
 Aboard!

COTTON. You mean *you* –?

VON EBERKOPF. I bag the whole caboodle. (*Goes down to the
 dinghy.*)

COTTON. I can't neglect my own interests.

     I'd better do the same.

TRUMPETERSTRAALE. The scoundrels!

BALLON. A bad business. *Mais enfin* – (*Follows the others.*)

TRUMPETERSTRAALE. I suppose I shall have to join them.

     But under protest![15] (*Follows.*)

SCENE TWO

Another part of the coast. Moonlight and drifting clouds. The yacht, a long way offshore, is under full steam. PEER GYNT *is running along the shore, now pinching his arm, now staring out to sea.*

PEER. I'm dreaming! It's a nightmare! I'll wake up soon.

     She's sailing away! And at full steam!

     It's a hallucination! I'm asleep! I'm drunk! I'm mad!

     Clenches his fists.

     I can't be going to die!

     Tears his hair.

     It's a dream. I insist it's a dream.

     Oh, this is dreadful! It's only too real! What monsters!

     Hear me, O Lord! You're so wise and so just! Judge!

     Stretches up his arms.

     It's me, Peter Gynt! Oh God, do pay attention!

     Protect me, Father, or I must perish!

     Make them turn the ship! Make them lower the sails!

     Stop the thieves! Make something go wrong!

     Oh, listen to me! Never mind other people.

     The world can take care of itself for a while.

     No, he's not listening. He's deaf as usual.

     That's charming! A God who won't help when you need him.

     Waves upwards.

     Psst! I've given up that nigger plantation!

     I've sent missionaries all the way to China.

     Surely one good turn is worth another!

     Oh, please help me to get on board—!

A jet of flame shoots into the air from the yacht, and thick smoke belches forth. A hollow explosion is heard. PEER GYNT *utters a shriek and sinks down on to the sand. Gradually the smoke dissipates. The ship has vanished.*

PEER (*pale and quiet*). The sword of vengeance!
    Gone to the bottom with every soul on board!
    Oh, what luck, what—!
    Moved.
    Luck? No, it was more than that.
    I was fated to be saved, and they to die.
    O all thanks and praise to Thee for preserving me
    In spite of all my sins!
    Emits a deep breath.
    What a wonderful feeling of peace and safety it gives
    To know that one is under special protection!
    But the desert! What about food and drink?
    Oh, I'll find something. He'll see to that.
    There's no need to be afraid.
    Loudly and ingratiatingly.
    He won't want a poor little sparrow like me
    To perish. Just be humble. And give Him time.
    Trust in the Lord and keep your courage up.
    Gives a frightened jump.
    Was that a lion growling in the reeds?
    His teeth chatter.
    No, it wasn't a lion.
    Plucks up his courage.
    [Well, what's a lion?
    Those beasts know it's best to keep out of the way
    And not try to mix things with their betters.
    Their instinct tells them not to play with elephants.]
    Still, I'd better find a tree. There's a grove
    Of palms and acacias over there.
    If I get up in them I'll be safe and cool.
    If only I knew a psalm or two!
    Climbs up into a tree.
    ['Morning is morning and night is night.'
    That's a text that has often been weighed and sifted.

Seats himself more comfortably.
How splendid to feel so spiritually uplifted.
Noble thoughts are more than silk and pearls.]
Just trust in him. [He knows how much
Of the chalice of suffering I have strength to drink.]
He keeps a fatherly eye on me.
Throws a glance out to sea and whispers with a sigh.
But he certainly isn't economical!

SCENE THREE

Night. A Moroccan encampment on the edge of the desert. Watch fires. WARRIORS *resting.*

A SLAVE (*enters, tearing his hair*). The Emperor's white charger
        is missing!

A SECOND SLAVE (*enters rending his clothes*). The Emperor's
        sacred robes have been stolen!

AN OVERSEER (*enters*). A hundred lashes of the bastinado
        For every man who fails to catch the thief!

        THE WARRIORS *mount their horses and gallop off in all
        directions.*

SCENE FOUR

Dawn. The grove of palms and acacias. PEER GYNT, *up in his tree
with a broken branch in his hand, is trying to ward off a swarm of
monkeys.*

PEER. Damnation! A most unpleasant night!
        Beasts around.
        Monkeys!
        You again! This is the bloody limit.
        Now they're throwing fruit. No, it isn't fruit.
        Filthy beasts! [How does the saying go?
        'Thou shalt keep watch and fight.' Well, I'm damned if I can.
        My eyes feel like lead.]
        They disturb him again. He says impatiently.

I must put a stop to this. I must try to catch
One of the brats and [hang him and] skin him
And dress myself up in his hairy coat,
So the others will think I'm one of them.
What are we mortals? Just motes of dust.
We've got to adapt ourselves a little.
Another crowd of them. Milling and swarming!
Be off with you! Shoo! They're acting like lunatics.
If only I had a false tail now,
Or something that made me a bit like an animal.
What now? Something's rustling over my head—
Glances up.
    It's the grandfather, with his fists full of filth—
*Huddles nervously and keeps still for a moment. The monkey makes
a movement.* PEER *begins coaxing him and talking to him gently as
though to a dog.*
    Hullo, old boy, is that you up there?
You're clever, aren't you? [You know what's what.]
You're not going to throw – no, of course you're not.
It's me. Pip-pip! We're good friends, aren't we?
Gives a couple of squeaks.
Do you hear, I can talk your language!
We're relatives. Tomorrow morning
I'll give you some sugar –! You filthy brute!
The whole lot down on my head! Ugh! Disgusting!
Or perhaps it was food. (*Tastes.*) I'm not sure.
But taste is a question of what you are used to.
[Who was it that said: 'One must spit and trust
In the power of habit'?] Oh, here come the young ones!
Beats around.
This is really too much, that Man, Lord of Creation,
Should be compelled to – ! No, stop it! Curse!
The old one was bad, but the young ones are worse!

SCENE FIVE

Early morning. A stony landscape, with a view over the desert. On one side a cleft in the mountain and a cave. A THIEF *and a* RECEIVER *are in the cleft with the Emperor's horse and cloak. The horse, richly caparisoned, is tied to a stone. Horsemen can be heard in the distance.*

THIEF. The tongues of the lances
    Are licking and playing.
    See! See!

RECEIVER. I can see my head
    Roll in the sand!
    Woe! Woe!

THIEF (*crosses his arms over his breast*). My father was a thief
    So his son must steal.

RECEIVER. My father was a receiver,
    So I must receive.

THIEF. Thou must bear thy lot.
    Thou must be thyself.

RECEIVER (*listens*). Footsteps [among the stones]!
    We must fly. But whither?

THIEF. The cave is deep
    And the Prophet is great.

They flee, leaving their loot behind them. The sound of horsemen dies away in the distance.

PEER (*enters, cutting a reed pipe*). What a beautiful morning!
    The dung-beetle's rolling his ball in the sand.
    The snail is creeping out of his house.
    Morning! Oh yes, it has gold in its mouth.
    Daylight has a wonderful power.
    One feels so safe, one's courage rises.
    I could fight a bull!
    Such silence everywhere! [Yes, these rustic pleasures!
    How extraordinary that I ever came to reject them.
    That man should choose to shut himself up in a city
    And be pestered by crowds on his doorstep.]

The lizard darts around, snapping and thinking of nothing.
What innocence in the life of beasts!
Each is himself, obeying his Maker's purpose;
[Preserving unspoiled his characteristic essence,
And being himself, whether playing or fighting,
As on the day when God first commanded. 'Be!']
Fixes his lorgnette on his nose.
A toad. In the middle of a [sandstone] rock.
[Stone all around him. Only his head is visible.]
There he sits, staring at life as through a window;
Being himself, and to Hell with the rest of the world!
To Hell with – ? Who said that?
[I expect I read it when I was a boy,
In some so-called great book.] Was it the Prayer Book?
[Or Solomon? Bad.] Every year my memory gets worse.
Sits down in the shade.
[Here's a cool place to rest and stretch my feet.
What's this? Ferns? Edible roots.
Tastes them.
They're probably all right for animals.
But it is written: 'Subdue thy nature,'
And also: 'He that is proud shall be brought low,
And he that abaseth himself shall be exalted.'
Uneasily.
Exalted? Yes, that'll happen to me.
I can't see any other solution.
Providence will help me to escape from this country
And arrange for me to continue on my way.
This is merely a trial. Salvation will follow,
Provided only the good Lord grants me strength.
*Puts these thoughts aside.] Lights a cigar, stretches himself and
gazes out over the desert.*
What a vast and limitless waste!
Far away over there an ostrich is strutting.
What is one to believe was God's intention
In creating all this emptiness and death?
[This desert, devoid of all sources of life,

Burnt and yielding profit to no man.
This fragment of the world, for ever fallow.
This corpse that, never since the earth was born,
Has given its Creator as much as thanks.
Why was it made?] Nature is unpractical.
Is that the sea shining over there in the east?
Glittering – ? No, it can't be. It's a mirage.
The sea's in the west behind me,
Dammed from the desert by a range of hills.
A thought strikes him.
Dammed? I wonder – ? Those hills are narrow.
Dammed? A little dynamite, a canal,
And the waters would rush like a life-giving river
In through the gap and fill the desert.
Soon this whole white-hot grave would lie
Fresh as a dimpled sea.
The oases would rise out of it like islands.
[Atlas grow green like our mountains in the north.]
The schooners, like migrating birds,
Would cut their way southwards on the caravan routes.
[The air of life will scatter these stuffy vapours,
And dew drop from the clouds.] Towns will arise,
And grass will grow around the swaying palms.
[The land to the south behind the Sahara's wall
Will become the coastland of a vital culture.
Steam will drive factories in Timbuctoo,
Bornu will speedily be colonized,
And scientists ride in their *wagons-lit*
Through Abyssinia to the Upper Nile.]
And in the midst of my sea, on a rich oasis,
I shall personally propagate the Norwegian race.
[The blood of our Northern valleys is – well, nearly royal,
And a little Arab mixture will do the rest.
Around a bay on rising sand
I'll found my capital, Peeropolis.]
The world's degenerate. Now comes the turn
Of Gyntiana,[16] my new land!

Jumps to his feet.
A little money and I could do it!
A golden key to the gate of the sea!
A crusade against Death! That mean old skinflint
Shall open the sack he lies brooding on!
[In every land the cry goes up for freedom.
Like the ass in the Ark I'll send my clarion call
Across the world, and bring the baptism of liberty
To the beautiful prisoned coasts that shall be born!]
I must do it! I must find capital!
My kingdom – well, half my kingdom for a horse!
The horse neighs in the cave.
A horse! And robes! And jewels! And a sword!
Goes closer.
It can't be. [Yes, it is. But – ? I have read
Somewhere, that human will can move mountains.
But a horse too – !] Well, it's a fact, here stands the horse.
[*Ab esse ad posse,* etcetera, etcetera.]
Puts on the cloak and looks himself up and down.
Sir Peter. A Turk from top to toe!
No, one never knows what fate will bring?
Gee-up now, Grane, my trusty steed!
Mounts into the saddle.
Golden stirrups! But of course!
You can tell a great man by the cut of his horse!
Gallops away into the desert.

SCENE SIX

The tent of an Arab chieftain, alone in an oasis. PEER GYNT, *in
Oriental costume, is reclining on cushions, drinking coffee and smoking
a long pipe.* ANITRA *and a group of girls are dancing and singing
for him.*

CHORUS OF GIRLS. The Prophet is come!
    The Prophet, the Master, [the Omniscient].
    To us is he come,

[Riding across the ocean of the sand.
The Prophet, the Master, the Infallible,
To us, to us is he come,]
Through the sand-ocean sailing.
[Let flute and drum hail him;]
The Prophet, the Prophet is come.

ANITRA. [His charger is white as the milk
That flows in the river of Paradise.]
Bend the knee! Bow the head!
His eyes are stars, shining and mild.
[But no earthborn child can endure
The brilliance of their light.]
Through the desert he came.
[Gold and pearls sprang forth on his breast.]
Where he rode, there was light.
Behind him all grew dark.
[Behind him drought and sandstorm reigned.]
He came, the Glorious One,
[Through the desert he came]
Dressed like a mortal.
[Kaba,[17]] Kaba stands empty.
He himself hath proclaimed it.

CHORUS OF GIRLS. [Let flute and drum hail him.]
The Prophet, the Prophet is come.
The GIRLS *dance to soft music.*

PEER. [I have read in print, and it's perfectly true:
'No man is a prophet in his own country.']
This is the life for me! [It's much better
Than the one over there among the Charleston shippers.
There was something hollow about all that,
Something foreign to me, something fishy behind it.]
I never felt at home among those shippers.
I never felt I was one of them.
Why did I ever get on to that wagon
To root around in the garbage cans of commerce?
[Now I think about it, I can't imagine why.

It just happened that way. That's the only answer.
To be oneself by the power of gold
Is simply to build one's house upon sand.
If you've a gold watch and a diamond ring
People will fawn and grovel before you.
They'll raise their hats to your glittering tiepin
But the ring and the pin are not the man.]
A prophet's position is much clearer.
[You know where you are. If you're a success]
It's you that they worship and not your money.
[One is what one is, and no nonsense about it.
One isn't a debtor to Chance or Fate,
And one has no need of licence or patent.
To be a prophet. That's something for me.]
And I tumbled into it quite by chance.
Simply galloping through the desert
I stumbled upon these children of nature.
Their Messiah had come; it was clear; [there was no doubt
  about it.]
I had no intention of deceiving them.
Prophetic utterances are not lies.
Besides, I can always revise my interpretations.
[I'm not bound at all. Things aren't too bad.
It's all a perfectly private matter.]
If it comes to the worst, I can leave as I came.
My horse stands ready.
In short, I am master of the situation.
ANITRA (*approaches*). Prophet and Master!
PEER. What would my slave?
ANITRA. The sons of the desert wait outside.
  They beg to be allowed to see thy face.
PEER. Stop! Tell them to keep their distance.
  Tell them I shall hear their prayers from there.
  No men are allowed in here.
  Men, my child, are a most untrustworthy race.
  Miserable bastards! You can't imagine [Anitra,]
  How they have cheated – hm – sinned, my child.

Well, that's all over. You may dance for me, maidens.
The Prophet would forget such painful memories.
CHORUS (*dancing*). The Prophet is good. The Prophet is grieved
    At the evil the sons of the dust have committed.
    The Prophet is merciful. Praised be his mercy!
    He opens to sinners the portals of Paradise.
PEER (*his eyes follow* ANITRA *as she dances*). [Her legs are as neat
      and nimble as drumsticks.]
    Mm. She's a nice piece of delicatessen, that girl.
    [A trifle extravagantly moulded. Not quite
    The classical formula. But what is Beauty?
    A mere convention. It changes like coin
    From country to country and age to age.
    But a little excess is a pleasant change
    When one has drunk normality to the dregs.
    You can't get intoxicated by what's average.
    They're either too fat or too thin, or else
    Disturbingly young or disgustingly old.
    And what lies between seems insipid.]
    Her feet aren't quite clean; nor are her arms.
    Especially one. Still, that's no great defect.
    It's almost an extra qualification.
    Anitra, my child! Listen to me.
ANITRA (*approaches*). Thy handmaiden listens.
PEER. My child, you attract me. The Prophet is stirred.
    If you don't believe me, I shall give you proof.
    I'll make you a Houri in Paradise.
ANITRA. Impossible, Lord.
PEER. What? You think I'm joking?
    I mean it, as truly as I am alive.
ANITRA. But I have no soul.
PEER. That can be arranged.
ANITRA. How, Lord?
PEER. You leave that to me.
    [I shall make it my personal task to educate you.
    No soul! Yes, indeed, you are, as the saying goes,
    Somewhat stupid. I've noticed it with distress.

But] the meanest creature has room for a soul.
Come here. Let me measure the size of your brain.
There's room, there's room. I knew I was right.
[You'll never become a profound thinker.]
Not very much room. Your soul will be small.
But what of that? You'll have enough.
ANITRA. The prophet is good –
PEER. You hesitate? Answer!
ANITRA. I'd rather –
PEER. Speak out. Don't be afraid.
ANITRA. I don't mind so much about a soul.
   I'd rather have –
PEER. What?
ANITRA (*points at his turban*). That beautiful opal.
PEER (*enraptured, hands her the jewel*). Anitra! O thou true
      daughter of Eve!
   How can I refuse you? I am but a man.
   [And, as a distinguished author has written:
   '*Das ewig weibliche ziehet uns an!*'[18]]

SCENE SEVEN

A moonlit night. A palm grove outside ANITRA'S *tent.* PEER GYNT
*is seated beneath a tree with an Arabian lute in his hand. His hair
and beard are clipped, and he looks noticeably younger.*
PEER (*plays and sings*). I locked the gate of Paradise
      And took away its key.
   I sailed towards the Southern Cross
   While lovely women mourned their loss
   On the salt shore of the sea.

   South like a bird I sped my way
   On wings of swift desire.
   At last, where palm trees proudly sway
   In a green wreath around the bay,
   I set my ship on fire.

[I stepped aboard the desert ship,
A four-legged bold corsair.
Beneath my whip it skimmed along.
O, catch me! I'm a bird in song.
A-twittering in the air.]

Anitra, thou art the palm-tree's sap,
A wine most dear to me.
Angora goat's-milk cheese, though fare
Fit for the gods, can scarce compare,
Anitra, ah, with thee!

Hangs his lute over his shoulder and goes nearer the tent.
Silence! Is my fair one listening?
Did she hear my little song?
Is she peeping through the curtain,
Veils etcetera cast aside?
[Hush! A sound! As of a cork
From a bottle gaily springing!
Now again! And yet again!
Sighs of passion? Love's sweet song?
No, it is the sound of snoring.
Heavenly sound! Anitra sleeps!
Nightingale, O cease thy scraping.
Woe and misery befall thee
If thou darest with gulp and gurgle –
Oh well, never mind, forget it.
Nightingale, thou art a singer.
Even such a one as I.
You, like me, bewitch with music
Gentle, tender, youthful hearts.
The cool night was made for music.
Music is our common sphere.
Music makes us what we are;
Peer Gynt and the nightingale.
And the fact that she lies sleeping
Makes my passion's bliss complete.
I poise my lips above the beaker,

The rich wine as yet untasted.]
No, bless my soul, here she comes.
[Well, after all, perhaps it's best.]
ANITRA (*from within the tent*). Dost thou call in the night, O
　　master?
PEER. I do indeed. The Prophet calls.
　　I was wakened by the cat
　　Uttering violent hunting-cries.
ANITRA. Oh, Master, those weren't hunting-cries.
　　[They were something much worse.]
PEER. What?
ANITRA. I dare not tell thee.
PEER. Speak!
ANITRA. I blush –
PEER (*comes closer*). The same passion that inspired me
　　When I gave you my great opal?
ANITRA (*horrified*). O treasure of the world, dost thou liken
　　thyself to an old tom-cat?
PEER. Child, torn by love tom-cats and prophets
　　Behave very much the same.
ANITRA. Jests flow like honey from thy lips, O Master.
PEER. My little friend, [you must not judge
　　Great men by their exteriors.]
　　I am at heart a jovial man,
　　Especially in private audience.
　　[I am bound by my position
　　To assume a solemn mask.
　　Daily duties cramp my style.
　　My numerous worries and anxieties
　　Make me sometimes rather surly.
　　But that's just my way of speaking.
　　Away with all that! *En tête-à-tête*
　　I'm Peer – I mean – well, whoever I am.]
　　Come on, let's forget the Prophet.
　　Here you see me as myself.
　　Sits under a tree and pulls her over to him.
　　[Come, Anitra, we will rest

Beneath the palm-tree's gentle fan.
I shall whisper, you shall smile.
Then we'll change parts, and your sweet lips
Will whisper love and make me smile.]

ANITRA (*lies down at his feet*). All thy words are sweet as song,
Though I understand little. Tell me, Master,
Can thy daughter get a soul by listening?

PEER. Soul, knowledge, spiritual enlightenment –
You shall have them
When in the East, on rosy streamers,
Letters of fire proclaim the day.
Then, my child, I'll give you lessons.
[You'll get your education.]
But now, in the night's sweet stillness,
Why should I act the schoolmaster
[With the threadbare remnants of my wisdom]?
The soul is not the most important thing.
The heart is what counts.

ANITRA. Speak, O Master. When thou speakest
I see a glimmer, as of opals.

PEER. Too much wisdom leads to folly.
[The bud of cowardice, forced to fullest bloom,
Swells into tyranny. Truth pushed to excess
Reads like a wise text written backwards.
Yes, my daughter, this world is full of people
So spiritually gorged that their eyes are blinded.
I knew such a fellow once, a pearl among men,
But he came to nothing, losing all sense in sound.
Do you see the desert surrounding this oasis?
Simply by flicking this turban, I could conjure
The seas of the world in to flood every acre.
But to create new lands and seas would be
Sheer madness.] Do you know the secret of life?

ANITRA. No, tell me.

PEER. [It is to float dry-shod down the river of time;]
To be oneself.
Only in the vigour of youth

Can I be myself, my child.
Age makes eagles lose their feathers,
Age makes old men shake and pine.
[Age makes women bald and toothless,]
Age gives misers withered hands.
Age shrinks hearts and withers souls.
Youth, ah! Youth! I shall rule
Like a Sultan, hot and strong!
Not on the shores of Gyntiana
Underneath the palms and vines,
But in the fresh and waving pastures
Of a maiden's virgin thoughts.
[So you see, my little girl, why
I have condescended to seduce you;
Why I chose your little heart
For my empire.
I shall rule your every longing,
Tyrant in my state of love!
You shall live for me alone.
I shall possess you, like a jewel.
Should we part, then life will cease –
That is, yours. So kindly note that.
Every inch and fibre of you
Must accept me as its master.
You shall have no will but mine.]
The midnight beauties of your hair,
All your rich loveliness, shall draw me
Like the Babylonian Gardens
To my royal trysting-place.
[So it's best your head is empty.
If one has a soul, one wastes so much time
In introspection. And while we're on the subject,
You can have a chain around your ankle.
Then we'll both be happy.]
My soul will do for both of us.
[In other respects, we'll maintain the *status quo*.]
ANITRA *snores.*

What? She's asleep! Has everything I've said
Been thrown away? No, that's another sign
Of my power. My talk of love bears her away
Like a river into dreamland.
Gets up and puts jewels in her lap.
Here are jewels! And here are more!
Sleep, Anitra! Dream of Peer!
Sleep. By sleeping you have set
The crown on my imperial brow.
Tonight, by force of personality,
Peer Gynt has won his greatest victory.

SCENE EIGHT

A caravan route. The oasis is visible far away in the background.
PEER GYNT, *on his white horse, is riding furiously through the*
desert with ANITRA *in front of him on his saddle-bow.*
ANITRA. Let me go! I'll bite you!
PEER. You little rogue!
ANITRA. What do you want?
PEER. What do I want? To play at hawk and dove.
 To carry you off! To play mad games with you!
ANITRA. Shame on you! An old prophet – !
PEER. Oh, rubbish. The Prophet isn't old, you little goose.
 Do you think this is a sign of age?
ANITRA. Let me go! I want to go home!
PEER. Now you're being a coquette.
 Home? To Daddy? A fine idea!
 [We're two wild birds that have flown from our cage.]
 We never dare enter his sight again.
 Besides, [my dear, one should never stay too long
 In the same place. The better people know you,
 The less they respect you. Especially when you're a prophet
 Or anything like that. One should come and go
 Fleetingly, like a vision;] it was time I moved on.
 [They're fickle fellows, these sons of the sand.]
 I was getting no incense or prayers in the end.

ANITRA. But are you a Prophet?

PEER. I am your Emperor! (*Tries to kiss her.*)

  My little woodpecker's being coy.

ANITRA. Give me that ring you've got on your finger.

PEER. Anitra, my dearest, take all I have.

ANITRA. Your words are music. [They bewitch me.]

PEER. It's wonderful to know that you love me so dearly.

  [I'll dismount, and lead your horse like a slave.

  Hands her the whip and dismounts.

  There now, my rose, my fairest flower.

  I'll trudge beside you through the sand

  Till I'm hit by sunstroke and meet my end.]

  I'm young, Anitra! Remember that.

  [So don't be alarmed if I seem to be frivolous.

  A sense of fun is inseparable from youth.

  If you had a few more brains in your head,

  My sweet little lily, you'd understand

  My playfulness is proof that I am young.]

ANITRA. Yes, you're young. Have you any more rings?

PEER. [Of course I am!] Catch! I can jump like a stag!

  If we had vine-leaves, I'd garland myself.

  Yes, of course I am young! Yoo-hoo! I'm going to dance!

  Dances and sings.

  I'm a happy little cock!

  Come and peck me, little hen!

  Yoo! Hup! Trippety-trip!

  I'm a happy little cock!

ANITRA. You're sweating, Prophet. I'm afraid you'll melt.

  Give me that heavy thing on your belt.

PEER. O tender care! Carry my purse for ever!

  [Hearts that love are happy without gold.

  Dances and sings again.

  Young Peer Gynt is a naughty madcap.

  He doesn't know his tummy from his toes.

  'Pish!' says Peer, 'Pish! Anything goes!'

  Young Peer Gynt is a naughty madcap.

ANITRA. How exalting to see the Prophet dance!

PEER. Never mind the Prophet.] Let's change clothes!
  Yoo-hoo! Take them off!
ANITRA. Your cloak would be too long, your belt too wide,
  And your stockings too tight.
PEER (*kneels*). Then inflict some ordeal on me!
  To a heart full of love, it is sweet to suffer.
  Listen. As soon as we get to my castle –
ANITRA. In Paradise. Have we far to ride?
PEER. O, a thousand miles!
ANITRA. Too far!
PEER. O listen! You shall have the soul I promised you –
ANITRA. Thanks, I'll manage without a soul.
  But you asked for an ordeal –
PEER (*gets up*). Yes, by Allah! Let it be short, but hard!
  A moment of exquisite pain!
ANITRA. Anitra obeys the Prophet! Farewell!
*She hits him sharply across the fingers and gallops back across the
desert.*
PEER (*stands for a long while as though thunderstruck*).
  Well, I'll be – !

SCENE NINE

The same, an hour later. PEER GYNT, *soberly and reflectively, is
removing his Turkish costume, garment by garment. Finally he takes
his little travelling-cap out of the pocket of his coat, puts it on, and
stands once again in European dress.*
PEER (*throws the turban far away*). There lies the Turk and here
        stand I!
  [This heathen life won't do at all.
  Thank goodness I only borrowed clothes
  And wasn't born to it. *Mon dieu, mon Dieu,
  Qu'allais-je faire dans cette galère?*][19]
  It's best, after all, to live as a Christian.
  [To put behind one all peacock pretensions
  And steer one's course by law and morality.

To be oneself and get at the end
A speech by the graveside and flowers on one's coffin.]
Walks a few paces.
That bitch. She was within an ace of turning my head.
[I'm damned if I'll ever understand
What it was that bemused me. Well, thank heavens it's
    over.]
I nearly made a fool of myself.
[It's lucky that joke was carried no further.
I have erred. That's true. But it wasn't my fault.
I was simply placed in a false situation.
It wasn't I myself who fell from grace.
This prophetic life is divorced from reality
And took its revenge with this show of bad taste.
It's a rotten profession, this being a prophet.
Its nature demands that you live in a mist.
As soon as you behave like a rational being
You're finished. I was only acting professionally
In pretending I was in love with that little goose.
All the same –
Bursts into laughter.

                                        Just fancy!
Trying to make time stop by dancing!
Trying to swim against the current
By fluttering my feathers and wagging my tail!
Playing on the lute, and caressing and sighing,
And ending by getting properly plucked!
Such conduct is truly prophetic madness.
Plucked! Yes, she's certainly plucked me clean.
Still, I have a little left here in my pocket;
And a bit more hidden away in America.]
I'm not a beggar yet. And maybe this halfway house
Is best; to be neither rich nor poor.
I'm not dependent on coachman or horses,
And don't need to bother with trunks or carriage.
In short, I am master of the situation,
As the saying is. Which path shall I choose?

Many lie open. [And it's the choice
That distinguishes the wise man from the fool.
My business life is a finished chapter.
My love-life is a cast-off shirt.]
I don't feel inclined to retreat like a crab.
'Forward or back, it's equally far.
Outside or in, I'm still confined.'
That's how it stands in some clever book,
[I think. Something new, then. Something noble.
A goal that's worth my money and labour.]
Suppose I wrote my autobiography?
[Candidly, to show people the way
And give them a lead to imitate?]
No, wait! [I've plenty of time on my hands.]
I might become a wandering scholar
And study the decline of man.
[Yes, that is the road for me!
I loved stories when I was a child.
And I've read a good deal of them since.] Yes, that's it!
I'll trace the path of the human race,
Float like a feather on the stream of time,
Re-live man's history, as in a dream;
See the great heroes wage their battles for truth
(As a spectator, from a safe distance);
I'll see thinkers perish, and martyrs bleed,
Empires founded and empires fall,
Mighty epochs growing from small beginnings –
In short, I shall skim the cream of history.
[I must try to get hold of a copy of Becker[20]
And arrange my travels chronologically.
Admittedly my knowledge isn't very thorough,
And the inner machinery of history is complicated –
But what of that? Original conclusions
Are often reached from the most unlikely starting-point.]
How fine to set oneself a goal
And drive one's way remorselessly towards it!

Quiet, moved.
To sever the bonds that bind one to one's [home
And] friends. To say farewell to earthly riches,
And bid the sweet joys of love goodnight,
All to seek out the mystery of truth.
Wipes a tear from his eye.
That is the test of the true scientist.
Oh, I feel so happy!
Now I have fathomed the riddle of my destiny
[And shall struggle towards it, however hard the road].
It is surely pardonable to feel a little proud;
And know that I am myself, Peer Gynt,
[Also called] Emperor of the Life of Man.
I shall hold the whole of the past in my hands.
I'll never more tread in the paths of the living.
The present is worthless. Man has no faith nor courage.
His soul is earthbound, his actions meaningless.
Shrugs his shoulders.
And as for women – they're not worth one's breath.
Goes.

SCENE TEN

*A summer day, far up in the North. A forest hut; the open door has
a large wooden bar on it. Reindeer's antlers over the door. A flock
of goats is grazing by the wall of the hut.* SOLVEIG, *now a middle-
aged woman, but still fair-haired and beautiful, is sitting outside in
the sunshine, spinning.*

SOLVEIG (*looks down the path and sings*). Winter may pass, and
            spring,
And summer too, and the whole long year.
But some time I know that you will come,
And I shall wait, as I promised I would
[When I saw you last, my dear.]
Calls the goats, then turns back to her spinning and singing.
God give you strength, wherever you may be.

God give you joy, if you stand before His footstool.
I shall wait here till you come back to me.
Looks upwards.
And if it's there you're waiting, we shall meet there, my
       friend.

SCENE ELEVEN

In Egypt. Dawn. The statue of Memnon[21] *stands in the sand.* PEER
GYNT *enters on foot and glances briefly around.*
PEER. The statue of Memnon.
       This would be a good place to start my travels.
       Now I'll become an Egyptian for a change.
       [But firmly based upon the Gyntian self.
       Afterwards I'll move on to Assyria.]
       I don't need to begin at Genesis.
       I'll go round all that Biblical stuff.
       [I'll probably come across the odd relic of it,
       But to investigate its seams, as the saying goes,]
       That's outside my plan. [It would overtax my strength.]
       Sits on a stone.
       Now I shall rest and wait patiently
       Till the Statue has sung its usual morning song.
       After breakfast I'll climb up the Pyramid,
       And glance inside it, if I have time.
       Then I'll journey by land round the Red Sea.
       I might find King Potiphar's grave.
       Then I'll turn Asiatic! In Babylon
       I'll look for the Hanging Gardens and the Concubines –
       Hm – I mean the chief traces of ancient culture.
       Then straight on to the walls of Troy.
       From Troy I can voyage directly by sea
       To great old Athens. [And there, on the very spot,
       I'll look at the pass Leonidas defended.
       I'll acquaint myself with the better philosophers,
       And find the prison where Socrates sacrificed

His life. Oh, no, I forgot – there's a war on there.
Well, my Hellenic phase will have to wait.]
Looks at his watch.
It's too bad, how long one has to sit around
Before the sun rises. My time is short.
Well, after Troy – that was where I'd got to –
Gets up and listens.
What's that curious whispering sound?
Sunrise.

MEMNON STATUE (*sings*). When I died, my mother begged Zeus
    to make me immortal.
Now from my ashes there rise, youth-renewing,
Birds ever singing.
Zeus the All-Knowing
Shaped them for battle everlasting.
O Owl of Wisdom, when will they find sleep?
You must solve the riddle of my song or die.

PEER. How strange! I really thought a sound
    Came from the Statue. The music of the past!
I heard a voice like stone rising and falling.
I must note that.
Writes in his notebook.
'The Statue sang. I heard the sound clearly,
But did not quite understand the words.
The whole thing was of course a hallucination.
Saw nothing else of interest today.'
He goes on.

SCENE TWELVE

*Near the village of Gizeh. The Great Sphinx carved out of the rock.
In the distance can be glimpsed the spires and minarets of Cairo.
PEER GYNT enters and studies the Sphinx closely, now through his
lorgnette, now through his hollowed hand.*

PEER. The Great Sphinx of Gizeh. Now where in the world
    Have I met before something like this monster?
Something I've half forgotten. [I've met it

Somewhere.] Was it a man? And if so, who?
That statue, Memnon, it struck me later,
Looked like [that character in the fairy books,
The one they call] the Old Man of the Mountains.
[Squatting up there, so stiff and still,
With a couple of columns supporting his rump.]
But this extraordinary mongrel,
This changeling, half woman and half lion,
Did I read about it in a story book too?
Or did I actually meet it somewhere?
[A story book?] Ah yes, now I remember.
[Of course!] It's the Boyg, that I hit on the head –
I mean, I dreamed I did. I was running a fever –
Goes closer.
The same eyes. And the selfsame lips.
Not quite so torpid. And a little more cunning.
But otherwise pretty much the same.
Hullo, old Boyg. So you look like a lion
When viewed from behind in the daylight.
Do you still talk riddles? We'll try.
Let's see if you answer the same as before.
Shouts at the Sphinx.
Hi, Boyg! Who are you?
A VOICE (*from behind the Sphinx*). *Ach, Sfinx, wer bist du?*
PEER. What was that? An echo in German? How strange!
VOICE. *Wer bist du?*
PEER. It speaks the language fluently.
    This observation is new, and mine.
    Writes in his notebook.
    'Echo in German. Dialect: Berlin.'
BEGRIFFENFELDT *emerges from behind the Sphinx.*
BEGRIFFENFELDT. A man!
PEER. [Oh, it was him talking.] (*Writes again.*)
    'Later came to another conclusion.'
BEGRIFFENFELDT (*making all kinds of restless gestures*).
    Excuse me, *mein Herr. Eine lebensfrage* –
    What makes you come here on this particular day?

PEER. I'm just visiting an old friend of my youth.

BEGRIFFENFELDT. What? The Sphinx –?

PEER (*nods*). Yes. I used to know him well when I was younger.

BEGRIFFENFELDT. *Wunderbar!* After such a night!
> My head is throbbing. It is ready to burst.
> You know him, man? Speak! Answer!
> Can you tell me who he is?

PEER. Who he is? That's easy enough. He is *himself*.

BEGRIFFENFELDT (*gives a jump*). Ha! In a flash, the answer to
> life's riddle!
> You are sure he is himself?

PEER. Yes. Well, he says so, anyway.

BEGRIFFENFELDT. Himself! Then the hour of revolution is at
> hand!
> *Takes off his hat.*
> Your name, *mein Herr?*

PEER. I was christened Peer Gynt.

BEGRIFFENFELDT (*in hushed admiration*). Peer Gynt! Allegorical!
> I might have expected it!
> Peer Gynt! That means The Unknown.
> The Messiah whose coming was revealed to me –

PEER. No, really? You've come here to meet –?

BEGRIFFENFELDT. Peer Gynt! What profundity! What mystery!
> What penetration!
> Each word is like the voice of infinity!
> What are you?

PEER (*modestly*). I have always tried to be myself.
> Here is my passport.

BEGRIFFENFELDT. That enigmatic word again!
> (*Seizes him by the wrist.*) To Cairo.
> The Emperor of Interpreters is found!

PEER. Emperor?

BEGRIFFENFELDT. Come!

PEER. People know of me –?

BEGRIFFENFELDT (*drags him away*). The Emperor of Inter-
> preters! The Prophet of Self!

SCENE THIRTEEN

In Cairo. A big courtyard surrounded by high walls and buildings.
Barred windows. Iron cages. THREE WARDERS *in the courtyard.*
A FOURTH WARDER *enters.*

FOURTH WARDER. Hi, Schafmann, where's the director?

ANOTHER WARDER. He went out this morning before daybreak.

FOURTH WARDER. I think something must have annoyed him.
      Last night he –

OTHER WARDER. Hush! There he is!

BEGRIFFENFELDT *enters, leading* PEER GYNT. *He locks the gate*
and pockets the key.

PEER (*to himself*). This is a very clever man.
      I can hardly understand a word he says.
      Looks round.
      So this is the Philosophers' Club you spoke of?

BEGRIFFENFELDT. Yes, here they are, every man of them.
      The Circle of the Seventy Interpreters;[22]
      Recently increased by a hundred and sixty.
      Shouts at the WARDERS.
      Mikkel, Schlingelberg, Schafmann, Fuchs!
      Get into your cages at once!

WARDERS. Us?

BEGRIFFENFELDT. Who else? Get in, get in!
      When the world turns over, we must do the same.
      Forces them into a cage.
      He's arrived this morning – the mighty Peer!
      You can guess the rest, I need say no more.
      Locks the cage and throws the key into a well.

PEER. But, my dear Doctor – director –

BEGRIFFENFELDT. Neither. I used to be – ! Herr Peer,
      Can you keep a secret? I must tell someone –

PEER (*increasingly uneasy*). What is it?

BEGRIFFENFELDT. Promise you won't get frightened?

PEER. I'll try –

BEGRIFFENFELDT (*drags him into a corner and whispers*).
Absolute Reason passed away at eleven o'clock last night.

PEER. God help me –!

BEGRIFFENFELDT. Yes, it's a terrible tragedy.
And especially unpleasant for me, in my position.
Up to now, this institution
Has been regarded as a madhouse.

PEER. A madhouse?

BEGRIFFENFELDT. Not now, you understand.

PEER (*pale, whispers*). Yes, I understand!
This man is mad, and no one knows it.
He edges away.

BEGRIFFENFELDT (*follows him*). I hope you don't misunderstand
me?
When I say he is dead, that isn't strictly true.
He's beside himself. Jumped out of his skin.
[Just like my compatriot Munchausen's fox.][23]

PEER. Excuse me a minute –

BEGRIFFENFELDT (*holds him back*). [No, not like a fox.]
Like an eel.
A needle through his eye, and he was squiggling on the
wall –

PEER. How am I going to get out – ?

BEGRIFFENFELDT. A razor round his neck, and pip! – out of his
skin!

PEER. He's mad! A raving lunatic!

BEGRIFFENFELDT. Now it's obvious that if Reason has jumped
out of his skin,
That must mean a complete revolution all over the world.
Those persons who were formerly regarded as mad
Became sane at eleven o'clock last night
[In accordance with this new phase of Reason].
Moreover, if one considers logically,
It is clear that at the hour I mentioned
The so-called sane began to rave.

PEER. You mentioned the hour. My time is rather short –

BEGRIFFENFELDT. Your time? Of course! That reminds me.
Opens a door and shouts.
   Come out, my children! The promised hour has come!
   Reason is dead! Long live Peer Gynt!
PEER. Now, my dear fellow –
THE LUNATICS *wander out into the courtyard.*
BEGRIFFENFELDT. Good morning! Come out here and greet the
        dawn
   Of liberation. Your Emperor is here!
PEER. Emperor?
BEGRIFFENFELDT. Of course.
PEER. But the honour is too great. Really too much –
BEGRIFFENFELDT. Oh, this is no time for false modesty.
PEER. But at least give me time! No, I'm not worthy –
   I am stupefied –
BEGRIFFENFELDT. A man who has solved the riddle of the
        Sphinx?
   A man who is himself!
PEER. That's just it. I *am* myself in everything.
   But here, as far as I can make out,
   The thing is to be beside oneself.
BEGRIFFENFELDT. Beside oneself? No, there you're quite
        mistaken.
   Here we are ourselves with a vengeance;
   Ourselves and nothing whatever but ourselves.
   [We go full steam through life under the pressure of self.]
   Each one shuts himself up in the cask of self,
   Sinks to the bottom by self-fermentation,
   Seals himself in with the bung of self,
   And seasons in the well of self.
   No one here weeps for the woes of others.
   No one here listens to anyone else's ideas.
   We are ourselves, in thought and in deed,
   Ourselves to the very limit of life's springboard.
   So, if we are to have an Emperor,
   It's obvious that you are just the man.
PEER. Oh, if only –!

BEGRIFFENFELDT. Don't be depressed. Everything seems new
    at first.
   'Oneself.' Come here, you shall see an example.
   We'll choose the first that comes. (*To a melancholy figure.*)
   Good morning, Huhu.[24] Well, my boy,
   Still wandering round so miserably?
HUHU. What else can I do when race after race
   Dies uninterpreted?
   To PEER.
   You're a stranger here. Will you listen to me?
PEER (*bows*). Certainly.
HUHU. Then lend me your ear.
   Far in the East, like garlands round a brow
   Lie the coasts of Malabar. [The Portuguese
   And Dutch have brought their culture to the land.]
   Many Malabaris still live there.
   But foreigners have messed the language up.
   And now they are masters of the land.
   But long ago, the orang-utang ruled.
   He was the forest's lord and master;
   [He was free to fight and to snarl in freedom]
   Grinning and gaping as Nature created him.
   He could fight and shriek in perfect freedom.
   [He was master in his own kingdom.]
   But then, alas, the foreigners came
   And stifled the original language of the jungle.
   [For four whole centuries the simian race
   Brooded in darkness. And, as is well known,
   Such long nights leave their mark upon a people.]
   Now the voice of the jungle is silenced.
   Grunts and growls are heard no more.
   Now we can only express our thoughts
   Through the medium of speech. How intolerably cramping!
   [Dutchmen and Portuguese, half-castes and Malabaris
   Suffer equally.] I have fought to restore
   Our native tongue, the primal speech of the jungle,
   Tried to resuscitate its corpse;

Fought for our right to shriek and snarl;
Have shrieked and snarled myself; [and proved the need
For shrieks and snarls if our folk literature
Is to survive] but my work has not been appreciated.
Now perhaps you understand my sorrow.
Thank you for lending me your ear.
If you have advice, let me hear it.

PEER (*to himself*). 'When surrounded by wolves it is best to howl.'
(*Aloud.*) My friend, I seem to remember that in Morocco
There live orang-utangs with no interpreter
[Or poet to speak for them]. Their language sounds
Like Malabari. Why don't you, like many great men,
Emigrate to serve your race?

HUHU. Thank you for your kind attention.
I will follow your advice.
Waves an arm impressively.
East, thou hast disowned thy singer.
Apes shall flourish in the West.
Goes.

BEGRIFFENFELDT. Well, wasn't he himself? I should have
thought so.
[He's full of his ego; he has no room for anything else.
He is himself in everything he says
And does. Himself, because he is beside himself.]
Come here! Now I'll show you another one
Who since last night has been equally reasonable.
To a FELLAH[25] *bearing a mummy on his back.*
King Apis! How goes it, mighty Lord?

FELLAH (*wildly, to* PEER). *Am* I King Apis?

PEER (*edges behind* BEGRIFFENFELDT). I must admit I'm afraid
I'm not fully acquainted
With the situation. But, to judge from your tone,
I should imagine –

FELLAH. Now you're lying, too.

BEGRIFFENFELDT. Your Majesty must explain to this gentleman.

FELLAH. Yes. I'll tell him my story.
Turns to PEER GYNT.

You see this man upon my back?
King Apis was his name.
But now he's just a mummy.
He's dead, for all his fame.

He sculpted the Great Sphinx, and built
The mighty Pyramid;
He fought the Roman and the Turk,
And brought them low, he did.

And therefore the Egyptians
Worshipped him as divine,
And fed with sacrifices
The Bull God in his shrine.

But I am this King Apis.
It is clear as noon.
If you don't understand me now,
You'll understand me soon.

King Apis while out hunting
Was taken short, poor man,
So squatted for a minute
On my ancestor's land.

Now the earth King Apis fertilized
Nourished *me* with its corn.
And if further proof were needed,
I have invisible horns.

So isn't it a scandal
That no one calls me King?
Though I was born an Apis,
I'm just a paltry thing.

Oh sir, can't you advise me?
Help me resolve my fate;

And make these damned fools realize
I *am* King Apis the Great!

PEER. Your Majesty must build a larger Sphinx
And better Pyramids.

FELLAH. Well, that's a fine suggestion!
A fellah! A starving louse!
I haven't got the strength to keep
The rats out of my house.

Quick, think of something better.
Now tell me what I lack.
What is it that will make me like
King Apis on my back?

PEER. How if Your Majesty hanged yourself?
Wound in a shroud so grim,
And hidden in the earth's dark womb,
You'd start to look like him.

FELLAH. I'll do it! Where's a rope?
The gallows'll settle the doubt.
We won't look quite alike at first,
But time will smooth that out.
Goes off and prepares to hang himself.

BEGRIFFENFELDT. Well, there's a real personality for you!
A man of method –

PEER. Yes, yes, I see.
But he's really hanged himself! My God!
I'm feeling dizzy! I'm going out of my mind – !

BEGRIFFENFELDT. A transitional state. It'll soon pass.

PEER. Transitional? To what?
Excuse me, I must be going –

BEGRIFFENFELDT (*holds him*). Are you mad?

PEER. Not yet. Mad? God forbid!

A commotion. HUSSEIN, *a cabinet minister, forces his way through the crowd.*

HUSSEIN. They tell me an Emperor has arrived today.
To PEER.
Is it you?

PEER (*desperately*). Apparently.

HUSSEIN. Good! Then you must have notes to be answered?

PEER (*tears his hair*). All right! Why not? The madder the
better!

HUSSEIN. Will you do me the honour of dipping me?
Bows low.
I am a pen.

PEER (*bows even lower*). And I am a piece of scrawled imperial
parchment.

HUSSEIN. My story, Your Majesty, is briefly this.
People think I'm blotting paper. But I'm not. I'm a pen.

PEER. My story, Imperial Pen, is equally brief.
I'm a blank sheet of paper that no one will write on.

HUSSEIN. Nobody understands where my talent lies.
They all want to use me to soak up ink.

PEER. I was a book with a silver clasp, that a girl
Held in her hands. Whether we're called mad or sane,
It is merely a printer's error.

HUSSEIN. Can you imagine a more frustrating life
Than to be a pen, and never taste the edge of a knife?

PEER (*jumps high in the air*). Imagine being a reindeer!
To jump down from a height!
Falling and falling, and never to feel the ground under your
hoof.

HUSSEIN. A knife! I am blunt! Come, cut me, slit me!
The world will perish if someone doesn't sharpen me!

PEER. Alas for the world, which our Lord thought so good!

BEGRIFFENFELDT. Here is a knife.

HUSSEIN (*seizes it*). Ah, how I shall lick up the ink!
What relief to cut oneself to a point!
Cuts his throat.

BEGRIFFENFELDT (*moves to one side*). Don't splash me.

PEER (*in increasing horror*). Hold him!

HUSSEIN. Hold me! Yes, that's the word! Hold me! Hold the
pen!
Put paper on the desk – !
Falls.

I'm worn out! My postscript – ! Don't forget it!
He lived and he died a pen guided by other hands!

PEER (*becomes dizzy*). What shall I – ? What am I? O Great One!
　　　Hold me safe!

I'm whatever you wish! I'm a Turk, a sinner,
A troll! Only help me! Something has burst!
Screams.
I can't remember Your name!
O help me, Thou, O Guardian of all madmen!
Sinks unconscious to the ground.

BEGRIFFENFELDT (*with a crown of straw in his hand, jumps and
　　　sits astride him*). [Ha! See him sitting enthroned in the
　　　mire!

Beside himself!] Crown him now!
Forces the crown on to his head and cries.
Hail, Emperor! Hail Emperor of Self!

[SCHAFMANN (*from his cage*). *Es lebe hoch der grosse Peer!*]

Act Five

SCENE ONE

*On board a ship in the North Sea, off the Norwegian coast. Sunset.
Stormy weather.* PEER GYNT, *a vigorous old man with grizzled
hair and beard, is standing aft on the poop. He is dressed partly in
sailor's clothes, with a seaman's jacket and long boots. His clothes are
somewhat worn, and bear the marks of hard use. He himself is
weather-beaten, and his face has grown harder.*

The CAPTAIN *of the ship is at the wheel beside the* STEERSMAN. *The
crew are forward.*

PEER (*leans his arms on the gunwale and gazes landward*).

There's Hallingskarv in his winter fur;
An old man pluming himself in the evening sun.
Jœkel, his brother, stands behind him,
Hooded still in his ice-green cloak.
Folgefaan lies so delicate,
Like a virgin in her white linen.
It's no use trying to turn your heads.
You'll never touch her, you old men of stone.

CAPTAIN (*shouts forward*). Another hand to the wheel, and hoist
the lantern!

PEER. She's blowing up hard.

CAPTAIN. We'll have a storm tonight.

PEER. Can you see the Ronde from the sea?

CAPTAIN. No, of course not. It's hidden behind the snowfield.

PEER. And Blaahœ?

CAPTAIN. No. But in clear weather

If you go aloft you can see Galdhœpiggen.

PEER. Where is Haarteig?

CAPTAIN (*points*). Over there.

PEER. Yes, of course.

CAPTAIN. You seem to know these parts.

PEER. When I sailed from Norway, I passed this way.

The dregs of memory stay in the glass.
Spits and gazes towards the coast.
[Up there, where the clefts and scars are blue,
And the mountain valley is black and narrow
Like a ditch; and below, along the open fjords,
The people live.
Looks at the CAPTAIN.
                    In this country
They build their houses far apart.

CAPTAIN. Yes, they're pretty scattered.]

PEER. Will we be in by daybreak?

CAPTAIN. Just about. If the night's not too bad.

PEER. It's thickening in the west.

CAPTAIN. It is.

PEER. Remind me when I settle with you,
    I'd like to give something to the crew.

[CAPTAIN. Thank you.

PEER. It won't be much. I made a bit
    Over there, but I lost most of it.
    Fate and I haven't quite hit it off.
    You know what I've got on board.
    Well, that's the lot. The rest – psst!

CAPTAIN. It's enough to make you a big man here.

PEER. I've no family.
    There's no one awaiting this rich old bastard.
    Well, at least I won't have to put up with any fuss on the
        quayside.

CAPTAIN. Here comes the storm.

PEER. Well, remember,
    If any of your men are really short –
    I'm not a man who looks closely at my money.]

CAPTAIN. That's generous of you. They're mostly poor men.
    They've all got wives and youngsters at home.
    [And their wages don't stretch far.]
    If they get a little extra, they'll not forget it.

PEER. What? Wives and children? Are they married?

CAPTAIN. Married? Yes, every man. [The cook's the poorest.
   There's always black hunger in his house.]
PEER. Married? Someone waiting to give them a good welcome?
CAPTAIN. Yes, as good as poor people can give.
PEER. When they come home, what'll happen?
CAPTAIN. Their wives'll give them a little extra something
   For once –
PEER. A candle on the table?
CAPTAIN. Maybe two. And a dram –
PEER. And they sit there snugly round the hearth
   With their children around them? All talking at once,
   [No one lets anyone finish a sentence]
   They're so happy –?
CAPTAIN. That's about it. So they'll bless you for your promise –
PEER (*bangs the gunwale with his fist*). I'll be damned if I will! Do
   you think I'm mad?
   Why should I pay for other men's children?
   I've had to work hard to earn my money.
   There's no one waiting for old Peer Gynt.
CAPTAIN. Well, well, do as you please. It's your money.
PEER. Yes! It's mine!
   Give me my bill when we cast anchor.
   My fare as cabin passenger from Panama,
   And a tot of rum for the crew. That's all.
   [If I give any more you can knock me down the hatchway.
CAPTAIN. It's my job as Captain to give you a receipt,
   Not a thrashing.] Excuse me. The storm's coming on.
*He goes forward. It has become dark. Lights are lit in the cabin. The
sea grows rougher. Thick mist and heavy clouds.*
PEER. [To have a home full of children; to be their joy.
   To be always in the forefront of their minds.
   To be followed on one's way by the thoughts of others –]
   There's no one who ever thinks of me.
   Candles on the table! I'll put out those candles!
   [I'll find some way!] I'll make them all drunk!
   Not one of those fools shall go ashore sober.
   They'll come home drunk to their wives and children.

They'll swear, and knock them about – all their love des-
troyed!
[They'll frighten their loved ones out of their wits.
Their wives'll scream and run from the house,
Dragging their children with them. That will be
A joyful homecoming!]

The ship heels violently. He staggers and has difficulty in keeping his balance.

That was a lurch!
The sea's still itself up here in the North!
[The old devil's working as though he'd been paid for
it.
It's always the same up in these Northern waters.
They're sullen and churlish. Always trying to thwart
you.]

THE WATCH (*forward*). Wreck to windward!
CAPTAIN (*amidships*). Helm hard to starboard! Keep her close
to the wind!
STEERSMAN. Anyone on the wreck?
WATCH (*screams*). I can see three!
PEER. Quick! Lower a boat!
CAPTAIN. She'd fill before we cast off. (*Goes forward.*)
PEER. Who cares about that?
        To some of the CREW.
                        If you're men, save them!
You're not afraid of getting wet, are you?
BOATSWAIN. It's impossible in a sea like this.
PEER. They're screaming again. Look, there's a lull!
You, cook! Will you try? I'll give you money!
COOK. Not if you gave me twenty pounds.
PEER. You dogs! You cowards! Don't you realize
These men have wives and children at home?
They are sitting, waiting for them – !
BOATSWAIN. Well, there's virtue in patience.
CAPTAIN. Bring her about!
STEERSMAN. The wreck's turned over.
PEER. How silent it is, suddenly!

BOATSWAIN. If they were married
　　This world's the richer by three new widows.
　　The storm grows. PEER GYNT *goes aft.*
PEER. There's no faith left among men any more.
　　[Christianity's only preached and written;
　　There's little charity and less prayer.]
　　They've no respect for the powers above.
　　On a night like this our Lord is dangerous.
　　[These brutes should take care and remember
　　That it's dangerous to play with elephants.
　　They simply thumb their noses at Him.]
　　I'm guiltless. [On the Day of Judgement] I can swear
　　I stood ready and willing [with money in my hand].
　　But what good is that? [They say
　　An easy conscience makes the softest pillow.
　　That may be so on dry land, but at sea,
　　Where an honest man's like a fish out of water,
　　It's not the same.] A man can never be
　　Himself at sea. He must sink or swim with the rest.
　　If vengeance should strike the boatswain or the cook
　　I'll be sucked down to my death with the rest of them.
　　[One's individual virtues are ignored.
　　You're just a bit of meat for the sausage machine.]
　　My mistake is this. I've been too meek,
　　And I've had no thanks for it. If I were younger,
　　I'd change my style [and start acting the boss].
　　Well, there's still time. They shall learn in the parish
　　Peer Gynt has come riding back over the sea!
　　I'll get back our farm by hook or by crook.
　　I'll rebuild it. It shall shine like a palace.
　　But they won't be allowed to enter the door.
　　They shall stand at the gate and twiddle their caps;
　　They shall beg and grovel – that they can do –
　　But not one shall get a farthing out of me.
　　[I've had to cringe under the whip of Fate,
　　And they'll find that I, too, can wield the lash.]

THE STRANGE PASSENGER (*stands in the darkness at* PEER'S *side and greets him amicably*). Good evening.

PEER. Good evening. What – ? Who are you?

STRANGE PASSENGER. Your fellow passenger.

PEER. I thought I was the only one.

STRANGE PASSENGER. A mistaken impression, now corrected.

PEER. But it's strange I should see you for the first time tonight.

STRANGE PASSENGER. I never appear in the daytime.

PEER. [Are you ill? You're as white as a sheet –

STRANGE PASSENGER. Thank you, no. I am in excellent health.]

PEER. What a storm!

STRANGE PASSENGER. Yes! Beautiful!

PEER. Beautiful?

STRANGE PASSENGER. The waves are running as high as houses.

It makes my mouth water. Think of the wrecks
There will be tonight. Think of the corpses drifting ashore.

PEER. God preserve us!

STRANGE PASSENGER. Have you ever seen a man strangled?
Or hanged – or drowned?

PEER. What – !

STRANGE PASSENGER. They laugh; but their laughter is forced.
Most of them bite out their tongues.

PEER. Get away from me!

STRANGE PASSENGER. Just one question. Suppose we, for example,
Should strike on a rock, and sink in the darkness –

PEER. You think there is a danger – ?

STRANGE PASSENGER. I don't really know what I ought to say.
But suppose, now, I should float and you should sink –

PEER. Oh, rubbish – !

STRANGE PASSENGER. It's just a hypothesis.
But when a man stands with one foot in the grave
He sometimes tends to be generous –

PEER (*puts his hand in his pocket*). Oh, money –

STRANGE PASSENGER. No, no. But if you would be so kind
    As to bequeath me your valuable body –
PEER. What!
STRANGE PASSENGER. Only your corpse, you understand.
    To help my researches –
PEER. Go away!
STRANGE PASSENGER. But, my dear sir, consider. It's to your
        advantage.
    I'll open you up and let in the light.
    I want to discover the source of your dreams.
    I want to find out how you're put together –
PEER. Away!
STRANGE PASSENGER. But, my dear sir! A drowned body – !
PEER. Blasphemous man!
    You're provoking the storm! Are you out of your mind?
    Look at the sea! [These waves are like mountains!]
    At any moment we may be killed.
    [And you're acting as though you can hardly wait for it.]
STRANGE PASSENGER. I see you're not in a mood for discussion.
    But time, they say, changes everything.
    Nods amicably.
    We'll meet when you're sinking, if not before.
    Perhaps you'll be more in the humour then.
    Goes into cabin.
PEER. Horrible fellows these scientists are!
    You damned freethinker!
    To the BOATSWAIN, *who is passing.*
                        A word with you, friend.
    That passenger. What kind of a madman's he?
BOATSWAIN. I know of no passenger except yourself.
PEER. No passenger – ? [This gets worse and worse.]
    To the CABIN BOY, *who has just come out of the cabin.*
    Who went into the cabin just now?
CABIN BOY. The ship's dog, sir. (*Goes past him.*)
WATCH (*shouts*). Land close ahead!
PEER. My trunk! My strong-box! Get my things on deck!
BOATSWAIN. We've more important things to do.

PEER. Captain – what I said just now –
   I was only joking. I'll help the cook –
CAPTAIN. The jib's blown away!
STEERSMAN. The foresail's gone!
BOATSWAIN (*shouts from forward*). Rocks under the bow!
CAPTAIN. She'll go to pieces!

   The ship strikes. Alarm and confusion.

SCENE TWO

*Close off shore, among rocks and surf. The ship is sinking. Through
the mist can be glimpsed the dinghy, with two men in it. A sea strikes
it. It heels over, there is a scream, then for a few moments all is
silent. Soon afterwards the boat comes to the surface bottom upwards.*
PEER GYNT'S *head appears close to it.*
PEER. Help! Help! A boat! Help! I'm drowning!
   O Lord, save me! [That's what the Bible says – !]
COOK (*comes up on the other side of the boat*). O Lord God! [For
      my children's sake!] Have mercy!
   Let me reach the land! (*Seizes hold of the keel.*)
PEER. Let go!
COOK. Let go!
PEER. I'll hit you!
COOK. I'll hit you!
PEER. [I'll break your bones!] I'll kick you down!
   [I'll hit you!] Let go! This boat won't take two!
COOK. No! Get off!
PEER. You get off!
COOK. No, no!
They fight. One of the COOK'S *hands is disabled, but he clings on
with the other.*
PEER. Off with that hand!
COOK. Spare me, sir! Think of my children at home!
PEER. I need my life more than you. I am still childless.
COOK. Let go! You've lived. I'm young.
PEER. Get on with it! Sink! You're dragging me down!

COOK. Have pity! For God's sake! No one will mourn for you – !
His hand slips. He screams.
I'm drowning!
PEER (*grips him by the hair*). I'll hold you by the hair. Say your
prayers quickly.
COOK. I can't remember – everything's going dark – !
PEER. [Say whatever's most important.] Come on!
COOK. 'Give us this day –'
PEER. [Never mind that, cook. You'll get all you need.
COOK. 'Give us this day –']
PEER. The same old song! It's clear what you were!
The COOK *slips from his grasp.*
COOK (*sinking*). 'Give us this day our –' (*Disappears.*)
PEER. Amen. You were yourself, to the very end.
Ah, well.
Draws himself up on to the keel.
                    While there's life there's hope.
STRANGE PASSENGER (*catches hold of the boat*). Good morning.
PEER. Ugh!
STRANGE PASSENGER. I heard shouting. How nice to find you.
Well, did I prophesy correctly?
PEER. Let go! Let go! It'll barely hold one!
STRANGE PASSENGER. I'm swimming with my left leg.
I'll stay afloat
If I can just hold on with my fingers
[To this little splinter]. Now about that corpse of yours –
PEER. Shut up!
STRANGE PASSENGER. It's all you have left.
PEER. Be quiet!
STRANGE PASSENGER. Just as you please.
Silence.
PEER. What are you doing?
STRANGE PASSENGER. [I'm being quiet.
PEER. Damn your tricks! What are you up to?]
STRANGE PASSENGER. Waiting.
PEER (*tears his hair*). I'm going mad. Who are you?
STRANGE PASSENGER (*nods*). A friend.

PEER. What else? Tell me!

STRANGE PASSENGER. What do you think? Do you know no one
        else like me?

PEER. The Devil – ?

STRANGE PASSENGER (*softly*). Is it his way to light the lantern
        On life's long pilgrimage of fear?

PEER. Ah! So you are a messenger of light?

STRANGE PASSENGER. My friend, have you even once a year
        Known the true anguish of the soul?

PEER. Of course one's afraid, when danger threatens –
        [But everything you say has another meaning.]

STRANGE PASSENGER. Yes, but have you once in life
        Won the victory that only defeat can bring?

PEER (*looks at him*). If you have come to open a door
        It was stupid not to come before.
        What's the good of coming now
        [When the sea's about to swallow me up]?

STRANGE PASSENGER. Would you have found that victory
        In the [warmth and] comfort of your hearthside?

PEER. Perhaps not. But I thought you were joking.
        [How could you think it would open my eyes?]

STRANGE PASSENGER. Where I come from, laughter is rated as
        high as tears.

[PEER. There's a time for everything. As the proverb says:
        'The publican's meat is the bishop's poison.'

STRANGE PASSENGER. Those whose dust sleeps in funeral urns
        would tell you:
        'The tragic mask is not for everyday wear.']

PEER. Get away! [You frighten me!] Leave me! [Go!]
        I must get ashore! I will not die!

STRANGE PASSENGER. Oh, don't worry.
        You won't die in the middle of the last act.
        Glides away.

PEER. [Well, at least I'm that much wiser.
        God, what a boring moralizer!]

SCENE THREE

A churchyard high up in the mountains. A funeral is in progress.
A PRIEST *and* VILLAGERS. *The last verse of a psalm is being*
sung.
PEER GYNT *comes past on the road outside.*
PEER (*at the gate*). Here's one of my countrymen gone the way of
    all flesh.

    Thank God it's not me.
PRIEST (*speaks at the graveside*). Now, as his soul moves blindly
    towards its judgement
And his poor dust rests here, an empty husk,
Now, my dear friends, let me remind you
About this dead man's pilgrimage on earth.

    He was not wealthy, neither was he clever;
His bearing was unmanly, his voice was weak,
Uncertain in expressing an opinion.
[He scarce seemed master even in his home.
He slunk into church as though he sought to beg
Permission to take his place with all the rest.

    He came, as you all know, from Gudsbrandsdal,
And moved here when he was no more than a boy.]
And, you remember, till the day he died,
He always kept his right hand in his pocket.

    [That right hand in his pocket was the thing
That stamped his image sharply on our minds;
And this strange shyness, this embarrassment.
Where'er he went, he seemed to dread being seen.]
But though he chose to tread his path alone,
And lived and died a stranger in our midst,
Yet you all know, although he sought to hide it,
That hand we never saw bore but three fingers.

    I well recall one morning, years ago;
Recruiting officers had come to Lunde.
It was in time of war. [All mouths discussed
Our country's sufferings, and its likely fate.

I stood and watched. An old grey-headed Captain
Sat with the sergeants and the Burgomaster
Behind a table.] Lad after lad was measured,
Given his shilling, and sworn in as a soldier.
The room was full, and in the yard outside
The winter air was filled with young men's laughter.
Then a name was called, and a new lad stepped in,
Pale as the snow that fringes a green glacier.
They called him closer. He faltered towards the table,
His right hand swathed in a bloodstained cloth.
He gasped and swallowed, trying to find words;
[But none would come, despite the Captain's questions]
Until at length, his thin young cheeks aflame,
[Now failing to find words, now gabbling fast]
He told some tale of an accident; a sickle had slipped
And cut off one of his fingers close to the stump.
    A silence filled the room.
Men looked at one another, and curled their lips,
Stoning his face with their dumb glances.
He felt their scorn although he did not see it.
Then the Captain, an old grey man, slowly rose.
He spat, pointed towards the door, and said: 'Go!'
    And as he walked, men shrank on either side,
So that he ran the gauntlet through their midst.
He reached the door, and then took to his heels
Through woods, up hills and the high tumbling screes,
Slipping and staggering,
His home lay far away among the mountains.
    Some six months later he came to live among us
[With his mother, his betrothed and a new-born child].
He leased a patch of land up in the hills
Where the waste ground slopes upwards towards Lomb.
He married, built his house, broke the hard ground.
Success attended him, as many a proud
Acre bore witness, waving tall and gold.
[In church he kept his right hand in his pocket,
But in his home I warrant those seven fingers

Toiled fully as hard as any other man's eight.]
Then the spring floods swept everything away.
　[They saved nothing except their lives.] Naked
And poor, he cleared another patch of land.
Before the autumn came, fresh wood-smoke rose
From a homestead newly built in safer lee.
[Safer? From floods, but not from avalanche.]
Two years later it lay, crushed by the snow.
　But even the avalanche could not break his spirit.
He dug, raked, carted, cleared the strangled earth.
And, ere the next winter's snows had come,
For the third time his humble home arose.
　[Three sons he had, strong and intelligent lads.
They had to go to school, but it lay far off.
They had to go where the mountain path could not,
Across the scar, narrow and steepling.
What did he do? The eldest had to manage
Alone, as best he might; where the slope was steepest
His father roped him to himself, and hauled him,
Bearing the second in his arms, the youngest
Upon his back. So, year by year, he toiled.
His sons grew, flourished, and in time became men.
Now he might surely look for some reward.
But three rich gentlemen in the New World
Have forgotten their father in Norway, and the slow journeys
　　to school.]
　His vision was narrow. Beyond the tiny circle
Of those who stood close to him, he saw nothing.
Those words that should have resounded in his heart
To him rang meaningless like tinkling cymbals.
[His race, his country, all we think great and glorious,
Were from his eyes veiled in perpetual mist.]
　But he was humble, humble was this man.
And from the day when the Captain rose, and spat,
And pointed, he carried his judgement on his brow,
[As surely as the brand of shame on his cheek]
And his three fingers hidden in his pocket.

A criminal in the eyes of the law? Perhaps.
But there is something that shines above the law
As surely as the highest mountain peak
Has clouds above it like yet loftier mountains.
This was no patriot. For Church and State
He was a barren tree. But on his mountainside,
In the narrow circle of home, where his work lay,
There he was great, because he was himself.
The metal of which God made him rang most true
Until the end. His life was as a lute
Whose strings are muted. Peace to thee, silent warrior,
Who strove and fell in thy small humble war.
　　It is not for us to search the heart and reins.
That is no task for dust, but for its Maker.
But freely I hope and firmly I believe
This man is not a cripple in the eyes of God.
The MOURNERS *disperse.* PEER GYNT *remains alone.*

PEER. [Now that's what I call Christianity.
There was nothing there that could distress anyone.
And the theme of the parson's sermon, that one must be
Inflexibly oneself, is edifying.]
Looks down into the grave.
Could this have been the lad who chopped off his finger
When I was felling wood that day in the forest?
Who knows? If I weren't standing here with my staff
By the graveside of this spiritual kinsman,
I could well believe it was I who lay here sleeping
And hearing, as in a vision, myself so praised.
[That's really a beautiful Christian custom
Charitably to reminisce
Over the life of the dear departed.]
I shouldn't mind accepting my judgement
At the hands of this good parish priest.
[Ah well, I've a few years yet before
The gravedigger comes and offers me lodging.
And as the Scripture says: 'What's best is best,'
And: 'Sufficient unto the day is the evil thereof.'

And: 'Don't cross your bridges before you come to them.'
Yes, the Church is the only true comforter.
I haven't fully appreciated it before.
But now I realize how good it is
To be assured by the voice of authority
'As a man sows, so shall he reap.'
One must be oneself and look after oneself
And one's own, in all things, whether great or small.
If your luck runs out, at least you've the honour
Of having lived your life in accordance with
The best principles.] Now home! Let the path
Be steep and narrow. Let Fate be spiteful to the end.
Yet old Peer Gynt will still go his own way
And remain, as always, poor but virtuous.
Goes.

SCENE FOUR

*A hill with a dried river bed. A ruined mill stands on the river bank.
The ground is torn up, and has a waste appearance. Higher up is a
large farmhouse, where an auction is taking place. A large crowd is
gathered there. There is drinking and much noise.* PEER GYNT *is
sitting on a heap of rubbish near the mill.*

PEER. Forward or back, it's equally far.
    Outside or in, I'm still confined.
    [Time wears on, and so does the river.]
    Go round, said the Boyg. I must do that here.
MAN IN MOURNING. There's only rubbish left now.
    Catches sight of PEER GYNT.
    Have we strangers, too? God save you, friend.
PEER. [Good day to you.] You're having a gay time.
    What is it, a christening or a wedding?
MAN IN MOURNING. More rightly a housewarming.
    The bride's at home to a host of worms.
PEER. And worms are fighting for what she's left.
MAN IN MOURNING. The song is over; the story's done.

PEER. Every story has the same ending,
And every song is an old song.
[I knew them all when I was a boy.]

A YOUTH OF TWENTY (*with a casting ladle*). Look at what I've
bought!
This is the ladle Peer Gynt used
To cast his silver buttons in!

ANOTHER YOUTH. I've done better than that!
Look! I've bought Peer Gynt's purse for a shilling!

[A THIRD. Is that all?
Only half a dollar for the pedlar's moneybags?]

PEER GYNT. Peer Gynt? Who was he?

MAN IN MOURNING. Cuckold to Death and to Aslak the smith.[26]

A MAN IN GREY. You're forgetting me! Are you drunk?

MAN IN MOURNING. You're forgetting the storehouse door at
Heggstad.

[MAN IN GREY. That's true. But you never used to be so
particular –]

MAN IN MOURNING. As long as she doesn't put horns on
Death –

MAN IN GREY. Come, cousin. A dram for kinship's sake.

MAN IN MOURNING. What the hell do you mean, kinship?
[You're drunk –]

MAN IN GREY. [Oh, nonsense. Be blood ever so thin,]
Everyone feels he's akin to Peer Gynt.
Wanders off with him.

PEER (*softly*). One meets old friends.

A BOY (*shouts after the* MAN IN MOURNING). Watch out, Aslak!
If you get drunk
My mother will rise from her grave and haunt you!

PEER (*gets to his feet*). They say: 'The deeper you dig, the better
it smells.'
Not so here.

[A LAD (*with a bearskin*). Look, the Cat of the Dovre![27]
Or anyway his skin!
It was he chased the trolls on Christmas Eve!]

ANOTHER LAD (*with a reindeer's antlers*). Here's the buck that
  carried Peer Gynt
  Along the crest of the Gjendin Edge!
A THIRD (*with a hammer, shouts to the* MAN IN MOURNING).
  Hi, Aslak, do you recognize this hammer?
  Was it this you used when the Devil split your walls?
A FOURTH (*his hands empty*). Mads Moen, here's the invisible
  cloak!
  The one Peer Gynt wore when he flew off with Ingrid!
PEER. Give me a drink lads. I'm feeling old.
  I think I'll put up my own rubbish for auction.[28]
A LAD. What have you got?
PEER. A palace!
  It lies in the Ronde. It's got strong walls.
THE LAD. I'll bid you a button.
PEER. I'll take a dram.
  It'd be a sin to offer me less.
ANOTHER LAD. He's a funny old boy!
  People gather round him.
PEER (*shouts*). My charger, Grane! Who'll make me a bid?
ONE OF THE CROWD. Where is he?
PEER. Far away in the west!
  Towards the sunset, lads! That horse can fly
  As fast, as fast as Peer Gynt can lie!
VOICES. What else have you got?
PEER. I've gold and I've scrap.
  I bought them with ruin. I'll sell at a loss.
A LAD. Put them up!
PEER. A dream of a book with a silver clasp.
  You can have that for a placket.
THE LAD. Who wants dreams?
PEER. My Empire!
  I'll throw it among you. You can fight for it.
THE LAD. Do we get a crown too?
PEER. Of the finest straw.
  It'll fit the first man who puts it on.
  Wait a moment, here's more. A rotten egg.

A madman's grey hairs. The Prophet's beard.
I'll give them all to the one who can show me
The signpost that says: 'Here lies the way.'
PARISH OFFICER (*enters*). Look, if you go on like this you'll get
    arrested.
PEER (*hat in hand*). Maybe. But, tell me, who was Peer Gynt?
PARISH OFFICER. What – ?
PEER. Oh, please [Your Honour]! I beg you humbly –
PARISH OFFICER. Well, they say he was a damned liar –
PEER. A liar – ?
PARISH OFFICER. Yes. All the great deeds he'd ever heard of,
    He pretended he'd done them. Well, excuse me,
    I've other business –
    Goes.
PEER. And where is he now, this remarkable man?
AN OLD MAN. He went away [to some foreign land]
    Across the sea. [Things went badly for him,
    As one might have foreseen.] He was hanged many years ago.
PEER. Hanged? Well, well! [I guessed as much].
    Poor old Peer Gynt! He remained himself
    To the very end.
    Bows.
    Goodbye [and thank you, kind sirs].
    Goes a few steps, and then stops.
    Well, my merry lads and lasses,
    Shall I repay your kindness with a story?
SEVERAL. Yes. Do you know any?
PEER. Why, yes. I do.
    Goes closer to them. A strange expression comes over his face.
    In San Francisco, once, I was digging for gold.
    The whole city was filled with mountebanks.
    One could play the violin with his toes.
    Another danced the bolero on his knees.
    [A third, they say, wrote poetry
    While someone bored a hole into his brain.]
    One day the Devil came and joined the circus.
    [He thought he'd try his luck like all the others.]

His trick was being able to grunt like a pig.
His personality impressed them all,
Though no one recognized him.
[The house was full, and anticipation ran high.]
He stepped on to the stage in a big flowing cloak.
[*Man muss sich drappieren*, as the Germans say.]
What they didn't know was that under the cloak
He'd hidden a real pig. [At length the performance started.]
The Devil pinched, and the pig let out a squeal.
[People accepted it as a fantasia
On our porcine existence, with its combination
Of liberty and bondage.] Then it gave
A screech as though its throat had been cut,
At which he bowed his thanks and went.
The experts discussed the performance and dissected it.
[Some praised it, some condemned.]
Some found the tone of the squeals too thin.
Others thought the death-shriek a trifle affected.
But on one point all were agreed. The actual grunting
Had been, throughout, decidedly exaggerated.
So the Devil got his due; a just reward
For over-estimating the intelligence of his audience.
He bows and goes. An uncertain silence falls on the CROWD.

SCENE FIVE

Whitsun Eve. Inside the forest. Behind, in a clearing, is a cabin, with reindeer antlers above the door. PEER GYNT *is crawling in the undergrowth gathering wild onions.*

PEER. Well, I've reached one resting-place. Where's the next?
    One must try them all, and choose the best.
    I've tried the lot. I started as Caesar.
    And I've come right down to Nebuchadnezzar.
    [I've gone back to the Bible after all;
    The old boy's had to crawl back to his mother.]
    Well, [the Scripture says: 'Of dust thou art made,'

And] the first thing in life is to fill one's belly.
Onions? That won't get me far.
I'll have to be cunning and lay some snares.
There's a river here, so I won't go thirsty.
[The beasts'll still regard me as their boss.]
When I have to die, as die I must,
I'll creep under a tree blown down by the wind.
I'll heap leaves all over me like a bear
And I'll carve on the bark in big bold letters:
'Here lies Peer Gynt. A decent chap,
Emperor of all the beasts of the forest'.
Emperor? (*Chuckles.*) You old fake!
You're no Emperor. You're just an onion.
Now then, little Peer, I'm going to peel you,
And you won't escape by weeping or praying.
Takes an onion and peels it layer by layer.
The outermost layer is withered and torn;
That's the shipwrecked man on the upturned keel.
Here, mean and thin, is the passenger;
But it still tastes a little of old Peer Gynt.
And inside that is the digger of gold;
Its juice is all gone, if it ever had any.
[Who's this coarse fellow with calloused skin?
Ah, he's the trapper from Hudson Bay.]
This next one's shaped like a crown. No, thank you!
We'll throw that away, and ask no questions.
Here's the student of history, short and tough;
And here is the Prophet, fresh and juicy;
[Like the man in the proverb] he stinks of lies
That would blind an honest man's eyes with tears.
This layer now that curls up so softly
Is the sybarite living for ease and pleasure.
The next one looks sick ; it's streaked with black.
That might mean a priest; or it might mean a nigger.
Peels off several at once.
What a terrible lot of layers there are!
Surely I'll soon get down to the heart?

Pulls the whole onion to pieces.
No – there isn't one! Just a series of shells
All the way through, getting smaller and smaller!
Nature is witty!
Throws the pieces away.
[I'm thinking too much. If you start going round
With your head in the clouds, you fall flat on your face.
Well, that's a danger I needn't worry about.
I'm safe on all fours.
Scratches his head.
Life is a fox. When you think you've got her
She slips through your grasp, and you're left holding
Something different, or nothing at all.]
He has come close to the cabin. He sees it and starts.
This hut? On the moor – !
Rubs his eyes.
I feel as though I'd seen it before.
Those antlers sprouting above the doorway –
[That mermaid, shaped like a fish from her navel –
It's a lie! There's no mermaid. Just nails and planks
To shut out nagging hobgoblin thoughts –]
SOLVEIG (*sings in the hut*). The house is ready for Pentecost.
My love is far away.
Come back, come back to me.
If your burden is heavy,
Take your time.
I will wait for you, my love.
PEER (*gets to his feet silently, pale as death*). One who remembered
        – and one who forgot.
One who kept what the other has lost.
And the game can never be played again.
Oh, here was my Empire and my crown!
Runs down the forest path.

SCENE SIX

Night. A moor, with pine trees. A forest fire has ravaged it. Charred tree-trunks can be seen for miles around. Here and there white mist patches hug the earth. PEER GYNT *is running across the moor.*

PEER. [Ashes, mist, and dust and wind!
    That's the stuff with which to build!
    Our palace shall be proud and fair
    As befits a sepulchre.

    Foolish dreams and stillborn wisdom
    Shall be our palace's foundation.
    Out of them it shall tower high.
    Every stone shall be a lie!

    Let fear of truth and of repentance
    Flame like fire upon the summit
    Sounding forth the trump of doom:
    Petrus Gyntus Caesar fecit!]

    What is this sound of children weeping?
    Weeping but halfway to song?
    Threadballs are rolling at my feet –
    Kicks them.
    Get away! You're blocking my path!
THREADBALLS[29] (*on the ground*). We are thoughts.
    You should have thought us.
    You should have given us
    Little feet.
PEER (*goes round them*). I gave birth to one.
    It was a monster with a twisted leg.
THREADBALLS. We should have flown
    Like children's voices.
    Here we roll on the ground,
    Grey balls of thread.

PEER (*stumbles*). Thread! Rubbish!
  Would you trip your father? (*Flees.*)
WITHERED LEAVES (*flying before the wind*). We are a trumpet-
    call.
  You should have sounded us.
  See how your sloth
  Has shrunk and withered us.
  The worm has gnawed us
  Through and through.
  We never wound
  Ourselves round fruit.
PEER. You weren't born in vain.
  Lie still. You'll make good manure.
A WHISPERING IN THE AIR. We are songs.
  You should have sung us.
  A thousand times
  You have stifled and strangled us.
  In the mine of your heart
  We have lain and waited.
  We were never summoned.
  Curse you! Curse you!
PEER. Curse you, fools!
  Did I have time to make up verses?
  Tries to take a short cut.
DEWDROPS (*dripping from the branches*). We are tears
  You never wept.
  We could have melted
  The sharp ice-spears.
  Now they fester
  Deep in your breast.
  The wound has closed.
  Our power has gone.
PEER. Thanks. I wept in the Troll King's palace.
  But I got a tail on me just the same.
BROKEN STRAWS. We are deeds
  You left undone.
  The strangler Doubt

Has broken and crippled us.
On the Day of Judgement
We shall be there
To tell our story.
Take care! Take care!

PEER. Dirty tricks!
Would you damn me for what I haven't done?
Hastens away.

AASE'S VOICE (*far away*). You're a fine driver!
Look where you've thrown me
Into a snowdrift!
I'm soaking and frozen.
You've come the wrong way!
Oh, Peer, where's the castle?
The Fiend's led you astray
[With the stick from the closet].

PEER. I think I'd better be running away.
If I have to carry the Devil's sins
Upon my shoulders, I shan't get far.
My own are heavy enough to bear.
Runs off.

SCENE SEVEN

Another part of the heath.
[PEER (*sings*). A gravedigger! A gravedigger! Where are you,
    dogs?
Open your mouths and let's hear you bray!
Let's see you girdle your hats with crêpe.
I've lots of corpses to bury today!]

THE BUTTON MOULDER *enters from a side path with his box
of tools and a large casting-ladle.*

BUTTON MOULDER. Well met, old man.

PEER. Good evening, friend.

BUTTON MOULDER. You're in a hurry. Where are you going?

PEER. To a funeral feast.

BUTTON MOULDER. Indeed? My eyes aren't too good, but –
    forgive me –
  Your name isn't by any chance Peer?
PEER. Peer Gynt, they call me.
BUTTON MOULDER. Well, that's lucky!
  You're the man I have to collect tonight.
PEER. Have to collect – ? What business have you with me?
BUTTON MOULDER. As you can see, I'm a button-moulder.
  You must go into my casting-ladle.
PEER. What for?
BUTTON MOULDER. To be melted down.
PEER. Melted?
BUTTON MOULDER. Yes. Look! It's clean and empty.
  Your grave is dug and your coffin is ready.
  Tonight the worms will feast in your body.
  But I have orders from my Master
  To collect your soul without delay.
PEER. But you can't! Without warning – !
BUTTON MOULDER. It's an ancient custom at funerals.
  As at christenings, one chooses the day,
  And the guest of honour receives no warning.
PEER. Yes, of course. My brain's in a whirl.
  Then you are – ?
BUTTON MOULDER. I told you. A button-moulder.
PEER. Of course.
  [One calls a favourite child by many names.]
  I see. So this is the end of my journey.
  But, my good man, this is most unfair.
  [I deserve more considerate handling than this.
  I'm not so bad as you seem to suppose.
  I've done quite a few good deeds in my life.
  At the worst I may possibly have been
  A bit of a fool.] I've never been a real sinner.
BUTTON MOULDER. [But, my dear sir!] That is just the point.
  [By the highest standards you aren't a sinner.
  So] you escape the horrors of torment
  And must go with others into the casting-ladle.

PEER. What does it matter what you call it,
   Casting-ladle or pool of fire?
   [They're the same vintage, just different bins.
   Get behind me, Satan!
BUTTON MOULDER. You're not so rude
   As to suggest that my feet are shaped like hoofs?
PEER. Whether you've hoofs or pads or claws]
   Be off with you, and take care what you do!
BUTTON MOULDER. My friend, you're labouring under a
      delusion.
   [We're both in a hurry, so to save time
   I'll explain the gist of the matter to you.]
   As you have told me with your own lips,
   You aren't what one could call a whole-hearted
   Sinner. You're scarcely even a minor one –
PEER. That's better. [Now you're beginning to talk sensibly –]
BUTTON MOULDER. Wait a moment! You are not virtuous
      either –
PEER. I'm not claiming that –
BUTTON MOULDER. You're [halfway between;] neither one nor
      the other.
   [Nowadays one hardly ever meets a sinner
   On the really grand scale.
   There's more to that than just scrabbling around in the mud.]
   A man needs strength and purpose to be a sinner.
PEER. Yes, one has to be ruthless and think of nothing else.
BUTTON MOULDER. But you weren't like that. You took your
      sinning lightly.
PEER. I just splashed about on the surface.
BUTTON MOULDER. Ah, we shall soon agree. The pool of fire
   Is not for those who splash about on the surface.
PEER. And therefore, my friend, I can go as I came?
BUTTON MOULDER. No. Therefore, my friend, I must melt you
      down.
[PEER. You've learned some new tricks while I've been abroad.
BUTTON MOULDER. The custom's as old as sin. It's merely
      designed

To prevent waste.] You've done it yourself.
You know that one occasionally moulds a button
That's useless. For example, without a loop.
What did you do in such a case?
PEER. Throw it away.
BUTTON MOULDER. Ah, yes. I had forgotten.
    John Gynt was famous for his improvidence
    [As long as he had anything in his purse].
    But the Master, you see, is a thrifty man.
    [That's why He's remained so prosperous.]
    He never rejects as worthless anything
    Which He can use again as raw material.
    Now you were meant to be a shining button
    On the waistcoat of the world. But your loop broke.
    So you must be thrown [into the rubbish bin,
    And go from there] back into the great pool.
PEER. You don't intend to melt me down with other dead
    men?
BUTTON MOULDER. That is precisely what I intend.
    [We've done it, you know, with quite a number of people.
    At the Royal Mint they do the same with coins
    That have got so worn you can't see the face on them.
PEER. But this is the most sordid parsimony!
    Oh, come on, be a sport and let me go!
    A button without a loop, a worn-out shilling –
    What are they to a man in your Master's position?
BUTTON MOULDER. Oh, as long as a man has some soul left
    He's always worth a little as scrap.]
PEER. No! I'll fight with all the strength I have!
    Anything but this!
BUTTON MOULDER. But what else is there? Be reasonable, now.
    You're hardly qualified to go to Heaven –
PEER. [Oh, I'm not aiming as high as that.] I'm easy to please.
    [But I'm not going to give up a jot of myself.]
    Give me the old-fashioned punishment.
    Send me down [for a while] to serve [a sentence]
    With Him with the Hoof – for a hundred years,

If need be – that's something a man can bear,
For they say the suffering's only spiritual.
And I think that ought to be fairly tolerable.
[It'll only be a transitional stage,
As the fox said when they started to skin him.[30]]
One will wait; then the hour of liberation
Will come, and I'll start another life,
And hope things will turn out somewhat better.
But this other business – to end one's days
As a speck of dirt in a stranger's body,
To be melted, and to be Peer Gynt no more –
It fills my soul with revulsion.

BUTTON MOULDER. But, my dear Peer, there's really no need
To get so upset. You have never been yourself.
What does it matter if you disappear?

PEER. I have never been – ? I could almost laugh!
Have I ever been anything but myself?
No, button moulder, you're guessing blindly.
If you could look into my heart
You'd find Peer Gynt and only him;
Nobody else, nothing less nor more.

BUTTON MOULDER. It's impossible. Here are my orders. Look,
It is written: 'Thou shalt claim Peer Gynt.
He has defied the Master's intention;
He is waste, and must go to the casting-ladle.'

PEER. [What nonsense!] He must mean somebody else.
Does it really say Peer? Not Rasmus or John?

BUTTON MOULDER. Oh, I melted them down long ago.
Now come along quietly, and don't waste my time.

PEER. No, I'm damned if I will! It'd be a fine thing
If it turned out tomorrow He meant someone else.
You'd better be careful, my good man.
[Consider the responsibility –]

BUTTON MOULDER. I have it in writing –

PEER. At least give me time!

BUTTON MOULDER. What good would that do?

PEER. I'll bring you proof

That I've been myself the whole of my life.
[And that's what we've been arguing about.]
BUTTON MOULDER. You'll prove it? How?
PEER. Witnesses and testimonials.
BUTTON MOULDER. I'm afraid the Master won't accept them.
PEER. [Oh, surely!] He must! [However:
'Sufficient unto the Day is the Evil thereof.']
My good man, let me offer myself as security.
I'll soon be back. One is only born once.
[And one doesn't want to face oblivion.]
Do you agree?
BUTTON MOULDER. Very well. If you wish.
But remember. We meet at the next crossroads.
PEER GYNT *runs away.*

SCENE EIGHT

Another part of the moor.
PEER (*runs in frantically*). [Time is money, as the Bible says.]
If I only knew where those crossroads were!
They may be near; or they may be far.
[The earth is burning my feet like fire.]
A witness! A witness! Where shall I find one?
[It's almost impossible here in the forest.
What a mess the world is! A fine state of affairs
When a man has to prove what's obviously his right.]
An OLD BENT MAN *plods by with a staff in his hand and a
pack on his back.*
OLD MAN (*stops*). Spare a penny, kind sir, for a homeless old
man.
PEER. I'm sorry, I don't have any change –
OLD MAN. Prince Peer! Well, well! So we meet again!
PEER. Who are you?
OLD MAN. Don't you remember the Old Man of the Mountains?
PEER. Surely you're not – ?

OLD MAN. The King of the Ronde, son.

PEER. [The King of the Ronde? Really?]

　　The King of the Ronde! [Answer me!]

OLD MAN. I'm afraid I've come down in the world –

PEER. Ruined?

OLD MAN. Robbed of every penny.

　　I tramp the roads, begging for food.

PEER. A witness!

　　My dear sir, men like you don't grow on trees –

OLD MAN. Your Highness has also aged since last we met.

PEER. [My dear father-in-law, the years take their toll.

　　But let's not waste time over private matters:

　　And above all, for God's sake, no family quarrels.]

　　I was a bit of a madcap in those days –

OLD MAN. Ah, well. Your Highness was young. [And youth will
　　　be youth.

　　But you did quite right to renounce your bride.

　　You saved yourself a lot of shame and bother.

　　She's turned out a bad one –

PEER. Has she?

OLD MAN. Gone completely to the dogs. Would you believe it?

　　She's gone off to live with that dreadful Trond.

PEER. Who is Trond?

OLD MAN. The troll of the Valfjeld.

PEER. Him? Oh, yes, I remember.

　　I once seduced three of his girls.

OLD MAN. My grandson's grown into a fine strong lad.

　　He's fathered children all over the country.

　　Fine kids, too –]

PEER. Dear father-in-law, [never mind all that.

　　There's something else I have on my mind.]

　　I've got into rather a difficult situation.

　　I need a witness [or anyway a testimonial].

　　Now you can help me better than anyone.

　　I might even raise you the price of a drink.

OLD MAN. You mean I can be of service to Your Highness?

　　And would you give me a reference in return?

PEER. Gladly. I'm a little short of ready cash.
    [And have to economize as much as possible.]
    Now listen, and I'll explain. You remember that night
    When I came as a suitor to your palace –
OLD MAN. Of course I do, [Your Highness].
PEER. [Oh, stop this Highness business.] Now, look. You remember
    You wanted to slit my eye and distort my sight,
    And turn me from Peer Gynt into a troll?
    And how did I react? I resisted you.
    [I swore that I would stand on my own two feet.]
    I renounced my chances of love and power and glory
    Simply so that I could remain myself.
    Now I want you to testify to this in court –
OLD MAN. No, I can't do that.
PEER. What do you mean?
OLD MAN. You surely wouldn't force me to lie?
    You can't have forgotten. You put on troll breeches
    And sampled our mead –
PEER. [Yes, you tricked me into that.] But I refused
    To take the decisive step. And that's the test.
    [It's the final verse of the song that matters.]
OLD MAN. But it was the opposite of what you say.
PEER. What on earth do you mean?
OLD MAN.   You left the Ronde
    With my motto branded on your brow.
PEER. What motto?
OLD MAN. Those words that divide us.
PEER. Which words?
OLD MAN. Those words that distinguish troll from man:
    'Be thyself – and to Hell with the rest of the world!'
PEER (*recoils*). 'To Hell with – !'
OLD MAN. Ever since then, with all your heart and soul,
    You have lived your life by that principle.
PEER. I? Peer Gynt?
OLD MAN (*weeps*). You're so ungrateful.

You've lived like a troll, but have always kept it secret.

It has made you a successful man,

And now you turn up your nose at it.

[At me and the motto to which you owe everything.]

PEER. Me a troll!

[It's all absolute nonsense. I'm sure of it.

OLD MAN (*pulls out a wad of old newspapers*). I suppose you
imagine we trolls don't have newspapers?

Wait a second, and I'll show you in black and red

How the *Bloksberg Express* has been lauding you to the skies,

And the *Heklefjelds Pictorial*, too, ever since you left us.

Would you care to read them, Peer? You can if you like.

There's an article here with the signature 'Stallion-Hoof,'

And another on 'The Importance of Troll Nationalism,'

In which the writer emphasizes the fact

That it isn't horns and a tail that make a troll,

It's the spirit that matters. The hallmark, he says, of trolldom,

Is really *believing*: 'To hell with the rest of the world!'

And he ends by quoting you as an example.

PEER. A mountain troll? I?]

OLD MAN. Most definitely.

PEER. You mean I could have stayed where I was,

Living in peace and luxury in the Ronde?

You mean all this worry and toil has been for nothing?

Peer Gynt a troll? It's nonsense! Be off with you.

[Here's a halfpenny. Buy yourself some tobacco.

OLD MAN. Oh, dear, kind Prince Peer – !

PEER. Let go! You're mad!

Or turning senile. Go to the workhouse!

OLD MAN. That's what I'm looking for. But my grandson's
children,

As I think I told you, are influential people,

And they're going round saying I only exist in legend.

They say there's nothing as nasty as an ungrateful child,

And now I'm learning the truth of that for my sins.

It's a bit of a blow to become a myth in one's lifetime –

PEER. Your're not the only person to whom that's happened.

OLD MAN. And we trolls don't have any Friendly Societies
        Or Savings Banks or National Assistance.
        Such institutions would never do in the Ronde.
PEER. No. The motto there was: 'Look after yourself!'
OLD MAN. Oh, Your Highness mustn't disparage that motto of
        ours.
        Though, if you could possibly see your way to –
PEER.   My man,
        You're barking up the wrong tree.] Anyway, I'm completely
        broke.
OLD MAN. No! Your Highness a beggar?
PEER. Yes. I've even had to pawn my [princely] self.
        And that's your fault, you and your bloody trolls.
        [It shows the danger of keeping bad company.]
OLD MAN. Oh dear, that's another hope gone.
        Well, goodbye. I'd best be moving on towards town.
PEER. What will you do there?
OLD MAN. Try to get on the stage.
        [I hear they're advertising for local talent.]
PEER. The best of luck! [You can give them a kiss from me!]
        If I get out of this, I'll come and join you.
        [I'll write them a farce both witty and profound. I –
        Yes! I think I'll call it *sic transit gloria mundi!*]
He runs off down the road. The OLD MAN *is left shouting after
him.*

SCENE NINE

At a crossroads.
[PEER. Well, my lad, you're really up against it now.
        That 'To Hell with the rest of the world' has fairly sunk you,
        Your ship's a wreck; you must find some straw to cling to.
        Anything rather than go into the waste bin.]
BUTTON MOULDER (*at the crossroads*). Well now, Peer.
        Have you found your witnesses?
PEER. A crossroads already? That didn't take long.

BUTTON MOULDER. I can see from your face that you've failed.
   [Your face is a poster telling me the news.
   I don't have to ask for a paper to find what's happened.]
PEER. I got tired of the hunt. One could lose one's way –
BUTTON MOULDER. Yes. And anyway, where does it lead?
[PEER. True enough; in the forest, at nightfall –]
BUTTON MOULDER. But there's an old man trudging along.
   Shall we call him?
PEER. No, let him go. He's drunk.
BUTTON MOULDER. But he might be able to –
PEER. Hush! No! Let him go!
BUTTON MOULDER. Well, shall we be off?
PEER. One question. What does it mean: 'To be oneself'?
BUTTON MOULDER. That's a strange question, from a man
   Who a moment ago –
PEER. Come on, answer me!
BUTTON MOULDER. To be oneself is: to kill oneself.
   But I suppose that explanation's wasted on you.
   Let us say: always to serve the Master's intention.
PEER. But what of a man who never learned
   What the Master intended him to be?
BUTTON MOULDER. His instinct should guide him.
PEER. But instinct can often lead you astray.
   [And then you're lost before you're halfway.]
BUTTON MOULDER. Very true, Peer Gynt. And in this bad
   instinct
   He with the Hoof has his best angel.
PEER. [This is a damnably complicated business.]
   Right. I abandon my claim of having been myself.
   [It might be difficult to get proof of that.
   I accept that part of my case as lost.]
   But a moment ago, when I was alone on the moor,
   [I felt the shoe of my conscience pinching me.]
   I said to myself: 'It's true. You are a sinner –'
BUTTON MOULDER. Now we're back where we started –
PEER. No, no. I mean a great sinner.

[Not merely in deed, but also in thought and word.
When I was abroad, I behaved very badly –]
BUTTON MOULDER. Maybe. I must ask you to show me the
    proof –
PEER. Yes, just give me time. I'll find a priest,
    Make a confession, and bring you a certificate –
BUTTON MOULDER. Yes, if you can bring me that
    You will certainly avoid the casting-ladle.
    But, Peer, I have my orders –
PEER. That paper's out of date. It was made out years ago
    [When I was leading a careless, lazy life,
    Playing the Prophet, pretending to be a Fatalist].
    Well, can I try?
BUTTON MOULDER. But –
PEER.   Please!
    Oh, please! I'm sure you can't be all that busy.
    [The air round here is excellent for the health.
    It lengthens people's lives considerably.
    You know what the priest at Justedal[31] once said:
    'Hardly anyone ever dies in this valley.']
BUTTON MOULDER. Till the next crossroads, then. But not a
    step farther.
PEER. I'll find a priest! If I have to drag him by his cassock – !
    He starts running.

SCENE TEN

*A hillside covered with heather. A path winds up towards the
mountains.*
[PEER. You never know what may turn out useful,
    As Esben said when he found the magpie's wing.[32]
    Who'd ever have guessed that a list of one's sins
    Could prove a man's salvation on his last night?
    Mind, the situation's still just as tricky.
    Would the ladle really be worse than the fire?

Ah, well. While there's life, they say there's hope.
That's a proverb that has stood the test of time.]

A THIN PERSON, *in a priest's cassock tucked high and with a fowling-net over his shoulder, comes running down the path.*

PEER. What's this? A priest [with a fowling-net]!
Hurrah! I'm in luck. Good evening, your Reverence.
Awkward going, isn't it?

THIN PERSON. Indeed. But what wouldn't one do for a soul?

PEER. Oh, is someone about to go to heaven?

THIN PERSON. I trust not.

PEER. May I accompany your Reverence for a little of the
way?

THIN PERSON. With pleasure. I am fond of company.

PEER. I should like to consult you –

THIN PERSON. Proceed.

PEER. I'm a good man. Always been law-abiding.
Never been inside. But you know how it is,
Sometimes a man puts his foot wrong and stumbles –

THIN PERSON. Ah, yes. That happens to the best of us.

PEER. Well, these trifles –

THIN PERSON. Trifles?

PEER. Yes, only trifles.
[I've never done anything really wicked –]

THIN PERSON. Then, my dear sir, you're wasting my time.
I'm not the person you seem to think me.
What are you looking at? [You find my fingers interesting?

PEER. Your nails are somewhat strikingly developed.

THIN PERSON. And now I see you're studying my feet.]

PEER (*points*). Is that hoof natural?[33]

THIN PERSON. So I flatter myself.

PEER (*raises his hat*). I thought you were only a priest.
And I have the honour – ! Well!
One mustn't look a gift horse in the – I mean, I'm delighted!
[If you find the front door open, why go through the back?
If the King puts his head out of the window
You can raise your fingers at the footman.]

THIN PERSON. Give me your hand. You seem remarkably
   unbiased.
   Now, my dear fellow, what can I do for you?
   [Er – you mustn't ask me to give you power or money.
   I couldn't do that if you put a noose round my neck.
   You can't imagine how dead business has been
   Lately. Trade has been completely at a standstill.
   There just aren't the souls. Just the odd stray now and then.
PEER. Has mankind taken a turn for the better, then?
THIN PERSON. Quite the contrary. They've deteriorated
   disgracefully.
   Most of them are only fit for the casting-ladle.
PEER. Yes, I've heard about that ladle. Actually
   That was what I wanted to talk to you about.]
THIN PERSON. You may open your heart to me.
PEER. If it isn't too much to ask, I'd like –
THIN PERSON. A place of refuge? Hm?
PEER. You've guessed [before I even opened my mouth.
   You said just now that business has been bad,
   So I thought you might conceivably stretch a point –
THIN PERSON. But, my dear sir –]
PEER. I don't ask much.
   I could even manage without a salary.
   Just decent treatment – as far as circumstances permit –
THIN PERSON. A warm room?
PEER. Not too warm.
   And, if possible, [freedom to come and go
   As I please; and especially] the right to leave
   If I get the offer of anything better.
THIN PERSON. My dear friend, it pains me to say this, but
   You can't imagine how many similar applications
   I receive from people departing their earthly life.
PEER. But think of the wicked life I've led!
   [Surely I am eminently qualified for admission?]
THIN PERSON. You said they were trifles –
PEER. Only in a sense. But, now I remember,
   I trafficked in slaves –

THIN PERSON. There are men who have trafficked in hearts and
       souls,
    [But they made a mess of the job] and failed to get in.
PEER. I shipped heathen idols to China.
THIN PERSON. Oh, [don't talk rubbish!] We laugh at such
       things!
    [There are people who set up much nastier idols
    In art and literature, and sermons for that matter;
    And even they don't get in.]
PEER. Yes, but wait a minute!
    Do you know, I once pretended to be a Prophet?
THIN PERSON. Who hasn't? [Most people's *Sehen ins Blaue*
    Ends in the casting-ladle.] No, I'm sorry.
    If you haven't any better credentials than these,
    I can't let you in [however much I might like to].
PEER. But listen! In a shipwreck
    [I was clinging to an upturned boat.
    There's a saying: 'A drowning man will clutch at a straw';
    But there's another: 'Charity begins at home,'
    And] I half robbed a poor cook of his life.
THIN PERSON. Would you expect me to be impressed if you told
    Me that you'd half-robbed a kitchen-maid of something else?
    [Don't waste my time with all this rubbish about halves.
    I'm sorry, but] do you think I can waste expensive fuel
    On people like you in difficult times like these?
    [Now, don't get angry. It's only your sins
    That I'm disparaging. I'm sure you'll forgive me
    For speaking out so straight. So, my dear fellow,]
    Put these ideas out of your head.
    Resign yourself to the casting-ladle. What good
    Would it be to you if I offered you board and lodging?
    Think a minute. You're a sensible man.
    You'd keep your memory, that's true enough,
    But what have you got to remember?
    I promise you, the memory of things past
    Would give you little joy.
    You'd find no cause for weeping or for laughter,

No cause for rejoicing or despair,
Nothing to fire your heart, or freeze your blood.
They'd merely be a source of irritation.
PEER. You may be right. [It isn't easy to know
    Where the shoe pinches when one hasn't got it on.]
THIN PERSON. [That's true. I myself, thanks to Never Mind
        Whom,
    Only need one shoe. Incidentally,
    It's lucky that you happened to mention shoes.
    That reminds me] I must be on my way.
    I've a joint to collect; a nice, juicy roast.
    [So I can't waste time exchanging pleasantries here.]
PEER. If one may ask, what sins made him grow fat?
THIN PERSON. I understand that all his life
    He has been himself. [Which of course qualifies him.]
PEER. Himself? You mean such people
    Are automatically your parishioners?
THIN PERSON. That depends. [The door is – left ajar.]
    There are two ways in which a man can be himself.
    A right way and a wrong way.
    You may know that a man in Paris
    Has discovered a way of taking portraits
    With the help of the sun. Either one can produce
    A direct picture, or else what they call a negative.
    In the latter, light and dark are reversed;
    And the result, to the ordinary eye, is ugly.
    But the image of the original is there.
    All that's required is to develop it.
    Now if a human soul, in the course of its life,
    Has created one of these negative portraits,
    The plate is not destroyed. They send it to me.
    [I give it treatment, and by suitable means
    Effect a metamorphosis.] I develop it.
    I steam it and dip it, I burn it and cleanse it
    With sulphur and similar ingredients,
    Till the picture appears which the plate was intended to give.
    [I mean, the one known as the positive.]

But when a soul like you has smudged himself out,
Even sulphur and potash can achieve nothing.

PEER. Then one must come to you as black as a raven
To be sent back as white as a dove? May I ask what name
Is scratched beneath this particular negative
[Which you are about to burn into a positive]?

THIN PERSON. The name is Peter Gynt.

PEER. Peter Gynt? Indeed? Is Mr. Gynt himself?

THIN PERSON. So he affirms.

PEER. Well, he's a reliable man.

THIN PERSON. You know him?

PEER. In a way.
[You know how it is. One knows so many people.]

THIN PERSON. [My time is short.] Where did you see him
last?

PEER. Down at the Cape.

THIN PERSON. Of Good Hope?

PEER. Yes, but I understand he's leaving very soon.

THIN PERSON. Then I must be off at once. I hope I'm in time
To catch him. I never liked that Cape of Good Hope.
It's always full of missionaries from Stavanger.
Runs off southwards.

PEER. The silly bastard! Look at him,
Running away with his tongue hanging out!
Well, I made a fool out of him.
[Putting on airs and acting big!]
A fat lot he's got to boast about!
[He won't get rich the way he's going.]
He'll be knocked off his perch. [And his whole show with
him.]
Hm. I'm not too safe myself.
I've been expelled from the privileged circle;
The exclusive club of men who are themselves.
A shooting star is seen. He nods after it.
Hail, brother star! A greeting from Peer Gynt!
We flash for a moment, then our light is quenched,
And we disappear into the void for ever.

He composes himself as though frightened, and goes deeper into the
mist. There is silence for a few moments, then he cries:

Is there no one, no one in all the Universe – ?

No one in the Abyss – no one in Heaven – ?

He comes forward again farther down, throws his hat down on the
road, and tears his hair. Gradually a calmness comes over him.

How unspeakably poor a soul can be
When it enters the mist and returns to nothing!
O beautiful earth, don't be angry with me
That I trod your sweet grass to no avail.
O beautiful sun, you have squandered
Your golden light upon an empty hut.
There was no one within to warm and comfort.
The owner, I know now, was never at home.
Beautiful sun and beautiful earth,
Why did you bear my mother and give her light?
The spirit is mean, and Nature is wasteful.
Life is a terrible price to pay for birth.
I want to climb, up to the highest peak.
I want to see the sun rise once again,
To gaze till I am tired at the promised land.
Then let the snow pile over me,
And let them write above: 'Here lies no one.'
And afterwards – let the world take its course.

CHURCHGOERS (*singing on the forest path*). O thrice blest morn,
      when tongues of fire
God's spirit did proclaim!
O Holy Ghost, our souls inspire
To sing in universal choir,
And praise God's glorious name!

PEER (*crouches in terror*). Never look there! That's waste and
      desert!

I was a dead man long before I died!

He tries to slink in among the bushes, but comes upon the crossroads.

BUTTON MOULDER. Good morning. Where is your list of
      sins?

PEER. I've shouted and whistled all over the heath.

BUTTON MOULDER. And met no one?

PEER. Only a [travelling] photographer.

BUTTON MOULDER. Well, your time is up.

PEER. Yes. Everything's up.

> The owl smells the light. Can you hear him hooting?

BUTTON MOULDER. It's the bell for mattins.

PEER (*points*). What's that shining over there?

BUTTON MOULDER. Only the light from a hut.

PEER. What is that sound I hear like sighing?

BUTTON MOULDER. A woman singing.

PEER. There! Yes! There I'll find my sins!

BUTTON MOULDER (*grips him*). Set thy house in order!

They have come out of the undergrowth and are standing by the cabin. Day breaks.

PEER. My house? It's there! Away! Begone!

> If your ladle were as large as a coffin
> It would be too small for me and my sins.

BUTTON MOULDER. Well, the third crossroads, Peer. But then – !

> *Turns aside, and goes.*

PEER (*approaches the cabin*). Forward or back it's equally far.

> Outside or in, I'm still confined.
> *Stops.*
> No! I hear like a wild, unending cry:
> 'Go in! Go back! Go home!'
> *Goes a few steps, then stops again.*
> 'Go round,' said the Boyg.
> *Hears the song from inside the cabin.*
> Ah! No! This time straight through,
> However narrow the path may be.

He runs towards the cabin. At the same moment, SOLVEIG *appears in the doorway, dressed for church, with a psalmbook wrapped in linen and a staff in her hand. She stands there, erect and gentle.*

PEER (*throws himself down on the threshold*). Judge this sinner!

> O, speak!

SOLVEIG. It is he! It is he! Oh, praise be to God!

> *She gropes for him.*

PEER. Cry out my sins!

SOLVEIG. You have sinned in nothing, my only child.
  Gropes for him again, and finds him.
BUTTON MOULDER (*behind the house*). The list, Peer Gynt?
PEER. Cry out my guilt!
SOLVEIG (*sits down beside him*). You have made my life into a
      song.
  Bless you for coming back to me at last.
  Blessed, oh, blessed be our meeting
  On this morning of Pentecost!
PEER. Then I am lost!
SOLVEIG. There is One Who rules all.
PEER (*laughs*). Lost! Unless you can solve riddles.
SOLVEIG. Tell me.
PEER. Tell you? Yes, I will!
  Can you tell me where Peer Gynt has been
  [Since you saw him last]?
SOLVEIG. Been?
PEER. With the mark of destiny on his brow
  As he sprang forth in the mind of God!
  Can you answer me that? If not, I must go
  To my home, down to the land of mists.
SOLVEIG (*smiles*). Oh, that riddle is easy.
PEER. Tell me, then!
  Where was my self, my whole self, my true self?
  The self that bore God's stamp upon its brow?
SOLVEIG. In my faith, in my hope, and in my love.
PEER (*starts back*). What do you say? Hush! Now you speak in
      riddles!
  Ah! *You* are the mother to that child?
SOLVEIG. Yes, I am. But who is its father?
  It is He Who forgives when the mother prays.
PEER (*bathed in light, cries*). My mother! My wife! O, thou pure
      woman!
  O hide me in your love! Hide me! Hide me!
*He clings tightly to her and buries his face in her lap. A long silence.
The sun rises.*

SOLVEIG (*sings softly*). Sleep, O sleep, my dearest boy.
   I will cradle you, I will guard you.
   Sleep, O sleep, my love, my joy.
   Sleep now, and rest.

   You've sat on my lap, we've played together.
   The life-long day you've lain on my breast.
   You've always been close to my heart.
   Now you're tired. You can rest.
   Hums
   Sleep, O sleep —
BUTTON MOULDER'S VOICE (*behind the house*). We shall meet
      at the last crossroads, Peer.
   [And then we'll see if – ! I'll say no more.]
SOLVEIG (*sings louder as the daylight grows*). I will cradle you, I
   will guard you.
   Sleep, sleep and dream.

Notes

1. *Changeling.* There is an old Norwegian superstition that changelings left by the fairies can be blown up the chimney.

2. *Master Cook.* A kind of master of ceremonies.

3. *Sæter.* A small mountain farm where the cattle are sent to pasture in summer.

4. *Be thyself – and to Hell with the rest of the world!* The phrase which Ibsen uses to formulate the philosophy of the trolls, *at være sig selv nok,* to be self-sufficient in a bad sense, was not, as many critics have assumed, created by Ibsen. The danger of self-sufficiency was a problem which was occupying people during the middle of the nineteenth century far outside the boundaries of Norway. English writers around this time were debating the reasons why the word self-sufficiency had acquired a pejorative significance; De Quincey suggested that *self-sufficingness* should be used to convey the original nobility of the Greek *autarkes* and the Latin *sibi sufficiens*; and Swinburne proposed *self-sufficience* as an alternative in, curiously enough, 1867, the very year in which Ibsen wrote *Peer Gynt.* The absence in modern English of any pejorative equivalent of self-sufficiency makes this vital phrase peculiarly difficult to translate. The usual: 'Troll, to thyself be enough' fails for this reason, apart from being deficient in any real impact.

5. *Salted herring.* The traditional remedy in Scandinavia for a hangover.

6. *Why, he's chopped his finger off!* This episode is based on a true incident of which Ibsen had read in the newspaper *Aftenbladet* on June 14, 1864. He had already used it in the epic version of *Brand,* of which he completed a considerable portion before abandoning it to treat the subject as a play. But there the boy had been a figure of shame; in *Peer Gynt* he appears as a man of honour, who had the courage to do what other men secretly wished

to do. It is difficult not to believe that Ibsen's preoccupation with this matter stemmed from the sense of guilt which we know he possessed for not having taken part in the Danish-German war, about which he felt so strongly.

The lines describing this incident may be cut in production because the audience is able to see it silently taking place.

7. *Soria-Moria.* The Arabic name for a group of islands beyond the Red Sea which were fabled to be the Islands of the Blest.

8. *Grane.* Sigurd Fafnirsbane's horse, descended from the god Odin's Sleipnir.

9. *Trumpeterstraale.* In the original, Herr Trumpeterstraale is a Swede, but since some of his remarks, about Charles XII's spurs and so forth, have no meaning for an English audience, we turned him, in the Old Vic production, into an American. This involved the alteration of a single line on page 99 (see footnote 13 below).

10. *A measure of spiritual contemplation* . . . This speech is deliberately obscure in the original, as a satire on the German tendency to talk abstract nonsense.

11. *Lippe-Detmold.* A tiny German principality.

12. *Your* Reich *last for a thousand years!* Literally: 'Our finest and most ancient Rhenish vintages!'

13. *Stand in history with Charlemagne!* Literally: 'And all the swords of Charles XII!'

14. *King Charles's spurs.* When King Charles XII of Sweden was fighting the Turks at Bender (in Bessarabia, on the Dniester) in 1713, his spurs are said to have tripped him and resulted in his capture. There is also a legend that he tore with these spurs the garments of the Turkish emissary who brought him the news that the Sultan had concluded a truce with their mutual enemy Peter the Great of Russia.

15. *But under protest.* This is probably a gibe at Count Manderström, the Swedish Foreign Minister who, when Germany had attacked Denmark in 1864, had written diplomatic notes of protest but had refrained from taking any positive action. Manderström is also supposed to have been the original of the minister

Hussein in the madhouse scene (see pp. 132–3). Ibsen had a particular contempt for him, and once drew a halter round his neck on a picture of him in an illustrated magazine in the Scandinavian Club in Rome. Manderström's nephew, Carl Snoilsky, later became one of Ibsen's closest friends.

16. *Gyntiana.* Ole Bull, Ibsen's old chief at the Bergen Theatre, had tried in 1852 to found an ideal Norwegian colony in Pennsylvania, on the model approved by the French Socialists. He called it Oleana; but it ended in financial disaster.

17. *Kaba.* A sacred building in Mecca, containing a black stone which pilgrims have to kiss.

18. *Das ewig weibliche ziehet uns an!* A deliberate misquotation of the last line of Goethe's *Faust.* Goethe's line reads: 'Woman eternally draws us upwards.' Peer says: 'Woman eternally draws us towards her.'

19. *Qu'allais-je faire dans cette galère?* A quotation, slightly wrong as always with Peer, from Molière's comedy, *Les Fourberies de Scapin:* 'What the devil was I doing in that boat?' Peer has already used this once, on page 110, where I have translated it: 'Why did I ever get on to that wagon?'

20. *Becker.* Becker's *Weltgeschichte* (1801–9) had been translated into Danish in the middle of the nineteenth century.

21. *Memnon.* Memnon was the god of the morning. When he died, his mother Aurora begged Jupiter to honour him. Jupiter answered her prayer by turning Memnon's ashes into birds that perpetually sang, fought and played. These lines are not, as has often been supposed, meaningless, nor does their significance seem to me obscure. The statue is telling Peer that the latter has sealed up his soul, and that unless he can unseal it he will die – as indeed he does. Whether Peer dies in the madhouse, or in the shipwreck, the last scenes of the play surely show us either his soul's passage through purgatory, or the film of his life, with its failures and errors, unreeling before his eyes in the moment of death. It is interesting to note that Ibsen had written of the Memnon Statue as early as 1855 in a prologue spoken from the stage at the Bergen Theatre.

22. *The Circle of the Seventy Interpreters.* Presumably a refer-

ence to the writers of the Septuagint, the Greek version of the Old Testament said to have been made by seventy translators around 270 B.C. Various unlikely suggestions have been put forward as to the meaning of Begriffenfeldt's next sentence, 'recently increased to a hundred and sixty,' but I think this is probably merely intended as an additional example of the German's lunacy.

23. *Munchausen's fox*. Baron Munchausen claimed to have nailed a fox to a tree by its tail, cut a slit in its forehead, and whipped it so that it jumped out of its skin.

24. *Huhu*. This character is a caricature of the Norwegian *maalstrævere*, 'a party,' to quote William Archer, 'which desired to substitute a language compounded of the various local dialects for the Norwegian of the bourgeoisie and of literature, which they called Danish, and declared to be practically a foreign tongue to the peasants and lower classes generally. The peasants, they argued (like Ibsen's orang-outangs), lived and died 'uninterpreted.' The movement attained no little force in the [eighteen-] sixties and seventies, and a considerable literature sprang up in the so-called *maal*, the work of such men as Ivar Aasen, A. O. Vinje, and Kristofer Janson.' Janson was furious when he read this scene and wrote a virulent attack on the play in *Aftenbladet*, expressing the hope that Ibsen would soon 'tire of spitting and scolding from his chimney corner.'

25. *Fellah*. A fellah is an Egyptian peasant. This character with the mummy on his back is an expression of a theme frequently to be found in Ibsen's work, especially of this period: man's bondage to his past. A few years later he was to write a poem on this theme entitled *The Corpse in the Cargo*; and it is, of course, the central *motif* of *Ghosts*. The Dovre kingdom and Aase's ruined farm are parallel symbols; but they should not be taken, as they have been, as referring specifically to Norway's, or Sweden's, glorification of her former greatness. The image of the Fellah and his mummy may have been based on the adulation shown by the Swedes towards the mummified body of Charles XII, and there are references in the troll scene which are aimed at Norwegian chauvinism; but it was humanity's bondage, not

Norway's, that troubled Ibsen most deeply.

26. *Cuckold to Death and to Aslak the smith.* Because Aslak and, now, Death have both slept with Ingrid since Peer seduced her on her wedding night; she is another person who has been destroyed by his greed. The Man in Grey is, of course, Mads Moen.

27. *The Cat of the Dovre.* The white bear which Peer Gynt took with him (in Asbjœrnsen's tale) to frighten the trolls on Christmas Eve.

28. *I think I'll put up my own rubbish for auction.* The word auction had painful associations for Ibsen. In a letter to Bjœrnson (undated, but probably written in October 1866, just before he started *Peer Gynt*), he expressed vehement indignation at the fact that his belongings in Norway had been auctioned without his authorization. 'It isn't so much the loss of my furniture, etc., that grieves me, but that my private letters, papers, drafts, etc., not to speak of many things that meant far more to me than their face value, should have found their way into the hands of any Tom, Dick or Harry, is a most bitter thought.'

29. *Threadballs.* Trolls in threadballs are a common idea in Norwegian folk lore.

30. *It'll only be a transitional stage, As the fox said when they started to skin him.* A reference to the Norwegian proverb: '"It'll be a change," as the fox said when they started to skin him.'

31. *Justedal.* Matthias Foss, a priest in Justedal in the middle of the eighteenth century, wrote in 1750 *A Short Description of Justedal*, which included the sentence: 'They [i.e., the people of Justedal] are exceedingly long-lived, so that it is seldom anyone dies there.'

32. *Esben.* Esben Askeladd is a character in a Norwegian folk tale who found a dead magpie which led to his winning the hand of a princess.

33. *Is that hoof natural?* The Devil is traditionally represented in Scandinavian folk lore as having a single hoof instead of a right foot.

Note on the Translation

Peer Gynt is the most difficult of Ibsen's plays to translate, because the style is continually changing. Although it is written in rhyme throughout, Ibsen employed half a dozen different measures. In the first three acts, where Peer is a peasant of twenty, the language resembles nothing so much as that of *The Playboy of the Western World*, with its ebullience, naïveté and extravagant imagery. In the fourth act, Peer is a middle-aged man of the world, and talks in a pretentious, would-be epigrammatical style like a character from one of Aldous Huxley's early novels; while the fifth act is – I had almost said Shakespearian, but that is not quite accurate; the conception is Shakespearian, but the style remains racy and colloquial; its characteristic quality, as Archer observed, is its vernacular ease and simplicity, so that when one reads the play in Norwegian one has no feeling of incongruity between the various sections. As with *Brand*, a free verse, with broken rhythms, seemed the only answer, apart from certain passages which demand rhyme.

Wherever I have had to choose between maintaining the rhythm and using the most effective phrase, I have not hesitated to prefer the latter. As long as each section is controlled by a general overall rhythm, the individual phrase or line can, and indeed, I believe, should break out of it. This translation was originally much more regular; a good deal of valuable fragmentation took place during rehearsal.

The text is presented complete and unabridged. Cuts made for the 1962 Old Vic production are indicated by square brackets.

The final 'e' is always pronounced in Norwegian names, like an abbreviated '-er'. Thus, Aase ('Awse'), Lunde, Ronde, Grane, etc., are all bisyllabic.

The Pretenders

Introduction

The Pretenders was Ibsen's first real success in the theatre; he wrote it in July and August of 1863, at the age of thirty-five.

His fortunes at this time were at their lowest ebb. Of his previous nine plays only two, *The Feast at Solhaug* and *The Vikings at Helgeland*, had received any recognition at all, and that very limited. The Norwegian Theatre in Christiania, where he had been artistic director since 1857, had gone bankrupt the previous summer, and his only employment since had been as literary adviser to the Danish-controlled Christiania Theatre; but this, too, was in such straits that the salaries of its staff were graded according to what came in, so that of his tiny stipend of one hundred crowns a month he received only a fraction. He was frequently penniless and forced to resort to money-lenders; his application in 1860 for a government grant had been rejected; and a further application early in 1863 had met a similar fate, while those of his fellow-poets, Bjœrnson and Vinje, had been granted. Worst of all, his most recent play, *Love's Comedy*, had been rejected by his own theatre, and had been poorly received when published as a New Year's Eve supplement to the magazine *Illustreret Nyhedsblad*. He had accomplished sadly little for a man half-way through his life. 'I was excommunicated; everyone was against me,' he wrote seven years later (28 October 1870) to Peter Hansen. 'And the fact that everyone was against me, that there was no uncommitted person who could be said to believe in me, could not but give rise to the strain of feeling which found utterance in *The Pretenders*.'

However, that June (1863) he received an invitation from some students to attend a choral festival at Bergen, at which over a thousand singers were to gather from various parts of Norway. Ibsen accepted the invitation, and wrote a song which the three choral groups from Christiania learned for the occasion. He left with them by ship on 12 June, and reached Bergen two days later. The voyage in their company, and the festival itself, had a remarkable effect on him.

Where before he had felt isolated and rejected, he now found himself surrounded by sympathy, friendship and admiration. He described his reaction in a letter which he wrote to his host at Bergen, a shipping agent named Randolph Nilsen, four days after his return to Christiania:

'It is eight days to the hour since we said goodbye, and, God be praised, I still carry within me the spirit of the festival, and I hope I shall long keep it. My hearty thanks to you and your good wife for all the indescribable warmth and friendliness you showed me. The festival up there, and the many dear and unforgettable people whom I met, are working on me like a good visit to church, and I sincerely hope that this mood will not pass. Everyone was so kind to me in Bergen. It is not so here, where there are many people who seek to hurt and wound me at every opportunity. This strong feeling of elevation, of being ennobled and purified in all one's thoughts, must I think have been common to all who attended the choral festival, and he would indeed have something hard and evil in his soul who could remain insensitive to such an atmosphere. . . .'

What particularly moved Ibsen was the generous public tribute which had been paid to him at a banquet on 16 June by his famous rival, Bjœrnsterne Bjœrnson. It is a little difficult, reading Bjœrnson's plays and novels today, to realize the immense influence that he wielded in Norway, and indeed throughout Scandinavia, for over half a century. He might have said, like Oscar Wilde, though the thought would hardly have occurred to him, that he put his genius into his life but only his talent into his writing. To Norway, a country struggling for political and cultural independence, he seemed at this time, and for the next forty years, the embodiment of noble patriotism; a kind of Parnell. Handsome, assured and a brilliant speaker, he had achieved the literary success that had eluded Ibsen, and the younger generation regarded him as their spokesman. Ibsen had directed two of Bjœrnson's plays, *King Sverre* and *Lame Hulda*, at the Christiania Norwegian Theatre, and must bitterly have noted the warmth of their reception compared with the indifference and hostility shown to his own work. 'In the world of art,' wrote Théophile Gautier, 'there stands always below each man of genius a man of talent, preferred to him'; and at every turn Ibsen found himself contrasted with Bjœrnson, to the latter's advantage.

At the festival banquet, however, Bjœrnson spoke out most

handsomely in admiration of Ibsen, and took the opportunity to
denounce those people who had tried, as critics will in every age that
contains writers of comparable stature, to turn them into adversaries.
'Have I not experienced,' he cried, 'that my friend Ibsen has been held
up against me for the purpose of disparaging me, and I against him,
to disparage him?' This speech was followed by the song which Ibsen
had written for the occasion, dealing, it so happened, with the
importance of naturally dissimilar people living in harmony – a
coincidence which Ibsen, no more than anyone else, can have missed.
Yet the contrast between his failure and Bjœrnson's success still
gnawed him, and it was the combination of this with the mood of
exhilaration and confidence induced by the festival that spurred him
to write *The Pretenders*, in which a man of great gifts invalidated by
self-distrust is defeated by a potentially lesser man who possesses the
supreme virtue of believing in himself. Bjœrnson was very much the
model for Haakon (whom incidentally he had praised in a speech at
Bergen as 'Norway's best king'), and Ibsen put much of himself into
Skule, and also, by his own admission, into the bard Jatgeir. 'I know
I have the fault' he wrote to Bjœrnson on 16 September 1864 from
Rome 'that I can't make close contact with those people who demand
that one should give oneself freely and completely. I am rather like
the bard Jatgeir in *The Pretenders*, I can never bring myself to strip
completely. I have the feeling that, where personal relationships are
concerned, I can only give false expression to what I feel deep down
inside, and that is why I prefer to shut it up within me, and why we
have sometimes stood as it were observing each other from a distance.'

Ibsen completed *The Pretenders* within two months of his return to
Christiania. He had in fact begun to plan a play on this theme as early
as five years previously, in the summer of 1858; the idea seems to have
come to him through reading Volume 3 of P.A. Munch's *History of
the Norwegian People*, which had appeared the previous year and
which dealt with the civil wars between the accession of King Sverre
in 1177 and the death of Duke Skule in 1240. But he had put the
project aside, and it needed the tonic effect of the Bergen festival and
the prolonged meeting with Bjœrnson to get him into the mood to
write it. Unfortunately no draft manuscripts or preliminary notes
relating to the play have survived, so that we do not know, as we do
with so many of his plays, exactly when he began and finished each
act, but from start to finish, excluding the fair-copying, it appears to

have taken him from six to eight weeks.

The Pretenders was published by the Christiania bookseller Johan Dahl towards the end of October 1863 (though by an error the year 1864 appears on the title page). Seven years later, in a letter to his Danish publisher Frederik Hegel of Gyldendal (who were to publish all the original editions of Ibsen's plays from *Brand* onwards), Ibsen described how Dahl acquired the rights. 'One day early in September 1863, with the fair copy of *The Pretenders* under my arm, I met Johan Dahl on the street in Christiania, told him I had written a new historical play, and offered it to him for publication. Dahl immediately expressed his willingness and agreed without demur to my request for an honorarium of 150 specie-dollars for the first edition. Dahl took the manuscript, the printing began forthwith, and on 15 September I signed the contract in Dahl's bookshop.'

The book was, on the whole, favourably received by the Norwegian newspapers, though Clemens Petersen, the doyen of the Danish critics and a future enemy of Ibsen's, voiced his disapproval. Unlike *Love's Comedy*, *The Pretenders* was at once accepted for production by the Christiania Theatre, and it received its first performance there on 17 January 1864. Ibsen directed it himself – the last time that he was to direct a performance of any of his plays. Halvdan Koht has described the premiere: 'It was not a really integrated performance. The young Sigvard Gundersen had not yet the strength and weight to give King Haakon the assurance of victory that is begotten of genius. The Danish actor Wolf played Duke Skule better than any role he had previously attempted . . . but in general it was the strong hero that he presented rather than the soul-sick doubter. . . . Nevertheless, the play gripped the public. Although it lasted for nearly five hours – later they managed to reduce the playing time to four – we are told that "from start to finish it was followed with excited attention," and that "after the fall of the curtain there was a general cry for the author who, when he appeared, was rewarded with thunderous applause." In less than two months, *The Pretenders* was performed eight times, a success unique for a play as long and serious as this in a town as small as the Christiania of those days. . . . Now for the first time he rested in a full and free confidence in his own ability to write, and in his calling as a poet.'

The Pretenders took some time to penetrate beyond Norway. It was not performed in Denmark until 1871, nor in Sweden until 1879. In

1876, however, it was the occasion of a notable production in Berlin by the famous Saxe-Meiningen company who had prepared it especially for their visit to the capital. Ibsen saw it, and was deeply impressed. 'At the beginning of this month', he wrote to the Swedish theatre manager Ludvig Josephson on 14 June 1876, 'I went to Berlin to attend the first performance of *The Pretenders* in a brilliant and spectacular presentation by the Duke of Meiningen's court ensemble. The play was received with great applause, and I was repeatedly called for. I don't think this much pleased the Berlin critics, most of whom are themselves playwrights. However, the play has run for nine successive performances, and would have continued longer if the Meiningers had not been scheduled to end their season on the 15th. After the opening performance, I was invited by the Duke to visit him at his summer place at Liebenstein in Meiningen, where I had been staying until I came back here the day before yesterday. On my departure he decorated me with the Knight Cross of the Saxon-Ernestine Order, first class. . . .'

Largely, one imagines, because of the supposed allergy of audiences to foreign history, *The Pretenders* has been performed comparatively seldom outside Norway, where it has remained a regular item in the national repertoire. It has, however, stimulated the imagination of several famous directors. In 1904, Max Reinhardt had a big success with it at the Neues Theater in Berlin; and in 1926 the Danish actor Johannes Poulsen winkled Edward Gordon Craig out of his Italian retirement to design and co-direct it at the Royal Theatre in Copenhagen. Craig has described the result in his book *A Production, 1926*, profusely illustrated with his designs for the sets and costumes, which are considerably more illuminating than his text. The first English production took place at the Haymarket Theatre in 1913. In 1927, Theodore Komisarjevsky staged it at Holyhead for the National Theatre of Wales, with an all-amateur cast, for a single performance attended by ten thousand people, and the following year Terence Gray directed it at the Festival Theatre, Cambridge. The Oxford University Dramatic Society presented it in 1922, and again in 1947 (with Kenneth Tynan as Bishop Nicholas); and in 1963 there was an exciting centenary production by Val May at the Bristol Old Vic, when Tynan acclaimed it in the *Observer* as Ibsen's 'first great play' and B.A. Young, in the *Financial Times*, wrote: 'It is hard to see why it has been so neglected.'

How accurate is *The Pretenders* historically? More than most people imagine. William Archer, who knew Norway well (he spent much of his childhood there, and was bilingual from an early age) noted: 'In *The Pretenders*, Ibsen stands much nearer to history than in any other play, except perhaps *Emperor and Galilean*. All the leading characters and many of the incidents of the drama are historical; but the poet has treated chronology with a very free hand, and has made use of psychological motives which are but faintly indicated, or not at all, in the sources from which he drew.' Archer went on to point out that the leading Norwegian historian of the day, J.E. Sars, writing thirteen years *after* the appearance of *The Pretenders*, assessed the characters of Haakon and Skule very similarly to Ibsen. Haakon was, says Sars, 'reared in the firm conviction of his right to the throne. . . . He owed his chief strength to the repose and equilibrium of mind which distinguished him, and had its root in the unwavering sense of having right and the people's will on his side.' Skule, on the other hand, according to Sars, 'was the centre of a hierarchic aristocratic party; but after its repeated defeats this party must have been lacking alike in numbers and confidence. . . . It was clear from the first that his attempt to reawaken the old wars of succession in Norway was undertaken in the spirit of the desperate gambler, who does not count the chances, but throws at random, in the blind hope that luck may befriend him. . . . Skule's enterprise thus had no support in opinion or in any prevailing interest, and one defeat was sufficient to crush him.' Historians in general condemned Skule; Ibsen tried to portray him sympathetically (as Strindberg was to do with Göran Persson in *Erik the Fourteenth*), while admitting that it was best for his country that he should be defeated.

Of Bishop Nicholas, Sars writes (I quote again from Archer's translation) that he 'represented rather the aristocracy . . . than the cloth to which he belonged. . . . During his long participation in the civil broils . . . we see in him a man to whose character any sort of religious or ecclesiastical enthusiasm must have been foreign, his leading motives being personal ambition and vengefulness rather than any care for general interests – a cold and calculating nature, shrewd but petty and without any impetus, of whom Haakon Haakonsson, in delivering his funeral speech . . . could find nothing better to say than that he had not his equal in worldly wisdom.' Archer continues: 'I cannot find that the Bishop played any such prominent part in the struggle between the King and the Earl as Ibsen assigns to him, and the only foundation for the great death-bed scene seems to be the following passage from *Haakon Haakonsson's Saga*, Cap. 138: "As Bishop Nicholas at this time lay very sick, he sent a messenger to the King praying him to come to him. The King had on this expedition seized certain letters, from which he gathered that the Bishop had not been true to him. With this he upbraided him, and the Bishop, confessing it, prayed the King to forgive him. The King replied that he did so willingly, for God's sake; and as he could discern that the Bishop lay near to death, he abode with him until God called him from the world." A chronological conspectus of the leading events referred to in *The Pretenders* (founded on P.A. Munch's *History of the Norwegian People*) will enable the reader to estimate for himself the extent of Ibsen's adherence to, and departure from history:

1189	Skule Baardsson born.
1204	Haakon Haakonsson born.
1206	Haakon is brought by the Birchlegs to King Inge.
1217	Haakon chosen King at the Oerething (national assembly).
1218	Haakon and Skule at Bergen. Inga undergoes the ordeal.
1219	Haakon betrothed to Skule's daughter, Margrete.
1219–20	Andres Skjaldarband and Vegard Væradal thanes of Halogaland.
1221	Vegard Væradal killed by Andres Skjaldarband's men (reason unknown).
1225	(January). Haakon's campaign in Värmland.
	(25 May). Haakon's marriage with Margrete.
	(7 November). Bishop Nicholas's death.
1227	Haakon's eldest son, Olaf, born.
1229	Andres Skjaldarband sets forth for Palestine.
1232	Haakon's second son, Haakon, born.
1235	Inga, the King's mother, dies.
1237	Skule created Duke. Dagfinn the Peasant dies.
1239	(6 November). Skule proclaims himself King at the Oerething.
1240	(6 March). Skule victorious at Laaka.
	(21 April). Haakon victorious at Oslo.
	(21 May). Skule's son Peter killed at Elgesæter.
	(24 May). Skule killed at Elgesæter, and the abbey burned.'

The Pretenders, as Ibsen wrote it, is a diffuse and unwieldy play which, uncut, would run for between four and five hours. After I had translated it *in toto*, Mr Val May, the director of the Bristol Old Vic, made certain cuts and transpositions for his production of the play there in 1963, and it is this version which is given here. Apart from occasional condensations, and transpositions for the sake of clarification, the main alterations have been as follows.

Act 1, Scene 1. The two minor Pretenders to the throne, Sigurd Ribbung and Guthorm Ingesson, have been cut, together with all references to them; also a good deal of historical background stuff. The arguments about the respective rights of Haakon and Skule have been condensed; and Skule has been given a line not in the original: 'Now *I* grasp the burning iron!'

Act 1, Scene 2. The sub-plot about the feud between Vegard Væradal and Andres Skjaldarband (Ingeborg's husband) has been cut; also Haakon's announcement that he is sending away his mistress, Kanga.

Act 2. All references to Sigurd Ribbung, and other digressions concerning the historical background, have been omitted; also the quarrel between the Earl's men and Ivar Bodde, resulting in the latter's departure from court, and the long passage about Skjaldarband's murder of Vegard Væradal.

Act 3, Scene 1. The scene in which Inga of Varteig brings Trond's letter to the Bishop has been cut. Instead, Peter hands over the letter; this involved the insertion of a short speech for him. The Bishop's deathbed monologues, which are of enormous length in the original, have been thinned down, and the short dialogue between Haakon and Skule after the Bishop's death has been cut.

Act 3, Scene 2. Skule's long monologue at the child's cradle, and the ensuing dialogue between him and Haakon, have been reduced. Inga of Varteig's melodramatic entrance at the end of the scene has been cut, and Haakon's change of heart towards Margaret condensed into a single speech.

Act 4, Scene 1. The opening of Jatgeir's song has been omitted: also part of the Skule-Jatgeir scene, in which certain transpositions were made, all references to Skule's men as the 'Wolfskins', and the discussion amongst them as to what booty they will take from their enemies. Skule's monologue after their departure, and the second Skule-Jatgeir dialogue, have been condensed; also the Skule-Ingeborg dialogue.

Act 4, Scene 2. Certain lines have been added to the crowd scene to clarify the course of the battle.

Act 5, Scene 1. No significant alterations.

Act 5, Scene 2. Much of the dialogue among the citizens after Skule's flight has been cut.

Act 5, Scene 3. The scene between Skule and the Bishop's Ghost has been reduced. (A myth has been handed down from commentator to commentator, starting, I fear, with Archer, that this scene is 'a blemish on the play,' etc. It is in fact superbly effective if properly done, and restores the balance temporarily upset by the Bishop's death in Act 3; it also makes the part more attractive to a star actor, a consideration which Ibsen is unlikely to have overlooked.) The name of the abbey where Skule seeks refuge, and which needs to be 'planted' in the audience's mind, has been altered from Elgesæter to St Stephen's.

Act 5, Scene 4. A few slight cuts only.

These amendments are not such a heresy as may be supposed, for it so happens that Ibsen put on record his awareness that some such treatment was desirable for future productions. On 20 January 1871 he wrote to Frederik Winkel-Horn from Dresden: 'You are wrong in assuming that I didn't want the play to be cut. On the contrary. During my stay in Copenhagen last summer, I explained to the director of the theatre that it neither could nor should be performed in its entirety. With his approval I therefore made an abridged version in which the Bishop's death-scene in particular was considerably reduced; moreover, I expressly urged that they should cut in rehearsal anything that they found to be superfluous.'

Stylistically, as well as structurally, *The Pretenders* marks an important stage in Ibsen's development as a dramatist. Of his previous eight plays (leaving aside the short comic opera, *Norma*), three (*Catiline*, *The Warrior's Barrow* and *Love's Comedy*) had been written in verse and three (*St. John's Eve*, *Lady Inger of Oestraat* and *The*

Vikings of Helgeland) in prose; while *The Feast at Solhaug* and *Olaf Liljekrans* had been composed in a mixture of the two. Although he had managed here and there to achieve a colloquial prose, he had limited it to his peasant and lower-class characters; his princes and chieftains had spoken a formal dialogue, and in his most recent prose play, *The Vikings at Helgeland*, he had deliberately imitated the antique language of the sagas. Bjœrnson had disapproved of this experiment, and Ibsen himself, in a review of Bjœrnson's historical drama *Sigurd Slembe*, had expressed his conviction that the language of a historical play should be living and colloquial, whoever might be speaking. In *The Pretenders* he attempted to create such a dialogue, retaining formal language only when the characters deliberately use a formal mode of address – as in the opening exchange between Haakon and Skule – and occasionally for special effect. He succeeded, not indeed completely, but to a considerable degree;[1] the play is full of terse, colloquial statements, such as Jatgeir's 'Buy a dog, my lord,' that we do not find in *Lady Inger* or *The Vikings*, and that shock by their unexpectedness. Parenthetically, it may be noted that Ibsen was surprised to find himself writing the play in prose at all. 'I am now working on a historical drama in five acts,' he wrote to Clemens Petersen on 10 August 1863, 'but in prose – I *cannot* write it in verse.' Within a few years, he was to renounce verse completely.

The Pretenders is full of anticipatory echoes of Ibsen's later plays; it makes a pleasant parlour game to look for them. Skule, like Brand, demands 'All or Nothing.' To Peter, like Solness to Hilde, he says: 'You are the one I've been needing.' and to Ingeborg, like Borkman to Ella: 'I left you, to gain power and riches. If you had stayed. . . .' The Bishop's Ghost promises Skule, as Rubek was to promise both Maja and Irene in *When We Dead Awaken*: 'I will lead you up on to a high mountain and show you all the glory of the world'; and this scene between the Ghost and Skule strongly anticipates the encounter in *Peer Gynt* between Peer and the Thin Person. The two priests, Aslak and Trond, whom we hear of but do not see in *The Pretenders*, were to reappear in *Peer Gynt* as a blacksmith and a troll respectively; so was the cowardly soldier of Bishop Nicholas's confession.

1. Not least in the delightfully easy rhymed verse given to the Bishop's Ghost in Act Five, and too glibly dismissed by some critics as 'doggerel'. If this is doggerel, so is much of *Peer Gynt*.

But it is not merely as apprentice work that *The Pretenders* demands attention. It stands solidly in its own right as a historical drama of epic sweep and intense poetic imagination, working remorselessly towards the superb climax in the abbey. It contains, in Skule, Haakon and Bishop Nicholas, three characters comparable in stature with anything that he created later; and, imaginatively directed, it works brilliantly. It should be regarded, not as an isolated range-finder, but as the first of the great epic quartet containing *Brand*, *Peer Gynt* and *Emperor and Galilean*. It was no mere apprentice work that fired the imagination of Reinhardt, Craig and Komisarjevsky.

Ibsen did not at the time intend *The Pretenders* to be his last play about Norwegian history. Soon after completing it, he made plans for a drama about Magnus Heineson, a Viking of the sixteenth century, and as late as 1870 he was meditating an opera about Sigurd Jorsalfar. But neither materialised. Nationalism began to lose its importance; other subjects, closer at hand, seemed more relevant than Norway's glorious past. The final speech of the Bishop's Ghost in Act Five was a formidable warning of what was to come.

MICHAEL MEYER

Characters

HAAKON HAAKONSSON, *chosen as King by the Birchlegs.*
INGA OF VARTEIG, *his mother.*
EARL SKULE, *regent of Norway during* HAAKON'S *minority.*
THE LADY RAGNHILD, EARL SKULE'S *wife.*
SIGRID, *his sister.*
MARGARET, *his daughter.*
NICHOLAS ARNESSON, *Bishop of Oslo.*
DAGFINN THE PEASANT, HAAKON'S *marshal.*
IVAR BODDE, HAAKON'S *chaplain.*
GREGORIOUS JONSSON } *followers of* EARL SKULE.
PAUL FLIDA
INGEBORG, *wife to a nobleman, Andres Skjaldarband.*
PETER, *her son, a young priest*
SIRA WILLIAM, *chaplain to* BISHOP NICHOLAS.
MASTER SIGARD OF BRABANT, *a doctor.*
JATGEIR, *an Icelandic bard.*
BAARD BRATTE, *a chieftain from the Trondheim district.*

CITIZENS *of Bergen, Oslo and Nidaros.*
PRIESTS, MONKS AND NUNS.
GUESTS, MEN-AT-ARMS, LADIES, SOLDIERS, *etc.*

The action takes place in Norway during the first half of the thirteenth century.

This translation of The Pretenders *was commissioned by the Old Vic Trust, and was first performed at the Theatre Royal, Bristol, on 12 February 1963. The cast was:*

HAAKON HAAKONSSON	David Sumner
INGA OF VARTEIG	Pauline Browne
EARL SKULE	John Phillips
THE LADY RAGNHILD	Barbara Leigh-Hunt
SIGRID	Hilary Hardiman
MARGARET	Monica Evans
BISHOP NICHOLAS	John Bennett
DAGFINN THE PEASANT	Stephen Thorne
IVAR BODDE	Terrence Hardiman
GREGORIUS JONSSON	Leader Hawkins
PAUL FLIDA	Christopher Benjamin
INGEBORG	Hilary Hardiman
PETER	Leo Maguire
SIRA WILLIAM	Roger Jerome
MASTER SIGARD	Gabriel Prendergast
JATGEIR	Terrence Hardiman
BAARD BRATTE	Peter Baldwin
NUNS	Cynthia Cowdell
	Marjorie Yorke
CITIZENS, SOLDIERS, PRIESTS, MONKS	Stanley Bates
	Patrick Black
	Alan Knight
	Gabriel Prendergast
	David Martin
	Cynthia Cowdell
	Marjorie Yorke
	Laurence Carter
	John Ainscough
	William Fisher
	Dirk Shoulder

Designed by Graham Barlow
Directed by Val May

Act One

The churchyard of Christ Church in Bergen. In the background is the church, with its main door facing the audience. Downstage left stand HAAKON HAAKONSSON, DAGFINN THE PEASANT, IVAR BODDE *and other thanes and chieftains. Facing them stand* EARL SKULE, GREGORIUS JONSSON, PAUL FLIDA, *and others of the* EARL's *followers. The approaches to the church are guarded by soldiers, and the churchyard is filled with people. Many of them are sitting up in trees or on the church wall. They all seem to be waiting tensely for something to happen. Bells can be heard from the steeples in the town, both near and in the distance.*

EARL SKULE (*impatiently, to* GREGORIUS JONSSON). Why are they so slow in there?

GREGORIUS JONSSON. Ssh! They're beginning the psalm!

From within the closed church can be heard a choir of MONKS *and* NUNS *singing* Domine coeli, *to the accompaniment of trumpets. As they sing, the church door is opened from inside and* BISHOP NICHOLAS *is seen in the entrance, surrounded by* PRIESTS *and* MONKS.

BISHOP NICHOLAS (*moves forward into the doorway and proclaims, with upraised staff*). Now Inga of Varteig is submitting to the ordeal on behalf of her son Haakon, pretender to the crown. If the white-hot iron leaves no mark on her hands, Haakon is her son by our lamented King.

The door is closed again. The singing continues within.

GREGORIUS JONSSON (*whispers to* EARL SKULE). Pray to the blessed St Olaf to defend your right.

EARL SKULE(*quickly, with a deprecating gesture*). Not now. Best not to put him in mind of me.

IVAR BODDE (*grips* HAAKON *by the arm*). Pray to the Lord your

God, Haakon Haakonsson.

HAAKON. There is no need. I am sure of Him.

The singing from the church grows louder. All bare their heads. Many fall on their knees and pray.

GREGORIUS JONSSON (*to* EARL SKULE). This is a fateful hour for you, and for many.

EARL SKULE (*gazes tensely at the church*). A fateful hour for Norway.

PAUL FLIDA (*close to* SKULE). Now she is holding the burning iron.

DAGFINN (*close to* HAAKON). They are coming down the nave.

IVAR BODDE. Christ protect thine innocent hands, Inga, mother of our King!

HAAKON. All my life I shall reward her for this hour.

EARL SKULE (*who has been listening intently, suddenly exclaims*). Was that a cry? Has she let the iron fall?

PAUL FLIDA (*moves towards the church*). I don't know what it was.

GREGORIUS JONSSON. The women are weeping in the antechapel.

CHOIR IN CHURCH (*bursts forth jubilantly*). *Gloria in excelsis deo!*

The door is thrown open. INGA OF VARTEIG comes out, followed by NUNS, MONKS *and* PRIESTS.

INGA (*on the steps of the church*). God has judged! Behold these hands! In them I have held the iron!

VOICES AMONG THE CROWD. They are as fair and white as before!

OTHER VOICES. Fairer still!

WHOLE CROWD. Haakon is the King's son!

HAAKON (*embraces her*). Thank you, most blessed mother! Bravest of women, thank you!

BISHOP NICHOLAS (*wanders past* EARL SKULE). It was foolish to insist on the ordeal of the iron.

EARL SKULE. No, my lord. We needed the voice of God.

HAAKON (*deeply moved, clasps* INGA *by the hand*). My whole being cried out against this deed, and my heart shrank from it. But now it is done. (*Turns to the* CROWD) By the ordeal of the iron

I have proved my birth, and proved my right in just succession to inherit the kingdom and the crown. Six years ago they named me King, but I was a child and Earl Skule became regent. (*Pauses and, looks at* SKULE) Little honour has been shown me in this time! But I have been patient, borne the humiliation, and waited. Now I can wait no longer – civil war is threatening our land, and this I must prevent. I might not have risked paying so dearly to prove my right – (*looks at* INGA) – if I had not felt the certainty of my calling. I feel it deep within me, burning like a flame, and I am not ashamed to declare it; I *know* that I alone can guide our country to its destiny.

EARL SKULE (*after a pause*). There are others here who have belief in themselves.

HAAKON. What do you mean, my lord?

EARL SKULE. I am the late King's brother, and the law supports me when I demand to enter into my inheritance.

DAGFINN (*mutters*). More treachery!

BISHOP NICHOLAS. Blessed St Olaf must be the judge.

HAAKON'*s men move closer together.*

HAAKON (*forces himself to be calm and takes a step towards the* EARL). I presume I have misunderstood you, my lord. Has not the ordeal just proved my right to the crown?

SEVERAL OF THE EARL'S MEN. No, no! We deny that!

EARL SKULE. It has proved only that you have a claim, and established your right to assert it against other claimants. It has not won you the crown itself.

HAAKON (*controls himself*). In short, you are saying that for six years I have falsely born the name of King, and that for six years you, my Lord, have unlawfully ruled the kingdom as my regent.

EARL SKULE. By no means. When my brother died, an heir had to be named. The Birchlegs were active in your cause, and elected you before my claim could be heard.

BISHOP NICHOLAS (*to* HAAKON). The Earl means that your election only gave you the right to use the name of King, not to wield royal power.

EARL SKULE. I believe that my right to the crown is at least as good as yours. Now let the law decide between us, and say which of us shall inherit it for himself and his descendants.

BISHOP NICHOLAS. The Earl certainly has grounds.

EARL SKULE. Moreover, if your right to the crown was already established six years ago, why did you consent to the ordeal today?

DAGFINN (*bitterly*). If my counsel had been heard, King Haakon would not have chosen hot iron but cold steel as his instrument of justice! Hear me now, men of the King! Draw your swords, and let them decide!

MANY OF HAAKON'S MEN-AT-ARMS (*storm forward*). To arms against the King's enemies!

EARL SKULE (*cries to his* MEN). Kill no one! Harm no one! Only defend yourselves!

HAAKON (*holds his men back*). Sheath your swords! Sheath them, I say. (*Calmly*). You injure my cause by such rashness. Men who are to rule a kingdom must first learn to rule themselves.

EARL SKULE. You see, Haakon, how every man stands with his sword at his neighbour's throat! It is so throughout the land. Norway is split into a hundred factions, and if you cherish peace and the lives of our countrymen, you know what you must do.

HAAKON (*pauses, then makes a decision*). Yes, now I know. My lords and justices, priests, chieftains, and men-at-arms. I hereby summon the Grand Council. The law shall judge, and the law alone. You Birchlegs, who six years ago elected me as King – I free you now from the oath you swore to me then. You, Dagfinn, are no longer my marshal. I shall not meet the Council with marshal or bodyguard, with royal men-at-arms or sworn warriors. I am a poor man; my inheritance consists only of a brooch and a gold bracelet. Take them, my mother, and God's blessings go with you for what you have done this day. Now, my fellow-claimant to the crown, we stand as equals. I want no advantage over you but the divine right I have from God. That I neither can nor will share with any man. Let the Council be summoned, and let the law decide!

He goes out left with his men. Horns and trumpets are sounded in the distance.

GREGORIUS JONSSON (*to* SKULE, *as the crowd disperses*). During the ordeal, I thought you seemed afraid; but now you look calm and almost joyful.

EARL SKULE (*contentedly*). Did you see? He had my brother's eyes as he spoke. Whether it be he or I, they will have chosen well.

GREGORIUS JONSSON (*uneasily*). Do not give way to him, though. Remember how many destinies are bound to yours.

EARL SKULE. I take my stand upon justice. Now *I* grasp the burning iron! (*Goes out left with his men.*)

BISHOP NICHOLAS (*hurries after* DAGFINN). It will be all right, my good Dagfinn, it will be all right. But if Haakon is chosen King, keep the Earl away from him! Keep him well away!

They all go out left behind the church.

SCENE TWO

A hall in the palace. Downstage left is a low window. To the right, an entrance door. Upstage, a larger door which leads to the King's Hall. By the window stands a table; elsewhere there are stools and benches. THE LADY RAGNHILD, *wife to* EARL SKULE, *and her daughter* MARGARET *enter through the smaller door. A few moments later,* SIGRID *follows them.*

RAGNHILD. In here, daughter.

MARGARET. Yes, it's darkest here.

RAGNHILD (goes to the window). We can watch them through the window.

MARGARET (*looks cautiously through the window*). Yes. There they are, a great crowd gathered by the church. Solemn and silent. Almost as though for a burial. (*Turns weeping*) Oh, God! How many of us will mourn this day!

RAGNHILD. It had to come. Just to be regent could never be enough for him.

MARGARET. Yes – it had to come. To be King in name alone could never be enough for him.

RAGNHILD. Whom do you mean?

MARGARET. Haakon.

RAGNHILD. I meant the Earl.

MARGARET (*almost to herself*). The two noblest men alive – my father, and the man I love! Why couldn't it be enough for them to rule together? Now one will be master in these halls tonight, but one will be his servant.

RAGNHILD. Look at Bishop Nicholas! How slyly he sits – just like a chained wolf!

MARGARET. Yes, look at him! With his hands crossed over his staff, and his chin resting on them.

RAGNHILD. Biting his beard and smiling!

MARGARET. How horribly he smiles, mother!

RAGNHILD. Ssh! Someone is speaking. Who is it?

MARGARET. Gunnar Grœnbak.

RAGNHILD. Is he for the Earl?

MARGARET. No, for the King.

RAGNHILD (*looks at her*). For whom, did you say?

MARGARET. For Haakon.

    Pause.

RAGNHILD. Who is speaking now?

MARGARET (*looks*). Tord Skolle, the thane of Ranafylke.

RAGNHILD. Is he for your father?

MARGARET. No – for Haakon.

RAGNHILD. How stilly the Earl sits and listens!

MARGARET. Haakon seems quiet and thoughtful – but how strong he looks! (*Excitedly.*) If a stranger stood here, he'd know those two among all the thousand others!

RAGNHILD. Look, Margaret. Dagfinn is bringing a gilded chair for Haakon –

MARGARET. Paul Flida is setting another behind the Earl –

RAGNHILD. Haakon's men are trying to stop him!

MARGARET. My father is clinging to the chair – !

RAGNHILD. Haakon is speaking angrily to him – oh, Jesus Christ!

Do you see how your father looks at him! His eyes – and the way he smiles! (*Turns from the window with a cry.*) No, that was never the Earl!

MARGARET (*has likewise turned in fear*). Nor Haakon either! Neither the Earl nor Haakon!

SIGRID (*at the window*). Oh, pity, pity!

MARGARET. Sigrid!

RAGNHILD. You here?

SIGRID. Must they stoop so low, to climb up to the throne?

MARGARET. Oh, God, please guide them!

RAGNHILD (*pale and fearful, to* SIGRID). Did you see him? Did you see my husband? Such eyes, such a smile – I would not have known him.

SIGRID. Did he smile like the Bishop?

RAGNHILD (*quietly*). Yes. He smiled like that.

SIGRID. Then we must pray!

RAGNHILD (*with despairing strength*). They *must* choose him King. Or I fear for his soul –

SIGRID (*more strongly*). Let us pray, then!

RAGNHILD. Ssh! What is that? (*At the window.*) A great shout! They have all risen! The flags and standards are waving in the wind.

SIGRID (*grips her arm*). Pray, woman. Pray for your husband.

RAGNHILD. Yes, blessed St Olaf, grant that he may be King!

SIGRID. Pray that he may not. Else he cannot be saved.

RAGNHILD. He must be King! All that is good in him will flower and blossom – ! Listen. Margaret, look!

MARGARET (*looks*). They have raised their hands in oath. They are swearing allegiance.

RAGNHILD. God and blessed St Olaf – to whom?

SIGRID. Pray!

MARGARET *listens and gestures to them to be silent.*

RAGNHILD (*after a moment*). To whom? (*Horns and trumpets sound loudly from the assembly.*) Whom have they named?

Short pause.

MARGARET (*turns her head and says*). They have chosen Haakon Haakonsson as King.

The music for the royal procession is heard, at first faintly, then gradually closer. RAGNHILD *clings weeping to* SIGRID, *who leads her quietly out right.* MARGARET *remains motionless, leaning against the window. The* KING'S SERVANTS *open the great doors, revealing the Hall, which gradually fills with the procession from the assembly.*

HAAKON (*turns in the doorway to* IVAR BODDE). Bring me a pen, and wax and silk. (*Moved and exultant, comes forward to the table and puts some parchment on it.*) Margaret, I am King!

MARGARET. I salute my lord and my King.

HAAKON (*looks at her and takes her hand*). Forgive me. I had forgotten that this must hurt you.

MARGARET (*takes away her hand*). No. You were born to be King, my lord.

HAAKON (*fervently*). Yes. Ever since I was born, it is as though God and His Saints had protected me – almost miraculously. When I was a year old, there was a plot to kill me, but I was carried to safety across the mountains in frost and storm through the midst of my enemies. In Nidaros they burned the town and I escaped unhurt while men were slain all around me. And today the ordeal – it has always been the same for me.

MARGARET. You have served a hard apprenticeship.

HAAKON (*looks earnestly at her*). Something tells me now that you might have made it less hard for me.

MARGARET. I?

HAAKON. You could have been a source of strength to me all the years we grew up together.

MARGARET. But things fell out differently.

HAAKON. Yes. Things fell out differently. We sat in the same hall, we looked at each other, each from our separate corners, but we seldom spoke. (*There is a pause.* HAAKON *looks at her, then turns impatiently away.*) Where is the pen and ink? (IVAR BODDE *enters with writing materials, followed by* BISHOP NICHOLAS.) You were slow. Give them to me.

He writes for a moment, then looks up at MARGARET.

HAAKON. Do you know what I am writing? It is a letter to my mother. I am sending her away to the east. She will live there, far from our affairs of state, quietly, but with all honour.

MARGARET. Will you not keep her with you at the palace?

HAAKON. She is too dear to me. A King must have no one by him who is near to his heart. A King must be free to act, he must stand alone, must never be swayed or influenced by affection. Then he can work with a single purpose – and there is much work to be done in Norway.

IVAR BODDE (*whispers to* BISHOP NICHOLAS). That was my counsel, to send away the King's mother.

BISHOP NICHOLAS. I recognised your touch.

IVAR BODDE. But you must keep your side of the bargain.

BISHOP NICHOLAS. Be patient. I shall not forget.

HAAKON (*hands the parchment to* IVAR BODDE). Fold this, and take it to her yourself, with my dearest greetings –

DAGFINN (*glances at the parchment*). My lord – must she sail today?

HAAKON. The wind is fair, and westerly.

MARGARET. Your Majesty – your mother did not sleep all last night. She spent it at the altar – in prayer and fasting –

DAGFINN. And the ordeal today –

HAAKON (*suddenly moved*). My blessed mother! (*Composes himself.*) Well, if she is tired, she may wait until tomorrow.

IVAR BODDE. Your Majesty's will shall be done. (*Puts a fresh parchment before the* KING. MARGARET *rises and moves towards the door*). And – the other matter, my lord?

BISHOP NICHOLAS (*who has meanwhile come closer*). Bind the Earl's hands now, King Haakon.

HAAKON (*softly*). You think I need to?

BISHOP NICHOLAS. You will never buy peace for Norway on cheaper terms.

HAAKON. I shall do it. Summon Earl Skule! (MARGARET *stops at the door and turns*). Give me the pen. (*Writes.*)

The BISHOP *whispers in his ear.* EARL SKULE *enters. The* BISHOP *moves away.*

EARL SKULE (*to the* BISHOP, *as the latter passes, right*). It seems you have the King's ear, my lord.

BISHOP NICHOLAS. To your advantage.

EARL SKULE. Indeed?

BISHOP NICHOLAS. You will thank me before evening. (*Moves further off.*)

HAAKON (*holds out the parchment to* SKULE). Read this, my lord.
The BISHOP *walks across to* HAAKON, *who is watching* SKULE.

BISHOP NICHOLAS (*hovers over* HAAKON'S *chair*). Your Majesty has taken a great step towards winning the Earl's friendship. Once his hands are bound, you need never fear again.

HAAKON (*tensely, to* SKULE). My lord, today I took the kingdom from you. But let your daughter share it with me.
MARGARET *catches her breath.* SKULE *slowly looks up from the parchment.*

HAAKON. Margaret – will you be my Queen? (MARGARET *is silent.* HAAKON *takes her hand.*) Answer me.

MARGARET. I will most gladly be your wife.
She looks at her father. Everyone waits for his reaction.

EARL SKULE (*finally speaks*). This is a noble action, Haakon. (*Presses his hand.*) Peace and friendship – from my heart!

HAAKON. Thank you!

IVAR BODDE (*to* DAGFINN). Heaven be praised! Now we shall have peace at last!

DAGFINN. I almost think so. I have never liked the Earl so well before.

BISHOP NICHOLAS (*behind him*). Stay on your guard, my good Dagfinn. Stay on your guard!

IVAR BODDE (*who has been waiting behind the* KING *with the parchments in his hand*). Here are the letters, my lord –

HAAKON. Good. Give them to the Earl.

IVAR BODDE. To the Earl? Will Your Majesty not seal them – ?

HAAKON. The Earl does that. He has the seal.

IVAR BODDE (*whispers*). While he was your regent, yes. But now –

HAAKON. Now as before. The Earl has the seal. (*Moves away.*)

EARL SKULE. Give me the letters, Ivar Bodde.

He goes over to the table with them, takes out the royal seal which he has kept hidden in his belt, and seals the letters during the ensuing dialogue.

BISHOP NICHOLAS (*half to himself*). Haakon is King – and the Earl has the seal. It will pass, it will pass.

HAAKON. What are you saying, my lord Bishop?

BISHOP NICHOLAS. I was saying? 'God and St Olaf watch over our Holy Church.' (*He moves away.*)

HAAKON (*goes over to* MARGARET). A wise Queen can do much for our land. I know you are wise, and that was what guided my choice.

MARGARET. Only that?

HAAKON. What do you mean?

MARGARET. Nothing, my lord, nothing.

HAAKON. And you will not hate me for making you renounce your fair hopes for my sake?

MARGARET. I have renounced nothing for your sake, my lord.

HAAKON. And you will stay close to me and give me good counsel?

MARGARET. I will most gladly stay close to you, my lord.

HAAKON. I shall be grateful. Every man needs a woman's counsel, and I shall have no one but you when my mother has gone.

MARGARET. No – she was too dear to you.

HAAKON. And I am King. Farewell then, Margaret! You are young, still; but our wedding shall take place next summer – and from that hour I swear to keep you by me, in trust and honour as befits a Queen.

MARGARET (*smiles sadly*). Yes. You will not send me away.

HAAKON (*startled*). Send you away? Of course not!

MARGARET (*with tears in her eyes*). No, the King only does that to those who are too dear to him. (*Goes towards the main door.* HAAKON *watches her thoughtfully.*) Thank you for the crown, my lord. I think I am glad, even of that. (*Goes out right.*)

BISHOP NICHOLAS. A wise deed, my lord. Now Your Majesty need never fear again.

HAAKON. You have counselled me well, Bishop Nicholas.

BISHOP NICHOLAS. Now at last you are King of Norway.

HAAKON (*takes a breath*). At last!

BISHOP NICHOLAS (*shouts*). Haakon is King!

ALL OUTSIDE (*in a great shout*). Haakon is King!

 HAAKON *moves towards the door to acknowledge the cry.*

EARL SKULE (*puts the seal in his belt*). But I rule the land.

Act Two

The banqueting hall in the royal palace at Bergen. In the centre of the rear wall is a large bow window. Along the length of this is a dais, with seats for the women. Against the left wall, the royal throne extends several feet into the hall; in the centre of the opposite wall is a big entrance door. Banners, standards, shields, coats-of-arms and embroidered tapestries hang from the pillars and from the hewn roofbeams. Around the hall stand drinking-tables, with pitchers, horns and beakers.

KING HAAKON *is seated on the dais, with* MARGARET, SIGRID, THE LADY RAGNHILD *and other noble women.* IVAR BODDE *stands behind the* KING. *At the drinking-tables sit the* KING'S MEN *and the* EARL'S MEN *on benches, with other* GUESTS. *At the first table, on the* KING'S *right, are, among others,* DAGFINN THE PEASANT, GREGORIUS JONSSON *and* PAUL FLIDA. EARL SKULE *and* BISHOP NICHOLAS *are playing chess at a table on the left.* THE EARL'S SERVANTS *go to and fro bearing drinks. From an adjacent room, music can be heard during the ensuing dialogue.*

DAGFINN. Five days of feasting, and the ale's still flowing! (*Calls to a* SERVANT.). Come on, fill these up!

DRUNKEN LORD. Don't worry, they will!

PAUL FLIDA. The Earl's never been one to stint his guests.

DAGFINN. So it seems. Norway has never known such a royal wedding feast.

PAUL FLIDA. Earl Skule has never given away a daughter before.

DAGFINN. True, true. The Earl's a mighty man, all right.

MAN-AT-ARMS. Haakon has given him a third of the kingdom. That's more than any man has ever had.

PAUL FLIDA. Except the King. The King has more.

MAN-AT-ARMS. The King has a right to more.

PAUL FLIDA (*flares up*). So has the Earl! And other rights besides – !

DAGFINN. Let's not discuss that now. We're all friends here

tonight. Let things be. (*Drinks to* PAUL FLIDA.) Let the King be King and the Earl Earl.

PAUL FLIDA (*laughs*). It's easy to tell you serve the King.

DAGFINN. It's every man's duty to serve the King.

PAUL FLIDA. We serve the Earl. We have sworn an oath to him, not to the King.

DAGFINN. Not yet. But it could happen.

BISHOP NICHOLAS (*whispers to the* EARL *as they play*). Did you hear what Dagfinn said?

EARL SKULE (*without looking up*). I heard.

GREGORIUS JONSSON (*looks at* DAGFINN). Is that the King's intention?

DAGFINN. No, no, let's forget it. Let's have no quarrels today.

BISHOP NICHOLAS. The King is planning to make your men swear the oath of allegiance to him, my lord.

GREGORIUS JONSSON (*more loudly*). Is that the King's intention, I asked?

DAGFINN. I'm not answering. Let's drink to peace and friendship between the King and the Earl. The ale is good.

PAUL FLIDA. It's had time to mature.

GREGORIUS JONSSON. Three times the Earl made ready for the wedding, three times the King promised to come – and three times he made his excuses.

DAGFINN. Blame the Earl for that. His rebels kept us busy in the north.

BISHOP NICHOLAS (*moves a piece and says, laughing, to* SKULE). Now I'm taking your castle, my lord.

EARL SKULE (*aloud*). Take it. I can spare a castle.

DAGFINN. Yes – as your men in the north found out.

Subdued laughter among the KING'S MEN. *The conversation is continued in quieter tones. After a few moments, a* MAN *enters and whispers to* GREGORIUS JONSSON.

BISHOP NICHOLAS. Now I move here; and you are mated.

EARL SKULE. So it seems.

BISHOP NICHOLAS (*leans back in his chair*). You didn't nurse your King.

EARL SKULE (*scatters the pieces and rises*). I've grown tired of nursing Kings.

GREGORIUS JONSSON (*approaches him and whispers*). My lord, Jostein Tamb says his ship is ready to sail. Have you the letter – ?

EARL SKULE (*takes out a sealed parchment and says quietly*). Here it is.

GREGORIUS JONSSON (*shakes his head*). My lord, my lord! Is this wise?

EARL SKULE. What?

GREGORIUS JONSSON. It bears the King's seal.

EARL SKULE. I am acting in the King's interest.

GREGORIUS JONSSON. Then let the King write the letter himself.

EARL SKULE. He won't if it's left to him. It is for the King's good.

GREGORIUS JONSSON. Perhaps. But this is dangerous –

EARL SKULE. Leave that to me. Take the letter and tell Jostein to sail at once.

GREGORIUS JONSSON. As you command, my lord.

He goes out right, and returns after a few moments.

BISHOP NICHOLAS (*to* EARL SKULE). It seems you have much to do.

EARL SKULE. But little thanks for my pains.

BISHOP NICHOLAS. The King has risen.

HAAKON *descends from the dais. All the* MEN *rise from the tables.*

HAAKON (*to the* BISHOP, *ignoring* SKULE). My lord Bishop, we are glad to have seen you looking so well and strong during these days of rejoicing.

BISHOP NICHOLAS. I feel a flicker of life in me now and then, Your Majesty; but the next draught may snuff it out. The winter has taken its toll of my strength.

HAAKON. You have lived a full life, rich in noble deeds.

BISHOP NICHOLAS (*shakes his head*). Too much is left undone, Your Majesty. If only I could be sure there was time to finish what I have begun.

HAAKON. The living must continue the work of the dead, reverend lord. We all have the same goal; the welfare and happiness of our country.

DAGFINN (*approaches*). Shall we sound the trumpets for the jousting, Your Majesty?

HAAKON. Good! Today let us be joyful. Tomorrow our work begins.

Trumpets. All bow except EARL SKULE. HAAKON *waits.* SKULE *slowly bows.* HAAKON *goes up on to the dais, offers his hand to* MARGARET *and leads her out right. The others follow in ones and twos.*

BISHOP NICHOLAS (*to* IVAR BODDE). A moment. Do you know a man called Jostein Tamb?

IVAR BODDE. There is a traveller here from Orkney of that name.

BISHOP NICHOLAS. From Orkney? Indeed. And now he is sailing home?

IVAR BODDE. So I have heard.

BISHOP NICHOLAS (*lowers his voice*). With a precious cargo, Ivar Bodde!

IVAR BODDE. Corn and cloth, I believe.

BISHOP NICHOLAS. And a letter from Earl Skule.

IVAR BODDE (*suspicious*). Yes?

BISHOP NICHOLAS. Sealed with the King's seal –

IVAR BODDE (*grips his arm*). My lord – is this true?

BISHOP NICHOLAS. Tsst! Don't involve me in this! (*Moves off.*)

IVAR BODDE. I must stop him at once – Dagfinn! Dagfinn! (*Forces his way through the crowd to the door.*)

BISHOP NICHOLAS (*sympathetically, to* GREGORIUS JONSSON). Every day it seems another innocent man loses his freedom. Now they are preventing some wretched traveller from leaving the country.

GREGORIUS JONSSON. Who is that?

BISHOP NICHOLAS. Jostein Tamb, I think his name was.

GREGORIUS JONSSON. Jostein – ?

BISHOP NICHOLAS. Dagfinn the Peasant is after him –

GREGORIUS JONSSON. Dagfinn – ?

BISHOP NICHOLAS. Yes, he's just gone to stop him sailing.

GREGORIUS JONSSON. Excuse me, my lord, I must hurry –

BISHOP NICHOLAS. Yes, do, my good lord. Dagfinn is such a

hasty man —

GREGORIUS *hurries out with the rest of the* GUESTS. *Only* EARL SKULE *and* BISHOP NICHOLAS *remain in the hall.*

EARL SKULE (*walks thoughtfully up and down. Suddenly it is as though he awakes. He looks round and says*). How quiet it is here suddenly!

BISHOP NICHOLAS. The King has gone.

EARL SKULE. And everyone followed him.

BISHOP NICHOLAS. Everyone except us.

EARL SKULE. It is a great thing to be King.

BISHOP NICHOLAS (*warily*). Would you like to try it, my lord?

EARL SKULE (*smiles seriously*). I have tried it. Every night when I sleep I am King of Norway.

BISHOP NICHOLAS. Dreams can be omens.

EARL SKULE. And tempters, too.

BISHOP NICHOLAS. Surely not to you. Not now, when you own a third of the kingdom, rule the land, and are the Queen's father —

EARL SKULE. Now most of all. Now most of all!

BISHOP NICHOLAS. Hide nothing. Confess. I see you are troubled by a great sorrow.

EARL SKULE. Now most of all, I say. That is the curse that hangs over my whole life. To stand so near to greatness — but with a gap between. Only a yard away — a single leap would do it — and there on the other side lie a crown and a purple cloak, a throne, power, everything! Every day I see them lying there — but I can never take the leap.

BISHOP NICHOLAS. True, my lord.

EARL SKULE. When they chose young Sigurd as King, I was in the full flower of manhood; and it was as though a cry sounded in my ear: 'Away with this child! I am the grown, strong man!' But Sigurd was the King's son. That was the gulf that lay between me and the throne then.

BISHOP NICHOLAS. So you waited?

EARL SKULE. I waited for Sigurd to die.

BISHOP NICHOLAS. And Sigurd died, and your brother became King.

EARL SKULE. And I waited for my brother to die. He was already sick; every morning when we met at Mass, I watched to see if the sickness might not take him. Every twist of pain that crossed his face was like a breath of wind in my sail, to carry me nearer to the throne. Every moan he uttered sounded in my ears like trumpets from a distant hill, summoning me to lead my people. I stifled every brotherly thought – and my brother died – and Haakon came – and the Birchlegs chose *him* King.

BISHOP NICHOLAS. And you waited.

EARL SKULE. I sensed the divine right in me, so I thought help must surely come from above. But I was growing older. Every day that passed was a day stolen from my life's work. Each night I thought – tomorrow a sign will come that will strike him down and set me on the empty throne.

BISHOP NICHOLAS. Haakon's power was weak then. He was only a child. You only had to take a single step. But you did not take it.

EARL SKULE. It was a hard step to take. It would have divided me from my family and from my friends.

BISHOP NICHOLAS. Yes. That is the curse that has dogged your whole life, Earl Skule. You have to leave every road open behind you. You dare not burn all your bridges except one, and stand on that alone, conquering or falling there. You lay snares for your enemy – dig pits for his feet, hang swords over his head, put poison in his dishes and set a hundred traps for him – but if he enters one of them you dare not spring it – if he reaches for the poison you think he had better fall by the sword – if he is about to be caught one morning you think it would be safer if it happened in the evening. That, Earl Skule, is your tragedy.

EARL SKULE (*after a short pause*). Then answer me one question, reverend lord. Why does Haakon never falter on his path? He is not wiser than I, nor bolder.

BISHOP NICHOLAS. Who accomplishes most in this world?

EARL SKULE. He who is greatest.

BISHOP NICHOLAS. But who is greatest?

EARL SKULE. He who is bravest.

BISHOP NICHOLAS. That is a soldier's answer. A priest would say, he who has the greatest faith – a philosopher, he who is wisest. But neither of these is right, my lord. The greatest man is he who has the most luck. This is the man who accomplishes the greatest deeds – the hunger of his age inflames him like a passion, it generates thoughts in him which he himself does not understand, but which point for him the way which leads he knows not whither, but which he follows, and must follow, until he hears the people cry in joy, and looks about him with distended eyes, and is amazed, and realises that he has performed a mighty deed.

EARL SKULE. Yes, that is Haakon. But I could be the same if I had his luck. (*At first thoughtful, then with rising emotion.*) Was he created from another dust than I? Was he born lucky? If not, why does everything turn out right for him? Why does everything bend to his will? Even the peasant notices it – he says that the trees bear fruit twice, and the birds breed twice, every summer now that Haakon is King. Blood and ashes fertilise the land when Haakon goes to war; the Lord renews the fields that Haakon tramples; the country which he burns and harries is bright again with new-built houses, and all the fields stand heavy with crops bending richly before the wind. It is as though the powers above hastened to blot out every trace of guilt that he leaves behind him. And how easily he strode to the throne! He needed my brother's death, and my brother died; he needed an army, and men flocked to him. He needed the proof of the ordeal and his mother underwent it for him.

BISHOP NICHOLAS (*bursts out involuntarily*). But we – we two – !

EARL SKULE. We?

BISHOP NICHOLAS. I mean you – you!

EARL SKULE. I stand in the shadow, doubting. (*Pause.*) Haakon has *right* on his side, my lord!

BISHOP NICHOLAS. Did you never see an old painting in the church at Nidaros? It shows the river of sin, swelling and rising over every mountain so that only one peak is left standing above it. Up to this peak has struggled a family, father and mother and son and the son's wife and children. The son has thrown his father down into the waters to gain a safer foothold, and he is trying to throw his mother down, and his wife and all his children, so that he may climb his way to the top – because up there is a square foot of rock on which he can survive for an hour. That, my lord, is the saga of wisdom, and the saga of every wise man.

EARL SKULE. But was he *right*?

BISHOP NICHOLAS. Of course he was right! He had the strength and the passion to live! Bow to your passion, and use your gifts. Every man has that right.

EARL SKULE. If the end is good.

BISHOP NICHOLAS. You play with words! There is no such thing as good or evil. Those are words you must forget, or you will never take that final step, never leap the gulf. (*Softly and persuasively*.) You must not hate a party or a cause because the party or the cause demands this and not that. But you must hate every man in any party who is against you, and you must hate every man who supports a cause if it does not advance your own. Everything that you can use is good. Everything that puts an obstacle in your path is evil. Don't you see that there is a stronger power than these Birchlegs behind Haakon, advancing his ambitions? He gets help from those above – from those – from those who oppose you. They were your enemies from the hour you were born! And you kneel before those enemies! Rise up, man! Straighten your back! Why else were you granted an immortal soul? Remember that the first great deed in history was performed by one who rebelled against a mighty King!

EARL SKULE. Who?

BISHOP NICHOLAS. The angel who rebelled against the light.

EARL SKULE. And was cast into a bottomless abyss –

BISHOP NICHOLAS (*passionately*). And created a kingdom there, and became a King, a mighty King – mightier than any of those ten thousand Earls who stayed above. (*Sinks down on to a bench by the drinking-table.*)

EARL SKULE (*gives him a long look and says*). Bishop Nicholas, are you a man? Or something less? Or something more?

BISHOP NICHOLAS (*smiles*). I am in a state of innocence. I do not know the difference between good and evil.

There is a pause. EARL SKULE *rises and walks agitatedly up and down.*

EARL SKULE. If only I had a son – if only I had a son who could inherit it all from me!

BISHOP NICHOLAS. If you had a son – ?

EARL SKULE. I could believe in myself. But I have none.

BISHOP NICHOLAS. Haakon will have sons.

EARL SKULE (*clenches his fists*). And is a King's son.

BISHOP NICHOLAS (*rises*). My lord – what if he were not – ?

EARL SKULE. He has proved it. The ordeal –

BISHOP NICHOLAS. But if he were not – despite the ordeal – ?

EARL SKULE. Are you saying that God lied?

BISHOP NICHOLAS. What was it that Inga begged God to witness?

EARL SKULE. That the child she bore was the son of the King.

BISHOP NICHOLAS (*nods, looks round, and says quietly*). And if Haakon were not that child?

EARL SKULE (*starts*). Almighty – ! (*Controls himself.*) That is unthinkable.

BISHOP NICHOLAS. Listen to me, my lord. I am seventy-six years old. I am beginning to wane, and I dare not take this secret with me –

EARL SKULE. Speak, speak! Is he not the King's son?

BISHOP NICHOLAS. Listen. When Inga found herself with child, it was kept secret. The King her lover had just died, and she was afraid of the new King, your brother, and of you. She bore the child secretly in the house of a priest named Trond. Nine days later she returned home. But the royal babe remained with the priest a whole year. She did not dare to visit it, and no one knew about it except Trond.

EARL SKULE. Yes, yes! And then?

BISHOP NICHOLAS. You will appreciate how dangerous it was for a humble priest to have the upbringing of a King's son. Therefore, soon after the baby was born, he revealed the truth in the confessional. His confessor counselled Trond secretly to exchange the child for another, send the true prince to a safe place, and give Inga the changeling, if she should ever claim her son.

EARL SKULE (*angrily*). Who was the dog who dared advise this?

BISHOP NICHOLAS. It was I.

EARL SKULE. You?

BISHOP NICHOLAS. I thought it would be unsafe for the prince to fall into your hands.

EARL SKULE. But the priest?

BISHOP NICHOLAS. Promised to do as I advised.

EARL SKULE (*grips his arm*). Then Haakon is the changeling?

BISHOP NICHOLAS. If the priest kept his promise.

EARL SKULE. *If* he kept it?

BISHOP NICHOLAS. A year later, Inga revealed the existence of her child, and a baby was brought from Trond's house to the royal palace which everyone assumed was hers. But that same winter, Trond left the country on a pilgrimage to the grave of Thomas Becket, and stayed in England until he died.

EARL SKULE. This proves he exchanged the child. He fled the country because he feared the revenge of the Birchlegs.

BISHOP NICHOLAS. Or he did not exchange it, and feared my revenge.

EARL SKULE. Which do you believe?

BISHOP NICHOLAS. Both are equally likely.

EARL SKULE. And Inga – ?

BISHOP NICHOLAS. Knows nothing, either of the priest's confession, or of the advice I gave him.

EARL SKULE. Her baby was only nine days old when she left him, you say?

BISHOP NICHOLAS. Yes. And the child she saw next was over a year old –

EARL SKULE. Then there is no one in the world who knows the

answer! (*Walks grimly up and down several times.*) Almighty
God, can it be true? Haakon an impostor! (*Goes to the window.*)
See how splendidly he sits his horse! No one looks as he does.
His eyes laugh and glitter like the sun, he looks at the day as
though he knew himself born to go forward, always forward!
The people gaze adoringly at him. In every eye shines the
unshakable belief that he is their rightful King.

BISHOP NICHOLAS. That is because *he* believes it, my lord. That
is his luck. That is where his strength lies. And yet, perhaps
he is not –

EARL SKULE. No. Perhaps not. (*Turns back violently to the
window.*)

BISHOP NICHOLAS. Hide the fact that you don't believe in
yourself. Look as though you did, speak as though you did.
Swear boldly and passionately that you do, and they will all
believe in *you*!

EARL SKULE (*at the window, starts and exclaims in surprise*).
What's this? Dagfinn has broken through the crowd. He's
whispering to the King.

BISHOP NICHOLAS (*looks out behind the* EARL). Haakon looks
angry. He's clenching his fist –

EARL SKULE. He's looking up here. What can it be? (*Turns to go.*)

BISHOP NICHOLAS (*holds him back*). My lord, listen to me. There
is a way to find whether Haakon is the rightful heir.

EARL SKULE. A way –?

BISHOP NICHOLAS. Before he died, Trond the priest wrote a
letter revealing what he had done, and swore upon the
sacrament that what he had written was the truth.

EARL SKULE. And this letter – in God's name, where is it?

BISHOP NICHOLAS. Well – (*Glances towards the door.*) Ssh, here
comes the King.

EARL SKULE. The letter, my lord, the letter!

BISHOP NICHOLAS. Here is the King.

> HAAKON *enters, followed by his* MEN-AT-ARMS *and many*
> GUESTS. *Immediately afterwards,* MARGARET *enters. She is in*
> *great distress, and tries to run to the* KING, *but is held back by*

THE LADY RAGNHILD *who, with several* WOMEN, *has accompanied her.* SIGRID *stands a little way apart, upstage. The* EARL'S MEN *look uneasy and gather on the right, near* SKULE, *but a little way behind him.*

HAAKON (*angrily but controlled*). Earl Skule, who is King in this land?

EARL SKULE. Who is King – ?

HAAKON. That was my question. I bear the name of King, but who wields the royal power?

EARL SKULE. Royal power should be wielded by the lawful King.

HAAKON. It should be so. But is it?

EARL SKULE. Are you accusing me – ?

HAAKON. I am. As is my royal right.

EARL SKULE. I am not afraid to answer for my actions.

HAAKON. Let us hope, for all our sakes, that you can. (*Steps up on to the dais where the throne stands and leans against the arm of the throne.*) I stand here as your King and ask you – do you know that Earl John of Orkney has rebelled against me?

EARL SKULE. Yes.

HAAKON. And is it true, my lord, that today you sent him a letter?

EARL SKULE. I did.

HAAKON. Bearing the King's seal?

EARL SKULE. Yes.

HAAKON. So you write to the King's enemies and seal your letters with the King's seal, although the King does not know what stands written there?

EARL SKULE. I have done so for many years, with your knowledge.

HAAKON. When you were my regent.

EARL SKULE. You never suffered by it, and will not suffer this time. Earl John wrote to me and asked me to mediate between him and you. He wanted peace, but on terms dishonourable to your Majesty.

HAAKON. The letter should have been shown to me. What did you write?

EARL SKULE. Read my letter.

HAAKON. Give it to me.

EARL SKULE (*turns to* GREGORIUS JONSSON). Gregorius, give the King the letter.

GREGORIUS JONSSON (*approaches uneasily*). My lord –!

EARL SKULE. What is it?

GREGORIUS JONSSON. You remember, my lord, you wrote sharp words of the King –

EARL SKULE. I can answer for them. Give me the letter.

GREGORIUS JONSSON. I have not got it.

EARL SKULE. Not got it?

GREGORIUS JONSSON. Dagfinn the Peasant was on our heels. I seized the letter from Jostein, tied a stone to it –

EARL SKULE. And –?

GREGORIUS JONSSON. It is lying at the bottom of the fjord.

EARL SKULE. You have done ill – ill!

HAAKON. I am waiting for the letter, my lord.

EARL SKULE. I cannot give it to you.

HAAKON. You *can* not? (*Pause.*) Are you defying me?

EARL SKULE. If you wish – yes, I am defying you.

IVAR BODDE (*angrily*). My lord, I think no man needs further proof than this.

HAAKON (*coldly to* SKULE). Earl Skule, I order you to surrender the royal seal. Give it to Ivar Bodde.

MARGARET (*runs, her hands clasped, to the dais where the* KING *is standing*). Haakon, be a gentle and merciful husband to me!
HAAKON *makes an imperious gesture towards her. She hides her face in her veil and goes back to her mother. Pause.*

EARL SKULE (*slowly moves towards* IVAR BODDE). Here is the seal.
Another pause. IVAR BODDE *goes towards* HAAKON *with it.*

PAUL FLIDA (*furiously to the* EARL'S MEN *around him*). Are we to endure this any longer?

GREGORIUS JONSSON (*steps forward*). We cannot and will not endure it! I say it plainly for all to hear – the Earl's men cannot serve the King with loyalty if the Earl does not keep the seal.

MANY OF THE EARL'S MEN. No, no! Give back the seal! The

Earl must have the seal!

IVAR BODDE (*proffers the seal to* HAAKON). Take it into your own
    hands, Your Majesty. It should have rested there long ago.

HAAKON *takes the seal. The crowd is hushed.*

IVAR BODDE. God bless and prosper all your undertakings.

HAAKON (*lowers his head, kisses the seal, and looks up at* SKULE).
    Now, my lord –

EARL SKULE. Evil angels are coming between us today. You must
    not ask more of me.

BISHOP NICHOLAS. The Earl is right, Your Majesty –

HAAKON. *You* say so, reverend lord? I say that justice must be
    done.

EARL SKULE. Your Majesty – more than one man's blood will be
    shed!

HAAKON. Perhaps. But treason must be punished. (*Draws his
    sword and says, calmly and firmly.*) All the Earl's men shall swear
    an oath of allegiance.

EARL SKULE (*vehemently*). You cannot mean this! (*Almost
    beseechingly.*) King Haakon, do not do this!

HAAKON. No man of the Earl's shall leave this palace until he has
    sworn allegiance to the King.

He goes with his bodyguard towards the door. As he reaches it,
    SIGRID *runs forward.*

SIGRID. My lord!

HAAKON *stops. She kneels before him.*

SIGRID. Grant me a boon, Your Majesty!

HAAKON. Rise, Sigrid. Whatever you ask shall be granted.

SIGRID. The nunnery at Rein will soon be consecrated. Write to
    the Archbishop and beg that I may become abbess there.

HAAKON. Why do you wish to enter a nunnery?

SIGRID (*rises*). Since the night at Nidaros, when they burned the
    city and murdered my husband at our wedding, the blood and
    fire have blinded my eyes to the outward world. But I have
    gained the power to see what other eyes cannot – and I see it
    now – a time of dreadful horror for our land!

EARL SKULE (*violently*). She is sick! Pay no heed to her!

SIGRID. A rich harvest shall ripen for him who reaps in the dark! Norway's women have but one task now – to kneel in the churches and the nunneries and pray – pray, day and night!

HAAKON (*shaken*). Take her away! The woman is mad! (*Goes out.*)

SIGRID (*to* EARL SKULE). Farewell, my brother. We shall meet once more. When you need me in your soul's extremity – when your peril is greatest – when you grasp the crown!

She goes out right with MARGARET, RAGNHILD *and the* WOMEN. THE BISHOP *and* EARL SKULE *are left alone.*

BISHOP NICHOLAS. The King has used you harshly today.

EARL SKULE *is silent and looks speechlessly after the* KING.

BISHOP NICHOLAS (*more strongly*). And he may be the son of a peasant.

EARL SKULE (*suddenly turns passionately to the* BISHOP *and grips his arm*). The priest's confession! Where is it?

BISHOP NICHOLAS. He sent it to me from England before he died. I don't know by whom, and I have not received it.

EARL SKULE. It must be found!

BISHOP NICHOLAS. I am sure it will be.

EARL SKULE. And you will place it in my hands?

BISHOP NICHOLAS. You shall have it.

EARL SKULE. You swear it by your soul's salvation?

BISHOP NICHOLAS. I swear it by my soul's salvation.

EARL SKULE. Good. Until then I shall work against Haakon wherever I can do so, quietly and in secret. He must not be more powerful than I am when the struggle begins.

BISHOP NICHOLAS. But if the letter should prove him to be the true heir to the crown – what then?

EARL SKULE. Then I shall beseech God for a humble spirit, to serve him loyally, and with all my strength.

BISHOP NICHOLAS. And if he is not?

EARL SKULE. Then he shall yield to me! His crown and his throne, his army and his bodyguard, his treasure and his fleet, his cities and his palaces – they shall all be mine!

BISHOP NICHOLAS. He will fly to his castle –

EARL SKULE. I shall hunt him from his castle!

BISHOP NICHOLAS. He will seek refuge in sanctuary –

EARL SKULE. I shall violate the sanctuary!

BISHOP NICHOLAS. He will flee to the altar and cling to St Olaf's shrine –

EARL SKULE. I shall drag him down from the altar, if I have to drag the Saint's shrine with him!

BISHOP NICHOLAS. But he will still have the crown on his head, my lord.

EARL SKULE. Then I shall strike the crown off with my sword!

BISHOP NICHOLAS. But if it sits too tightly, my lord – ?

EARL SKULE. Then in God's name, or in Satan's – I shall strike his head off with it! (*He goes out right.*)

BISHOP NICHOLAS (*looks after him, nods slowly, and says*). Yes – yes! This way I like the Earl!

Act Three

SCENE ONE

A room in the BISHOP'S *palace in Oslo. To the right, an entrance door. Upstage, a small door, standing open, leads into the chapel, which is illuminated. A door covered by a curtain in the left-hand wall leads into the* BISHOP'S *bedchamber. Downstage on the same side is a padded couch. Over to the right is a desk, on which are letters, documents and a lighted lamp.*

At first, the room is empty. From behind the curtain on the left can be heard MONKS *singing. After a few moments,* PAUL FLIDA *enters right in travelling clothes, stops inside the door, waits, looks around, and then strikes three times on the floor with his staff.*

SIRA WILLIAM (*enters left and exclaims, keeping his voice low*). Paul Flida! God be praised! Then the Earl is not far off?

PAUL FLIDA. His ships are past the cape. He sent me ahead. How is the Bishop?

SIRA WILLIAM. He is receiving the last sacrament. They say he cannot survive the night.

PAUL FLIDA. Then we have come too late.

SIRA WILLIAM. No, no. He is fully conscious, and has a little strength left. Every minute he asks when the Earl will be here.

PAUL FLIDA. You still call him Earl. Don't you know the King has made him a Duke?

SIRA WILLIAM. Yes, yes, of course. I'd forgotten. Ssh!

He and PAUL FLIDA *make the sign of the cross, and bow. From the* BISHOP'S *bedchamber enter two* ACOLYTES *with candles, followed by two more with censers, and* PRIESTS *carrying chalice, paten and crucifix. Behind them follows a procession of* PRIESTS *and* MONKS. ACOLYTES *with candles and censers bring up the rear of the procession, which winds slowly into the chapel. The door of it is closed behind them.*

PAUL FLIDA. So; the old man has settled his account with this world.

SIRA WILLIAM. Can I tell him that Duke Skule will be here soon?

PAUL FLIDA. He will come straight here from the harbour. Goodbye.

He goes. Several PRIESTS, *including* PETER, *and* SERVANTS *of the* BISHOP, *enter left with fur rugs, cushions and a large brazier.*

SIRA WILLIAM. What are these for?

PRIEST (*making the couch ready*). The Bishop wishes to lie out here.

SIRA WILLIAM. But is that wise?

PRIEST. The doctors say we must humour him. Here he is.

BISHOP NICHOLAS *enters, supported by* MASTER SIGARD *and a* PRIEST. *He is in his episcopal robes, but without his staff and mitre.*

BISHOP NICHOLAS. Light more candles! (*He is carried to the couch, placed on it in a sitting position close to the brazier, and covered with furs.*) William! I have received absolution for my sins. They have all been taken from me. I feel so light now!

SIRA WILLIAM. Duke Skule has sent word to you, my lord. He will be here at any moment.

BISHOP NICHOLAS. That's good, very good! The King will be here soon too, surely. I've been a sinful dog in my time, William. I have sinned grievously against the King. The priests in here said all my sins would be forgiven me – that's all very well, it's easy for them to promise – I haven't sinned against them. No, no – I'd best have pardon from the King's own lips. (*Shouts angrily.*) Lights, I say! It's so dark in here!

SIRA WILLIAM. The candles are lit, my lord –

SIGRID (*silences him with a gesture and goes closer to the* BISHOP). How do you feel, my lord?

BISHOP NICHOLAS. So-so, so-so. My hands and feet are cold.

MASTER SIGARD *glances at* SIRA WILLIAM *and moves the brazier closer.*

BISHOP NICHOLAS (*fretfully, to* SIRA WILLIAM). I've ordered eight monks to sing and pray for me in the chapel tonight. Keep an eye on them. They're lazy dogs, some of them.

SIRA WILLIAM *points silently towards the chapel, from which can be heard singing that continues throughout the following dialogue.*

BISHOP NICHOLAS. So much still undone – and to have to leave it all! So much undone, William!

SIRA WILLIAM. Think of Heaven, my lord!

BISHOP NICHOLAS. There's no hurry. The doctor says I've got till morning –

SIRA WILLIAM. My lord, my lord –

BISHOP NICHOLAS. Give me my mitre and my staff! You're right – I must try to think of – ! (*A* PRIEST *brings them.*) No, put the mitre here, it's too heavy for me. Place my staff in my hand. There, now I am armed. A Bishop! The Evil One dare not touch me now! Leave me, all of you!

All go out right except PETER, *who remains in the shadows by the door.*

PETER (*quietly*). My lord.

BISHOP NICHOLAS (*starts*). Who's that? Who's there?

PETER. Peter, my lord.

BISHOP NICHOLAS. Why do you stay behind?

PETER. I have a letter for you, my lord.

BISHOP NICHOLAS. A letter?

PETER. It was given to me by a priest, newly arrived from England. He made me promise to deliver it to you in secret. He said it was from someone named Trond.
Pause.

BISHOP NICHOLAS. Give it to me. (PETER *does so and moves away. Pause.*) Peter.

PETER (*approaches*). My lord?

BISHOP NICHOLAS. Have you ever seen an old man die?

PETER. No.

BISHOP NICHOLAS. They're all afraid, I'll swear to that! Are they singing in there?

PETER. Yes, my lord.

BISHOP NICHOLAS. Eight big fellows, with throats like trumpets – that must help a little, mustn't it?

PETER. My lord, my lord, let me pray too!

BISHOP NICHOLAS. Ah, Peter. You've always been a comfort to me. Is your mother well?

PETER. Yes, my lord.

BISHOP NICHOLAS. Did you give her my message?

PETER. Yes, my lord – but let me pray!

BISHOP NICHOLAS. The message! Did you give her my message?

PETER. I did, my lord.

BISHOP NICHOLAS. I've left too much unfinished, Peter. Life is too short – (*Doubles up in pain.*)

PETER. Are you in great pain?

BISHOP NICHOLAS. There is a ringing in my ears – a light flickers in my eyes –

PETER. It is the bells of Heaven ringing you home. And the light is the altar candles which God's angels have lit for you.

BISHOP NICHOLAS. Yes, yes, of course. There's nothing to fear, as long as they go on praying in there. Leave me. I am not afraid to be alone.

PETER. Farewell, my lord. We shall meet again when the bells of Heaven have sounded for me too. (*Goes out right.*)

BISHOP NICHOLAS. The bells of Heaven! Yes, it's easy to talk like that when you're young and healthy. So much left undone! (*Pause.*) Trond's confession! So it's come after all! I swore to the Duke on my soul's salvation to give it to him if I ever received it. And here it is, lying in my hand. One should never swear anything on one's soul's salvation when one's as old as I am. If I'd time left, I'd find a way out of the oath; but tonight, my last night – no, that wouldn't be wise. But how can I keep it? That would mean risking everything I've worked for all my life. If the Duke knew for sure, he would conquer or yield; and either way, one of them would become the mightiest man ever to have lived in Norway. No, no! What I can't have, no one else shall have! He must remain uncertain; then the strife will go on for ever. Towns will be burned, whole regions laid waste – neither shall profit by the other's defeat. He must never know! (*Whispers.*) Oh, if only I could cheat the Evil One, just once more! (*Hides the letter under his pillow. There is distant thunder.*)

What's that? (*Frightened.*) Mercy, mercy! I am the one who is guilty! I started it all! I drove them on! (*More thunder. He cries.*) William, William!

SIRA WILLIAM *enters right.*

BISHOP NICHOLAS. What's that horrible sighing and moaning?

SIRA WILLIAM. There's a storm blowing up.

BISHOP NICHOLAS. A storm! A storm, you say? Are they singing in there.

SIRA WILLIAM. Yes.

BISHOP NICHOLAS. Tell them to sing harder. Especially Brother Aslak. He always says such short prayers – he's a shirker, he misses bits out, the dog! (*Strikes the floor with his staff.*) Go in and tell him this is my last night. He must be diligent, or I will come and haunt him!

SIRA WILLIAM. My lord, had I not better fetch the doctor?

BISHOP NICHOLAS. Go in, I tell you!

SIRA WILLIAM *goes into the chapel. The* BISHOP *takes out the letter from beneath the pillow.*

It must be Heaven's will that I shall reconcile the King and the Duke. This is a hard thing, Nicholas – to destroy your life's work at a single blow. But this time I must obey His will. (*Opens the letter.*) I can't read a word – a mist drifts before my eyes – and I daren't let anyone else read it to me. I must, I *shall* live longer! (*Bangs with his staff. A* PRIEST *enters right.*) Bid Master Sigard come! (*The* PRIEST *goes. The* BISHOP *crumples the letter in his hand.*) Here, beneath this thin seal, rests Norway's history for the next hundred years. It lies here dreaming, like an unborn chick in its egg. (*Clasps the letter to his chest.*) Oh, if only I had time, I would hatch you into a hawk that would cast the shadow of fear over the whole land, and sink its sharp claws into every human heart! (*Starts.*) But the judgement – the punishment – ! (*Cries.*) No, no! You shall be a swan, a white swan! (*Throws the letter across the room, and cries.*) Master Sigard, Master Sigard!

SIGARD (*enters right*). What is it, my lord?

BISHOP NICHOLAS. Master Sigard, sell me three days life!

SIGARD. I have told you –

BISHOP NICHOLAS. I'll pay well. Three days of life, Master Sigard, only three days!

SIGARD. If I had to die with you, my lord, I could not add three days to your span.

BISHOP NICHOLAS. One day, then – just one day! Let it be daylight, let the sun be shining, when I depart! Listen, Sigard! (*Beckons him over and draws him down on the couch.*) I've given nearly all my gold and silver to the Church, to have great masses read when I am gone. I'll revoke my will – you shall have it all! What, Sigard, shall we fool those fellows in there – just the two of us? He, he, he! You'll be rich, Sigard! (MASTER SIGARD *feels his pulse. The* BISHOP *cries in anguish.*) Well, why don't you answer?

SIGARD (*gets up*). I have no time, my lord. I will prepare a drink which may ease you a little at the last.

BISHOP NICHOLAS. No, wait!

SIGARD. I have no time. The drink must be ready within an hour. (*Goes out right.*)

BISHOP NICHOLAS. Within an hour! (*Knocks furiously on the floor with his staff.*) William! William!

SIRA WILLIAM *enters from the chapel.*

BISHOP NICHOLAS. Get more people to sing in there! Eight aren't enough.

SIRA WILLIAM. My lord – ?

BISHOP NICHOLAS. More, I say! Brother Kolbein has been sick in bed for five weeks – he can't have sinned much in that time –

SIRA WILLIAM. He went to confession yesterday.

BISHOP NICHOLAS. He'll do, then. Get him. (SIRA WILLIAM *goes back into the chapel.*) Within an hour! (*Wipes the sweat from his brow.*) Ugh, it's stifling in here! The dog, what's the use of all his learning if he can't give me another hour? He sits there in his room all day, fiddling with little wheels and weights and levers, trying to make something that will go on for ever, round and round and never stop. *Perpetuum mobile*, he calls it. Why doesn't he use his knowledge to make men do that? (*Stops and*

thinks. His eyes light up.) *Perpetuum mobile!* Round and round
till the end of time. What if I could set wheels and weights and
levers working in the King's heart, and the Duke's – set them
going so that no power on earth could stop them? If I can do
that, I shall go on living, and survive through my work!
Perhaps that's what's meant by immortality. O cool and
comforting thoughts, to ease an old man's heart! (*Emits a deep
breath, and settles himself more comfortably on the coach.*) The
Devil's been after me tonight! It's all this lying idle – *otium est
pulvis – pulveris* – no, damn that Latin! The Devil shan't get
his claws into me again – I'll go on working to the end! (*Knocks
on the floor, shouts.*) Stop that din in there! I'm trying to think!

SIRA WILLIAM (*enters*). My lord, you asked for them to – ?

BISHOP NICHOLAS. Tell them to keep quiet. They're distracting
me.

SIRA WILLIAM (*turns to go*). Very well, my lord.

BISHOP NICHOLAS. Wait a moment. Give me that letter.

SIRA WILLIAM (*goes to the desk*). Which one, my lord?

BISHOP NICHOLAS. The one that's lying on the floor. Good. Now
go and tell them to keep quiet. (SIRA WILLIAM *goes.*) To die,
and yet to rule in Norway! To die, and make sure that no man
will ever raise his head above the rest! How? (*Pause.*) But of
course! It's so easy! I shall keep the oath – the Duke shall hold
the letter in his hands – and the King – hm! – the King shall
know it too – he shall feel the sting of doubt in his heart. His
faith in himself shall falter. Both shall believe and doubt, see-
saw up and down, never feel firm ground beneath them – round
and round – *perpetuum mobile!* (*Breathes a sigh of content.*) My
spirit feels young again. I shall work on my last night! Work
– till the light goes out –

DUKE SKULE (*enters right and goes over to the* BISHOP). Peace and
greetings, reverend lord! How goes it with you – ?

BISHOP NICHOLAS. I am a corpse in bud, Your Grace. Tonight
I shall flower; tomorrow you shall know my perfume.

DUKE SKULE. Tonight?

BISHOP NICHOLAS. So Master Sigard says. Within an hour.

DUKE SKULE. And the priest's letter – ?

BISHOP NICHOLAS. Do you still think about that?

DUKE SKULE. It never leaves my mind.

BISHOP NICHOLAS. The King has made you a Duke. No man has ever held that rank in Norway before.

DUKE SKULE. It is not enough. If Haakon is not the rightful King, I must have everything.

BISHOP NICHOLAS. Ugh, it's cold in here. It bites through my limbs –

DUKE SKULE. The letter, my lord! In the name of God, tell me – has it come?

Pause.

BISHOP NICHOLAS. I know where it can be found.

DUKE SKULE. Then tell me, tell me!

The BISHOP *leans forward.*

SIRA WILLIAM (*enters right*). The King is coming! We can see his torches –

BISHOP NICHOLAS. He shall be made welcome. (SIRA WILLIAM *goes.*) Your Grace, in return I crave a lost favour of you. When I am dead, avenge me against my enemies. (*Takes out the letter.*) I have written their names. Those at the top I should like hanged, if it could be arranged so.

DUKE SKULE. Do not think of revenge now. You have no time.

BISHOP NICHOLAS. Not revenge – punishment! Swear you will punish all my enemies when I am gone. They are as jealous of you as they were of me. When you are King, you can punish them. Swear you will do it!

DUKE SKULE. Very well. I swear it. But the letter – ?

BISHOP NICHOLAS. I will tell you. (*Beckons him close.*) Not yet. Here comes the King. Hide the list of our enemies.

The DUKE *hides the paper. As he does so,* HAAKON *enters right.*

BISHOP NICHOLAS. Welcome to this funeral feast, Your Majesty.

HAAKON. Greetings, my lord Bishop. (*Turns and sees* SKULE. *Starts angrily.*) Why is the Duke here?

DUKE SKULE. My lord Bishop, will you assure King Haakon upon my faith and honour that I did not know he was coming here until I set foot on Oslo quay?

BISHOP NICHOLAS. Alas, alas! The blame is mine. I have been bedridden these last months – I thought all was now well between you noble kinsmen.

HAAKON. My friendship with the Duke prospers best when we do not see each other. Therefore, farewell, Bishop Nicholas. You have been my enemy, but Death settles all accounts, and I forgive you. God be with you, whithersoever you are bound. (*Turns to go.*)

DUKE SKULE (*whispers uneasily*). My lord, my lord, he is going!

BISHOP NICHOLAS (*suddenly and, with passionate strength*). Stay, King Haakon!

HAAKON (*involuntarily lays his hand on his sword and says to the* DUKE). What trap is this? Where are your warriors?

DUKE SKULE. I did not call you back.

BISHOP NICHOLAS. Your Majesty shall not leave this room before old Bishop Nicholas has delivered his last sermon. Where there is a funeral in the house, the dead man is King. It is he who commands. My sight is dimmed, but before my inward eye, my life unfolds most clearly. Mark and learn, King! My family was the greatest in the land. Many mighty chieftains issued from it. I wanted to be King. I hungered for great deeds when I was a boy – I felt I could hardly wait for manhood. Then came the day of my first battle. The sun shone, and its light flashed from a thousand polished swords. The trumpets sounded, and our ranks moved forward as though to a game. I alone felt a tightening round my heart. Our army fought bravely forward – but I could not follow. I fled across the mountain, ran and ran, and did not stop until I had reached the fjord, far from the battle. Many men washed their bloody clothes in Trondheim fjord that night. I had to wash mine too, but not of blood. Yes, King, I was afraid! Born in love with greatness, and afraid! It smote me like a thunderbolt. I prayed secretly in the churches. I wept and knelt before the altars, I made rich offerings and sacred vows. I tried to fight, in battle after battle, always in vain. They laughed when I stepped forth in my armour. Since then, I have hated – because I could not love. Women – ah, I could devour them even now, with glistening eyes! I am eighty years old, and still I yearn to destroy men and possess women. But it was the same in love as in battle – only the will, only the desire! Impotent from birth – tormented with the seething gift of love, and yet a cripple! So I became a priest. He who wishes to rule must either be a King or a priest! (*Laughs.*) I, a priest! A man of God! Well, Heaven had fitted me for one holy office – to sing high notes – to lead with a woman's voice at the great church festivals! A half-man – not sinning, but sinned against. Let Heaven stand in the dock! I am the accuser!

DUKE SKULE (*whispers*). My lord, the letter! You have not long left.

HAAKON. Think of your soul, and humble yourself!

BISHOP NICHOLAS. A man's life-work is his soul, and my life-work shall not die! But you, King Haakon – take care! For, just as Heaven has opposed me and suffered by it, so you oppose the man who holds the welfare of our country in his hand –

HAAKON. Enough – !

BISHOP NICHOLAS (*to* HAAKON). He will oppose you as long as his head sits on his shoulders. Share with him. I shall find no peace in my coffin, I shall walk, unless you share. Neither of you must stand on the other's shoulders – there must be no giants in Norway – for I was never one. Share, share! (*Sinks feebly back upon the couch.*)

DUKE SKULE (*throws himself on his knees beside the couch and cries to* HAAKON). Get help. For God's sake, get help! The Bishop must not die yet.

BISHOP NICHOLAS. It's getting dark. I can't see – ! King, for the last time – will you share with the Duke?

HAAKON. I shall not part with one fragment of what God has given me.

BISHOP NICHOLAS. Very well. (*Whispers to himself.*) Then I will split you in two myself. (*Shouts.*) William!

DUKE SKULE (*whispers*). The letter, the letter!

BISHOP NICHOLAS (*not listening to him*). William! (SIRA
  WILLIAM *comes in. The* BISHOP *draws him close, and whispers.*)
  When I received the last sacrament, all my sins were forgiven
  me?

SIRA WILLIAM. All your sins, from birth until unction.

BISHOP NICHOLAS. Only till then?

SIRA WILLIAM. My lord, you cannot sin tonight.

BISHOP NICHOLAS. Hm – who knows – ? Take the golden
  chalice I had from Bishop Absalom – give it to the church – and
  read seven more masses.

SIRA WILLIAM. My lord, God will be merciful.

BISHOP NICHOLAS. Seven more masses, I say! For the sin I shall
  commit tonight. Go, go! (SIRA WILLIAM *goes. The* BISHOP
  turns to SKULE.) Your Grace, when you read the priest's letter,
  if it reveals that Haakon is the rightful King – what will you
  do? Search every corner of your heart. Answer as though you
  stood before your judge. What will you do, if you know he is
  the King?

DUKE SKULE. Bow my knee and serve him.

BISHOP NICHOLAS (*mutters*). Then take the consequences. (*To*
  SKULE.) Your Grace, I am weak and weary. I feel moved by
  a spirit of mercy and forgiveness –

DUKE SKULE. God's death – the letter! Where is it?

BISHOP NICHOLAS. Something else first. I gave you a list of my
  enemies –

DUKE SKULE (*impatiently*). Yes, yes. I shall avenge you –

BISHOP NICHOLAS. No, I feel so peaceful now. I want to forgive,
  as the good book says we should. As you renounce power, so
  I renounce revenge. Burn the list.

DUKE SKULE. Yes, yes, as you wish.

BISHOP NICHOLAS. Here in the brazier, so that I can see it –

DUKE SKULE (*throws the paper in the fire*). Look, there it burns.
  And now, speak, speak! Thousands of lives may perish if you
  do not speak now!

BISHOP NICHOLAS (*his eyes sparkle*). Thousands of lives! (*Cries.*)
  Light! Air!

HAAKON (*runs to the door and shouts*). Bring help! The Bishop is dying!

SIRA WILLIAM *and others of the* BISHOP'S *men come in.*

DUKE SKULE (*shakes the* BISHOP'S *arm*). Norway's glory for centuries – perhaps her greatness for all eternity – !

BISHOP NICHOLAS. For all eternity! (*Triumphantly.*) *Perpetuum mobile!*

DUKE SKULE. By your soul's salvation – where is the priest's letter?

BISHOP NICHOLAS (*cries*). Seven more masses, William!

DUKE SKULE (*desperately*). The letter! The letter!

BISHOP NICHOLAS (*smiles in his death agony*). You have burned it, most noble Duke! (*Falls back upon the couch and dies.*)

DUKE SKULE (*emits an involuntary cry as he starts back and covers his face with his hands*). Ah – Almighty God – !

The MONKS *flee in from the chapel.*

SOME OF THEM. Evil spirits are loose tonight!

OTHERS. One laughed from the corner! It cried: 'We have him!' All the candles were quenched!

HAAKON. Bishop Nicholas is dead.

The MONKS *flee out right. Their chanting fades.*

SCENE TWO

A room in the palace. In the background is the entrance door. Small doors in each of the side walls. Downstage right, a window. A lamp burns in the ceiling. Close by the door on the left stands a couch, and farther back a cradle, in which the baby prince is sleeping. MARGARET *is kneeling beside the child.*

MARGARET.   (*sings as she rocks the cradle*):

> Above the rafters of the hall,
> Among the stars in peaceful skies,
> In answer to the angels' call
> In dreams my little Haakon flies.

Out of your crib a ladder leads
Your gentle thoughts to peace above.
May all your mighty manhood deeds
Be just as gentle, filled with love.

God's little angels watch your rest
To keep all evil far from you.
God bless you, little golden child.
Your mother watches over you.

A short pause. DUKE SKULE *enters upstage.*

MARGARET (*jumps up with a cry of joy and runs to greet him*). Father!
Oh, how I've longed to see you!

DUKE SKULE. God's peace be with you, Margaret. Where is the
King?

MARGARET. Ssh! Come! Come here and look – ! (*Takes his hand
and leads him across to the cradle.*)

DUKE SKULE. Your child!

MARGARET. Yes. This beautiful child is mine! Isn't he
wonderful? His name's Haakon, like the King. Look at his eyes
– no, you can't see them now – he's sleeping – but he has great
blue eyes. And he knows me already – he laughs, and stretches
out his hands to touch me. (*Arranges the child's clothes about
him.*)

DUKE SKULE. Haakon will have sons, the Bishop prophesied.

MARGARET. I can hardly believe I'm so happy! I sleep with the
cradle close by my bed every night, so that if I wake I can reach
out my hand and touch it to make sure it isn't a dream.

DUKE SKULE (*listens and goes to the window*). Is that the King?

MARGARET. Yes. I'll go and fetch him. (*Takes her father's hand
and leads him playfully back to the cradle.*) Duke Skule! You
must stand guard over the Prince while I'm away! Yes, it's hard
to get used to, but that's what he is – a Prince! If he wakes, you
must bow low and salute him as you would a King. Now I'll
fetch Haakon. When you see him, won't you try to settle your
differences and become friends, as in the old days? Every day

I pray to God that it may happen. (*Goes out right.*)

DUKE SKULE (*walks a few steps across the room, and suddenly stops by the cradle*). The King's son! What a pretty forehead – ! He is dreaming. (*Settles the coverlet more comfortably over the child and looks long at it.*) A little one like you could lead a man's soul from despair. I have no son. (*Bends down over the cradle.*) He looks like Haakon. (*Suddenly shrinks back.*) 'Bow low and salute him as you would a King', she said. If Haakon dies before me, this child will be set upon the throne – and I – I shall stand at his footstool, bowing before him, saluting him as King, white-haired and bent with age, seeing my life-work sleep unborn. (*Pause.*) 'Burn all your bridges but one!' the Bishop said. That was three years ago, and what have I done? Left every bridge open – divided and wasted my strength. (*Sharply.*) Now I must do as he says – now or never! I have more men than Haakon – there is a storm blowing tonight, the wind is sweeping down the fjord – ! What if I seized the Prince? I can count on the citizens here. What could Haakon do if his son were in my power? So be it! Let the step be taken, let the gulf be leaped! But if I did win the crown, would not doubt still consume me, gnawing and devouring me until it bored right through my brain? Yes, yes – but it is better to sit on the throne and doubt oneself than to stand below in the crowd and doubt him who sits up there. I must settle things once and for all! For once I have the advantage. I must exploit it. (*Hesitantly.*) But now – ? Tonight – ? (*Leans over the cradle.*) If only I could see whether you have the old King's eyes! He is asleep. I cannot tell. (*Pause.*) Sleep is a sentinel. Sleep in peace, little pretender. (*Goes over to the table.*) I shall speak to Haakon once more. He shall decide what is to be.

MARGARET (*enters with the* KING *right*). The Bishop dead! Oh, believe me – all our troubles will die with him.

HAAKON. Go to bed, Margaret. You must be tired after your journey.

MARGARET. Yes, yes. (*To the* DUKE.) Father, be gentle and yielding. Haakon has promised to be. Goodnight, both of you!

(Waves to them in the doorway left, and goes. Two SERVANTS *take the cradle after her.)*

DUKE SKULE. King Haakon, this time we must not part as enemies. Evil will follow. It will be a time of dreadful horror for our land.

HAAKON. Duke Skule, when I became King I gave you a third of the kingdom. You thirsted for more. I increased your share. Now you own half the country. You still demanded more. I made you a Duke – a title no man in Norway has ever held before –

DUKE SKULE. But you are King. There must be no King above me! I was not born to serve you.

HAAKON *(looks at him for a moment and says coldly).* Heaven protect your reason, my lord. Goodnight. *(Turns to go.)*

DUKE SKULE. Listen to me! Remember the Bishop's words. Let us share. Divide the kingdom. It has happened before. We will be friends and allies –

HAAKON. Every rock on our coasts is a stone in the house our forefathers built! And you want me to break their work asunder? Never!

DUKE SKULE. Well, then, let us rule in turn!

HAAKON. Do you think my crown would fit your forehead?

DUKE SKULE. No crown is too broad for me!

HAAKON. A man must be called by God before he can wear a crown.

DUKE SKULE. And you are sure that God has called you?

HAAKON. I know he has.

DUKE SKULE. Very well, then. Let us fight, man against man, sword against sword, to the death!

HAAKON. Blind man! I pity you. Can't you see that it is your own pride that lures you towards the throne, not God's calling? What is it that tempts you? The golden circlet, the purple cloak, the right to sit with your chair three inches above the floor? They are nothing, nothing. If *that* were to be King, I would toss the kingdom into your hat as I throw a penny to a beggar. You have all the gifts of the mind – shrewdness, and courage. But you were born to stand next to the King, not to be King yourself.

DUKE SKULE. That is what we shall prove!

HAAKON. In all the years you ruled the country for me, name me one deed that you accomplished worthy of a King. The land was harried by rebel fractions, but did you bring a single one to heel? Yet you were the mature man. I was young and inexperienced when I took power, but they all submitted to me. There are no rebels left.

DUKE SKULE. That is the last thing you should boast about, for therein lies your greatest danger. Party must vie with party, interest with interest, district with district, if the King is to stay powerful. Every region, every faction must either need the King, or fear him. If you root out all dissension, you undermine your power.

HAAKON. How can you hold a belief like that and think yourself fitted to rule? Fifty years ago, you could have been a worthy chieftain; but that time is past. Don't you see that the kingdom of Norway is like a church that has still to be consecrated? The walls stand high on strong foundations, the vaulted roof spans wide, the spire points upwards like a forest pine; but there is no life in it, no beating heart, no blood pulsing in its veins. God's spirit has not breathed into it. *I* shall consecrate our country. Norway has been a kingdom; it shall become a people! The men of Trondheim warred with the men of the Vik, the men of Bergen with those of Oslo; henceforth all shall be one, and shall rejoice in their unity. That is the task which God has set upon my shoulders; that is the promise of our land, the mission of future Kings. And it is a task which you, my lord, would never accomplish; for, to speak plainly, you have not the gift for it.

DUKE SKULE (*bewildered*). Unite – ? Unite all Norway? (*Incredulously.*) But that's impossible! Such a thing has never been known, even in legend!

HAAKON. For *you* it is impossible. You can only re-tell the old sagas. But for me it is as easy as for the hawk to cleave the clouds.

DUKE SKULE (*uneasily moved*). To unite the whole people – to make them know they are one? Where did you find such a thought? It freezes my blood, and sets my soul aflame! (*Bursts out.*) You have it from the Devil, Haakon! It shall never be done, as long as I have the strength to set a helm upon my brow!

HAAKON. The idea is from God, and I shall not abandon it as long as I wear St Olaf's crown.

DUKE SKULE. Then the crown must fall!

HAAKON. By whose hand?

DUKE SKULE. Mine, if no other. Haakon! Do not tempt God. Do not drive me to the brink of the abyss!

HAAKON (*points to the door*). Go, my lord. And let us forget that we spoke with sharp tongues tonight.

DUKE SKULE (*looks at him proudly for a moment, and says*). We shall speak with sharper tongues when next we meet. (*Goes out upstage.*)

HAAKON (*after a short pause*). He cannot mean to threaten me. He is overwrought. He must, he shall obey me. I need that strong arm and that shrewd brain. God has given him those gifts that he may serve me. To defy me is to defy Heaven.

DAGFINN (*enters upstage*). My lord, be on your guard tonight. I fear the Duke intends some mischief.

HAAKON. What?

DAGFINN. I don't know; but I saw him whispering to Paul Flida and Gregorius. I am sure something is afoot.

HAAKON. Can he be planning to attack us? Impossible, impossible.

DAGFINN (*goes to the window and looks out*). He is going on board his ship. They are hoisting sail.

HAAKON. Go and find out what is happening.

DAGFINN *goes.*

HAAKON. It's unthinkable. He would never rebel. God would not allow it. I must have peace now, peace to begin my work. I hear God's urgent voice crying within me: 'Thou shalt achieve a mighty deed for Norway!'

GREGORIUS JONSSON (*enters upstage*). My lord and King!

HAAKON. Gregorius! You?

GREGORIUS JONSSON. I come to offer myself as your liegeman. Thus far I have followed the Duke. Now I dare follow him no longer.

HAAKON. What has happened?

GREGORIUS JONSSON. Something no man will believe –

HAAKON. Speak, speak!

GREGORIUS JONSSON. I dread to hear the sound of my own words. Know then – ! (*Takes him by the arm and whispers.*)

HAAKON (*starts back with a cry*). What? You are mad!

GREGORIUS JONSSON. Would to God I were!

HAAKON. Impossible! It cannot be – !

GREGORIUS JONSSON. By the precious blood of Christ, it is.

HAAKON. Go, go. Bid them sound the trumpets. Call my bodyguard! Summon all my men!

GREGORIUS JONSSON *goes.*

HAAKON (*walks up and down several times, then goes quickly over to the door of* MARGARET'S *bedchamber, knocks, walks up and down a couple more times, goes back to the door, knocks again and cries*). Margaret! (*He continues to pace to and fro.*)

MARGARET (*appears in the doorway to her room, dressed for bed, with her hair half down. About her shoulders she wears a red cloak, which she clasps tight across her breast*). Haakon! Is it you?

HAAKON. Yes, yes. Come in here.

MARGARET. Then you mustn't look at me. I'd just gone to bed.

HAAKON. You are wise, Margaret. I need your counsel.

MARGARET. What has happened?

HAAKON. I have just heard the worse news that ever reached my ears.

MARGARET (*alarmed*). What news?

HAAKON. There are two Kings in Norway now.

MARGARET. Two Kings – ? Haakon, where is my father?

HAAKON. He has proclaimed himself King on board his ship. He is sailing to Nidaros to be crowned.

MARGARET. Oh, Almighty God – ! (*Sinks down on the coach, covers her face with her hands, and weeps.*)

HAAKON. Two Kings in the land!

MARGARET. My husband one – and my father the other!

HAAKON (*paces restlessly up and down*). What shall I do, Margaret?
Cross the mountains, get there before him, and prevent the
coronation? No, impossible. He is stronger than I in the north.
I have too few men for that. What shall I do? How can I kill
him before he gets there?

MARGARET (*pleadingly, with clasped hands*). Haakon, Haakon!

HAAKON. Why does God chastise me like this? Skule is the most
dangerous enemy I could have. I must kill him! Help me,
Margaret. Help me to think of a way to kill him!

MARGARET (*sobs violently*). He is my father!

HAAKON (*stops suddenly*). Yes. Your father. I had forgotten.

   MARGARET *weeps passionately.* HAAKON *slowly approaches her.*

HAAKON (*gently*). Don't cry, Margaret. Comfort yourself. (*Raises
her and holds her.*) Why should you suffer for this madness? I
ask why God punishes me – and I have my answer. I have
sinned grievously against you. I have shunned your feelings,
and closed my heart to you – you, who have given me so much
love. Forgive me, Margaret, I need you. I need your warmth
and light –

MARGARET (*throws her arms around his neck*). Oh, Haakon, my
beloved husband! Am I near to you at last?

HAAKON. Yes, yes. Now you stand close to me. Not to give me
wise counsel, but to light my path. If there are two Kings in
Norway, there is only one in Heaven. And He will guide us.

Act Four

SCENE ONE

The great hall in Oslo Palace. KING SKULE *is feasting with his* MEN-AT-ARMS *and his* CHIEFTAINS. *Downstage left stands the high seat, on which* KING SKULE *sits, richly robed, with a purple cloak and a crown on his head. The supper table, at which the* GUESTS *are seated, stretches upstage from the high seat. Opposite* SKULE *sit* PAUL FLIDA *and* BAARD BRATTE. *Some of the humbler guests are standing on the right. It is late evening; the hall is brightly lit. The feast is drawing towards its close. The* GUESTS *are merry and partly drunk. They toast each other, laugh and converse. The bard* JATGEIR *is singing a ballad in the middle of the room.*

JATGEIR *(sings.)*

> . . . And this is sure. Since the days of yore
> Was never so fierce a fight.
> The plain, like warriors' winding-sheets,
> Grew red, that before was white.
>
> And ere the battle yet was won,
> They fled, the Birchlegs bold.
> But many could not turn and run,
> For they lay and were icy cold.
>
> Where Haakon hides no man can state.
> King Skule holds fort and town.
> Hail, King! Long, long mayst thou be great,
> And wear proud Norway's crown!

SKULE'S MEN *(jump to their feet cheering, raise their cups and goblets above their heads, clash their swords and repeat).*

> Hail, King! Long, long mayst thou be great,
> And wear proud Norway's crown!

KING SKULE. Thank you for your song, good Jatgeir. I like a song that praises warriors.

JATGEIR. To praise your warriors is to praise you, Your Majesty.

KING SKULE. Take this bracelet as a reward. Stay with me, and be my friend. I would have many poets about me.

JATGEIR. They will be needed, my lord, if songs are to be written in praise of all your great deeds.

KING SKULE. I shall be thrice as bountiful as Haakon. Poets shall be rewarded as richly as warriors while I am King. Sit; you are now a courtier. All that you need shall be freely given you.

JATGEIR (*sits*). Your Majesty will soon run short of what I need most.

KING SKULE. What is that?

JATGEIR. Enemies, whose flight and fall I may celebrate.

MANY OF THE GUESTS (*amid laughter and applause*). Well spoken, Icelander!

JATGEIR. I promise you, my lord, I shall compose a great ode to you when you kill the Sleeper.

KING SKULE. The Sleeper?

JATGEIR. That is what they have called Haakon ever since you beat him at Laaka. He has lain in Nidaros like a man paralysed.

BAARD BRATTE. With his eyes closed, they say. I suppose he's dreaming that he is still King!

KING SKULE. Let him dream. He will never dream himself back to the throne.

PAUL FLIDA. They say he has renounced the Church and all that is holy. He refused to attend mass on New Year's Day.

BAARD BRATTE. He had a good excuse. He spent the whole day chopping up his silver plates and cups – he had nothing else to pay his men with!

Laughter and loud comments from the GUESTS.

KING SKULE. I drink to you, Baard Bratte, and I thank you and all my new men. You fought bravely for me at Laaka.

BAARD BRATTE. We soon found how easy it was to conquer with such a chieftain riding at our head. It was a pity we killed so many of them. I fear it will be a long time before they show their faces again.

KING SKULE. Wait till the spring comes. When they think they are strong enough, we shall hear from them.

BAARD BRATTE. They won't dare.

KING SKULE. Then we shall lure them out by guile.

MANY VOICES. Yes, yes!

BAARD BRATTE. You have a good store of cunning, King Skule. Your enemies never know where you are until you are upon them. You will enter Nidaros in triumph, Your Majesty, and this time the monks will not dare refuse to bring the shrine from the church. You will be proclaimed beside it in the marketplace, and then you will be King of all Norway.

KING SKULE. But the shrine must be brought out. My coronation must be lawful. (*Turns to his* MEN.) My good men, I make you all a promise. After our next battle, each of you shall have the weapons and clothes, the gold and silver, the land and the inheritance of the men he kills; and he shall take the title that his victim held. He who kills a knight shall become a knight – he who kills a judge shall take the judge's seat upon the bench –

THE MEN (*leap to their feet in wild excitement*). Hail, hail, King Skule! Lead us against the Birchlegs!

BAARD BRATTE. Now you are sure of victory!

KING SKULE. Go to your beds now, my good men. We have sat late at the tables tonight.

MEN-AT-ARMS (*as the others prepare to go*). Tomorrow we'll cast lots for the Birchlegs' goods!

ANOTHER. No, let's grab what we can get.

There is a bubble of excited disagreement as they go out.

BAARD BRATTE. Now the wolves are fighting for the bear's pelt.

PAUL FLIDA. Before they have killed him.

They all go out upstage except KING SKULE.

KING SKULE (*waits till his* GUESTS *are gone. Then his face relaxes, and he sinks down on one of the benches.*) How tired I am. Tired to death! Day in and day out to stand amidst this crowd, smiling as though I were certain of my cause, and without one friend in whom I can confide my fears. (*Rises in terror.*) Haakon sent his army against me. And the impossible happened – Haakon lost, and I won! And yet I am still afraid. When the question comes to me unawares: 'Which of us is the rightful King?', my heart always answers 'he', and never 'I'. To see myself as King I have to use art, build a throne of imagination, a crown of dreams – I have to chase away memories, and possess faith by force. *Why?* Is it because the Bishop burned the letter? No – that only made my doubt eternal – it did not increase it. (*Sits, right.*) Then what *is* it? Ha, that's strange – it dances on the tip of my tongue, like a forgotten word. (*Jumps up.*) Ah – now I remember! 'Norway has been a kingdom – it shall become a people. All shall be one, and shall rejoice in their unity!' Since Haakon spoke those madman's words, I see him clearly as the rightful King. (*Stares vacantly in anguish, and whispers.*) Did those words reveal God's calling? Has He chosen Haakon to be His prophet?

PAUL FLIDA (*enters upstage*). Your Majesty, I have news.

KING SKULE. News?

PAUL FLIDA. A man from down the fjord says the Birchlegs have put out to sea, and that many strangers have entered Oslo during the last few days.

KING SKULE. We will deal with them. Tomorrow, perhaps.

PAUL FLIDA. My lord, perhaps they are planning to surprise us.

KING SKULE. We shall beat them, as we did at Laaka.

PAUL FLIDA. My lord, it is not so easy to beat the Birchlegs twice in succession.

KING SKULE. Why not?

PAUL FLIDA. Because our country's saga tells us that such a thing has never happened before. Should I not send scouts to Head Isle?

KING SKULE. There is no need. It is a dark night, and misty.

PAUL FLIDA. Well, Your Majesty knows best. But remember, the citizens of Oslo hate you, and if the Birchlegs come they will make common cause with them.

KING SKULE (*on an impulse*). Paul Flida, isn't it possible that the people of Oslo might support me?

PAUL FLIDA (*looks at him amazed and shakes his head*). No, my lord, that is unthinkable.

KING SKULE. Why?

PAUL FLIDA. Because the people of Trondheim are on your side.

KING SKULE. I want to have both!

PAUL FLIDA. No, my lord, that is impossible.

KING SKULE. Unthinkable – impossible! Why? Why shouldn't they?

PAUL FLIDA. Because the people of Trondheim are the people of Trondheim, and the men of Oslo are the men of Oslo, and because the sagas tell us that that is so, and because it has always been so.

KING SKULE. Yes, yes. You are right. Go.

PAUL FLIDA. Shall I not send scouts?

KING SKULE. Wait till daybreak. (PAUL FLIDA *goes*.) The sagas of Norway tell us that it is so, and it has always been so. He answers me as I answered Haakon. Has God given Haakon the power to see what I cannot see? (*Pause. He walks broodingly up and down; then stops.*) Can a man rob another of that power, as he can take arms and gold from the enemy he has slain? Can a pretender put on the divine calling like a purple cloak? Can the oak felled for ship's timber say: 'I shall be the mast, I shall perform the task of the pine, point straight and shining towards the sky, fly a golden pennant at my head, arch in the sunshine with my white, bellying sails and be seen by people far, far away?' No, no, old heavy, knotted oak – your place is beneath the keel; you must lie there and do your duty, silent and unseen. Your task is to keep the ship from heeling over when the storm comes. The mast with the golden pennant and the bellying sails shall carry it forward towards the new, towards the unknown, towards the strange shore and the saga that is to come! (*Passionately.*) Since Haakon spoke of his great ideal, I can think of nothing else. Why should I not make it mine and fulfil it myself? (*Pensively.*) If it is beyond my power, why do I love it so?

JATGEIR (*enters upstage*). Forgive me, Your Majesty –

KING SKULE. You are welcome, poet.

JATGEIR. I thought it my duty to tell you – there are rumours in the town –

KING SKULE. Tell me, poet. You have travelled far and wide – have you ever seen a woman love a child that was not her own? Love it with her heart and soul?

JATGEIR. Only women with no children of their own do that.

KING SKULE. Only those?

JATGEIR. Especially women who are barren.

KING SKULE. Barren? Do they?

JATGEIR. Often.

KING SKULE. And does a barren woman ever kill someone else's child because she has none of her own?

JATGEIR. Oh, yes. But that's a foolish thing to do.

KING SKULE. Why foolish?

JATGEIR. Because then she gives the other woman something priceless. The gift of sorrow.

KING SKULE. Is that so precious?

JATGEIR. Yes, my lord.

KING SKULE (*looks earnestly at him*). There seem to dwell two men in you, Icelander. When you sit among the warriors at a feast, you draw cap and cloak over every thought. But when a man is alone with you, you seem the kind of man one would choose to have as a friend. Why is this?

JATGEIR. When you go to swim in the river, my lord, you do not undress where the people walk to church. You seek out a lonely place.

KING SKULE. Of course.

JATGEIR. My soul is shy. So I do not bare it when the hall is full.

KING SKULE (*short pause*). Tell me, Jatgeir, how did you come to be a singer? From whom did you learn your art?

JATGEIR. The art of song cannot be learned, my lord.

KING SKULE. Then how did you acquire it?

JATGEIR. I received the gift of sorrow, and found myself a singer.

KING SKULE. Is that what a singer needs?

JATGEIR. I needed sorrow. Others may need faith – or joy – or doubt –

KING SKULE. Doubt too?

JATGEIR. Yes. But then he who doubts must be strong.

KING SKULE. And whom would you call a weak doubter?

JATGEIR. He who doubts his own doubt.

KING SKULE (*slowly*). That sounds to me like death.

JATGEIR. It is worse. It is twilight.

KING SKULE (*suddenly, as though casting aside his thoughts*). Where is my sword? I want to fight – not think. What did you come to tell me?

JATGEIR. The people at the inn are whispering among themselves. They ask if we are quite sure that King Haakon is still hiding in the west. They're pleased about something.

KING SKULE. The people of Oslo have always been against me.

JATGEIR. They mock you because the monks refused to bring St Olaf's holy shrine out of the church when you were proclaimed. They say it is an evil omen.

KING SKULE. Next time I sail to Nidaros, the shrine shall be brought out. It shall stand in the square for all to see, if I have to batter the church to rubble!

JATGEIR. That will be a great deed. But I shall write a poem to match it.

KING SKULE. Have you many unsung poems in your head, Jatgeir?

JATGEIR. No. But I have many that are unborn. One by one they are freed, and so take life.

KING SKULE. If I had you killed, would all those unborn poems die within you?

JATGEIR. My lord, it is a sin to kill a beautiful thought.

KING SKULE. I am not asking if it is a sin. I am asking if it could be done.

JATGEIR. I do not know.

KING SKULE. Have you never had another poet as your friend, and has he never told you of a great and noble poem that he wished to write?

JATGEIR. Yes, my lord.

KING SKULE. Didn't you wish you could kill him, so that you might steal his thought and write the poem yourself?

JATGEIR. My lord, I am not barren. I have children of my own. I do not need to covet those of other men. (*Turns to go.*)

KING SKULE. Jatgeir! (JATGEIR *stops*). Who gave you the gift of sorrow?

JATGEIR. The one I loved.

KING SKULE. She died?

JATGEIR. No. She played me false.

KING SKULE. And so you became a poet?

JATGEIR. Yes. I became a poet.

KING SKULE (*grips him by the arm*). What gift do *I* need to become King?

JATGEIR. Not the gift of doubt, or you would not have asked.

KING SKULE. What gift do I need?

JATGEIR. My lord, you *are* King.

KING SKULE. Are you always sure that you are a poet?

JATGEIR (*looks at him silently for a moment, then asks*). Have you never loved?

KING SKULE. Yes, once. Passionately, beautifully – sinfully.

JATGEIR. You have a wife.

KING SKULE. I took her because I wanted a son.

JATGEIR. But you have a daughter, my lord. A gentle and noble daughter.

KING SKULE. If my daughter had been a son, I would not have asked you what gift I needed. (*Passionately.*) I must have someone by me who will obey me instinctively, believe in me unflinchingly, stand close by me through good days and evil, live only to give light and warmth to my life – someone who, when I fall, must die! What shall I do, Jatgeir?

JATGEIR. Buy a dog, my lord.

PAUL FLIDA (*runs in*). To arms, Your Majesty! Haakon is lying off Elkness with all his fleet!

KING SKULE. Off Elkness! He has made good speed.

JATGEIR. To arms, my lord! If there is to be killing here tonight,

I will gladly be the first to die for you!

KING SKULE. Can you not live for me? Be a son to me – live for my life-work, and believe in me!

JATGEIR. A man can die for another's life-work. But if he is to go on living, he must live for his own. (*Goes.*)

PAUL FLIDA (*impatiently*). What are your orders, my lord? The Birchlegs will be in Oslo within an hour!

KING SKULE. We must go to blessed Thomas Becket's grave. He has helped many souls in their hour of need.

PAUL FLIDA (*more loudly*). My lord! I tell you the Birchlegs are upon us!

KING SKULE. Let all the churches be opened. We must seek sanctuary.

PAUL FLIDA. My lord! You have the chance to destroy your enemies at a blow! This is no time to speak of churches!

KING SKULE. Yes, yes. Keep all the churches open.

PAUL FLIDA. Haakon will violate the sanctuary!

KING SKULE. No. God will guard him against such a sin. God always guards Haakon.

PAUL FLIDA (*takes him aside and whispers*). My lord, the men will hear you. They will ask: 'Who is King in this land?'

KING SKULE (*smiles sadly*). Yes, Paul Flida, that is the great question. Who is King in this land?

PAUL FLIDA (*pleadingly*). You are sick tonight, my lord. Let me act for you.

KING SKULE. Yes, yes, do so.

PAUL FLIDA (*going towards the door*). First we must burn all the bridges.

KING SKULE. Madman! Stop! Burn all the bridges? Don't you know what that means? Beware of doing that!

PAUL FLIDA. Every second is precious now, Your Majesty! (*Seizes his hand.*) King Skule, let us burn all the bridges, fight like wolves and trust in Heaven!

KING SKULE (*whispers*). Heaven will not trust me. I dare not trust in Heaven.

PAUL FLIDA. Our saga has been short, King Skule. (*Goes out upstage.*)

KING SKULE. A hundred wise heads, a thousand armed men –
these I command. But not one loyal and loving heart. Such is
the poverty of Kings.

SKULE *sits down pensively right. After a few moments, a* WOMAN
IN BLACK *enters. She is wearing a long cloak, a hood and a thick
veil which hides her face. A* PRIEST *enters after her and remains
by the door.*

KING SKULE. Who are you?

WOMAN. One whom you loved.

KING SKULE *(shakes his head).* Who are you, I ask?

WOMAN. One who loves you.

KING SKULE. Then you must have come from the dead.

WOMAN *(comes closer and whispers passionately).* Skule Baardsson!

KING SKULE *(with a cry).* Ingeborg!

INGEBORG. You know me now, Skule?

KING SKULE. Ingeborg – Ingeborg!

INGEBORG. Oh, let me look at you! For a long, long time! *(Clasps
his hands. Pause.)* How I loved you! Why were you false to me?

KING SKULE. Take off your veil. Look at me with those eyes
which were once as clear and as blue as Heaven.

INGEBORG. Those eyes have been a clouded Heaven these twenty
years. You would not recognise them; and you will never see
them again.

KING SKULE. But your voice is still fresh, and soft, and young,
as it used to be.

INGEBORG. I have only used it to whisper your name, to impress
your greatness on a young heart, and to pray to the God of
mercy to forgive us for our sinful love. That is why my voice
is still young.

KING SKULE. A lifetime lies between us. I have put aside every
memory of that fair time. Yet you have stayed in the cold
loneliness of the north, keeping those memories.

INGEBORG. They have been my happiness.

KING SKULE. And I left you, to win power and riches. If you had
stayed by my side, how much easier things might have been – !

INGEBORG. God prevented it. My soul needed a great sin, to turn it towards remorse and penitence.

KING SKULE. And now –?

INGEBORG. I come to you a widow.

KING SKULE. Your husband is dead?

INGEBORG. He took my guilt upon his strong and loving shoulders. He went to fight in the Holy Land, and died on the road from Jerusalem, bleeding for my sins.

KING SKULE (*quietly*). Did he know everything?

INGEBORG. From the first. Bishop Nicholas knew, too, for I confessed to him.

KING SKULE. And why do you come to me now?

INGEBORG. To make the final sacrifice.

KING SKULE. What do you mean?

INGEBORG (*points to the* PRIEST *standing by the door*). There he is. Peter, my son, come here.

KING SKULE. Your son –?

INGEBORG. And yours, King Skule.

KING SKULE. Ingeborg!

PETER *comes to them, silent and bewildered, and kneels before* KING SKULE.

INGEBORG. Take him. He has been the light and comfort of my life for twenty years. Now you are Norway's King. The King's son must enter into his inheritance. I have no right to him any longer.

KING SKULE (*raises him joyfully*). Come to my heart! Oh, I have longed for you so burningly! (*Embraces him tightly, releases him, looks at him for a moment, and embraces him again.*) My son! My son! I have a son! (*Roars with laughter.*) Who can withstand me now? (*Goes across to* INGEBORG *and clasps her hand.*) You will not take back your word, Ingeborg?

INGEBORG. Bishop Nicholas enjoined me to make this sacrifice. He sent him to me from his deathbed, imploring this penance for all my sins.

KING SKULE. Then our sin is wiped out; and now he is mine alone!

INGEBORG. Yes. But I ask one promise of you.

KING SKULE. Ask what you will!

INGEBORG. I give him into your hands, as pure as the lamb of God. But the path that leads to the throne is dangerous. Do not let his soul be stained. You hear, King Skule? Do not let my son's soul be corrupted.

KING SKULE. I promise and swear it.

INGEBORG (*clasps his arm*). Let him rather die!

KING SKULE. He shall rather die. I swear it.

INGEBORG. Then I can go north to my home in peace. Beg God to call me; and when we meet before God, he will come to his mother pure and unstained.

KING SKULE. Pure and unstained.

INGEBORG (*to herself*). To love, to sacrifice everything, and to be forgotten. That has been my saga. (*Goes silently out upstage.*)

KING SKULE (*turns to* PETER). Let me look at you. Yes, you have your mother's eyes. You are the one I have been needing.

PETER. My father! My great and noble father! Let me live and fight for you. Whatever be your cause, I shall know that I am fighting for what is right.

KING SKULE. You shall renounce your vows and march beside me. The King's son must carry a sword.

PETER. We will go forward together!

KING SKULE (*clasps him to him*). Yes, together! And when we have gained the kingdom, it shall be yours after me. Peter, my son – listen! You and I shall perform a noble deed for Norway. We shall awake the people and unite them. North and south, mountains and valleys – all shall become one mighty people, and then our country shall grow great!

PETER. Through the great thought of a great King!

KING SKULE. Do you grasp it?

PETER. Yes – yes! Clearly!

KING SKULE. And do you believe in it?

PETER. Yes! Yes – because I believe in you!

KING SKULE (*passionately*). Haakon Haakonsson shall die!

  Distant trumpets are heard.

PAUL FLIDA (*enters and cries*). Our hour has struck, King Skule!

The Birchlegs are swarming in thousands down from the hills!

KING SKULE. Sound the trumpets! Call the men to arms! How shall we meet them?

PAUL FLIDA. All the churches stand open for us.

KING SKULE. The churches – ? But the Birchlegs – ?

PAUL FLIDA. All the bridges stand open for them.

KING SKULE. Accursed man, what have you done?

PAUL FLIDA. Obeyed my King.

KING SKULE. My son, my son! I have cast away your kingdom!

PETER. No! You will win! So great an idea cannot die!

SCENE TWO

A street in Oslo. On either side, low modern houses with porches. In the background lies St Hallvard's churchyard, enclosed by a high wall with a gate. To the left, at the end of the wall, can be seen the church, the door of which is standing open. It is still night; gradually, the day begins to dawn. The alarm bell is ringing. Far away to the right can be heard distant war-cries and confused alarums.

KING SKULE'S TRUMPETER (*enters right, sounds his trumpet and cries*). To arms! To arms, all King Skule's men! More is at stake here than life and death! To arms! (*He sounds his trumpet again and goes on. After a few moments he is heard sounding his trumpet and shouting in the next street.*)

A WOMAN (*comes out of a house on the right*). Merciful God! What's happening?

A CITIZEN (*emerges half-dressed from a house on the other side of the street*). The Birchlegs are in the town! Now God will punish Skule for all he has done!

2ND CITIZEN (*runs down a side street left with several others*). Where are they?

3RD CITIZEN (*from a house on the right*). I don't know.

4TH CITIZEN. They're storming the bridge!

OTHERS. To the bridge! To the bridge! (*They all run out.*)

WOMAN. The Saints preserve us! It is the Birchlegs?

2ND CITIZEN. It's them all right. King Haakon's with them. His whole fleet's sailing into the harbour. He's already landed with his best men.

1ST CITIZEN. He'll avenge his losses at Laaka!

2ND CITIZEN. I'll wager he will!

1ST CITIZEN. Look! Skule's men are fleeing already!

A CROWD OF KING SKULE'S MEN *enters fleeing from the right.*

ONE OF THEM. Into the church! Into the church! The Birchlegs are fighting like devils from Hell tonight!

They run into the church and close the door from inside.

2ND CITIZEN (*looks away right*). Look! King Haakon's banner! They've taken the bridge!

5TH CITIZEN. They're charging up the hill!

1ST CITIZEN. Look, look! Skule's men are on the run!

More of KING SKULE'S MEN *enter from the right.*

KING SKULE'S MEN. Sanctuary! Sanctuary! To the church! Sanctuary! (*They rush towards the door.*) It is shut! It is shut! They've barred the door!

ONE OF THEM. Up to the mountains, then!

ANOTHER. Where is King Skule?

A THIRD. Yes, where's the King?

THE FIRST. He's abandoned us! Away! There's Haakon's banner!

They flee out left past the church. HAAKON *enters right with his* STANDARD-BEARER, GREGORIUS JONSSON, DAGFINN THE PEASANT *and several others.*

DAGFINN. Do you hear that war-cry? Skule is rallying his men!

1ST CITIZEN. They're behind the churchyard!

2ND CITIZEN. Some are fleeing up the mountain!

DAGFINN. Follow them!

OLD CITIZEN (*shouts from his loft to* HAAKON). Take care, my dear lord! Skule's men are desperate tonight! They're fighting for their lives!

HAAKON. Is it you, old friend? You fought for my father, and his father.

OLD MAN. Would to God I could fight for you too!

HAAKON. There's no need. Go back to your fireside – you have played your part. The whole town has risen to join me.

DAGFINN (*points over the wall, right*). Here comes the Duke's banner!

GREGORIUS JONSSON. The Duke himself! He's riding on his white charger!

DAGFINN. Don't let him get through the gate!

HAAKON (*to his* TRUMPETER). Blow, blow! (*The* TRUMPETER *blows.*) Dog, you blew louder than that when you played for money on Bergen Bridge!

The TRUMPETER *blows again, louder. Many people come.*

ONE OF SKULE'S MEN (*enters right, fleeing towards the church, pursued by a* BIRCHLEG). Spare my life! Spare my life!

BIRCHLEG. Not if you were sitting on the altar! (*Cuts him down.*) That's a fine cloak you have. I can use that. (*Bends down to take it but utters a cry and flings away his sword.*) My brother! My brother! King Haakon, I have killed my own brother!

HAAKON (*to* DAGFINN). Is it true?

DAGFINN. Yes. I knew them both.

HAAKON (*shaken*). Brother against brother, father against son. Almighty God, let there be an end to this!

GREGORIUS JONSSON. Here comes the Duke!

DAGFINN. Bar the gate against him!

The combatants come into sight within the wall. KING SKULE'S MEN *fight their way towards the left, driving the* BIRCHLEGS *back step by step.* KING SKULE, *his sword drawn, is riding his white charger.* PETER *walks at his side, holding the horse's bridle, a crucifix raised in his left hand.* PAUL FLIDA *is carrying* KING SKULE'S *standard, which is blue with a golden lion rampant, but without the axe.*

KING SKULE. Cut them down! Spare no one! Norway has a new heir to the throne!

HAAKON. Skule Baardsson, let us share the kingdom!

KING SKULE. All or nothing!

HAAKON. Think of your daughter! Think of the Queen!

KING SKULE. I have a son! I have a son!

HAAKON. I have a son too. If I die, he will inherit my crown.

KING SKULE. Kill the Prince, wherever you find him! Kill him on the throne! Kill him on the altar! Kill him, kill him in the Queen's arms!

HAAKON. You have pronounced your own death!

KING SKULE (*hews about him*). Kill, kill! King Skule has a son! Kill, kill! (*The battle moves off left.*)

GREGORIUS JONSSON. They are fighting their way through!

DAGFINN. Only to flee.

GREGORIUS JONSSON. Yes, by Heaven! The other gate is open. They are escaping!

DAGFINN. Up the mountains! (*Shouts.*) After them, after them! Avenge our brothers who died at Laaka!

HAAKON. You heard him. He condemned my son. My innocent child, the heir to Norway's crown.

HAAKON'S MEN. We heard him.

HAAKON. And what is the punishment for such a crime?

THE MEN. Death!

HAAKON. Then he too shall die. (*Raises his hand in an oath.*) I hereby swear it. Skule Baardsson shall die, wherever he be met on unconsecrated ground.

DAGFINN. It is every loyal man's duty to kill him.

BIRCHLEG (*from the left*). Duke Skule is fleeing!

CITIZEN. The Birchlegs have won!

HAAKON. Which way?

BIRCHLEG. Up the mountains.

HAAKON. God be thanked for His help! Where is the Queen?

GREGORIUS JONSSON (*points right*). She is here, my lord. See!

HAAKON (*to those nearest him*). My heaviest task is still before me. She loves her father. Listen. No word to her about the danger to her child. Swear to me, all of you, protect your King's son; but no word to her.

THE MEN (*softly*). We swear.

MARGARET (*enters with* ATTENDANTS *right*). Haakon, my husband! Heaven has protected you! You have won, you are unharmed.

HAAKON. Yes, I have won. Where is our son?

MARGARET. On board your ship, in safe hands.

HAAKON. Go down there, some of you.
  Several of the MEN *go.*

MARGARET. Haakon, where is – Duke Skule?

HAAKON. He has fled into the hills.

MARGARET. Then he is alive! Oh, my husband – may I thank God for preserving him?

HAAKON (*struggling with himself*). Listen to me, Margaret. You have been a loyal wife to me. You have followed me in good times and evil, you have given me your love unceasingly. Now I must cause you great grief. I would have avoided it. But I am King, and therefore I *must* –

MARGARET (*tensely*). Is it – the Duke?

HAAKON. Yes. I could suffer no greater punishment than to have to live without you – but if, after what I am going to tell you, you decide that it must be so – if you feel you can no longer stay at my side, no longer look at me without turning pale – well, then we must part, and live alone, and I shall not blame you for it.

MARGARET. Part from you? How can you think of such a thing? Give me your hand –

HAAKON. Do not touch it. I have just raised it in an oath –

MARGARET. An oath?

HAAKON. An oath that sealed a death sentence.

MARGARET (*cries*). My father! Oh, my father! (*Staggers. Two of the* WOMEN *run forward and hold her.*)

HAAKON. Yes, Margaret. As King, I have condemned your father to death. (*Pause.*) If you now decide that we must part, so be it.

MARGARET (*comes closer and says calmly*). We can never part. I am your wife, and nothing else. Only your wife.

HAAKON. Did you hear and understand? I have condemned your father.

MARGARET. I heard and understood. You have condemned my father.

HAAKON. And you do not ask to know his crime?

MARGARET. It is enough that you know.

HAAKON. But I have condemned him to death.

MARGARET (*kneels before the* KING *and kisses his hand*). My husband and most mighty lord, your judgement is just.

Act Five

SCENE ONE

A room in the palace at Nidaros. The entrance door is on the right. Downstage on the same side is a window. On the left, a smaller door. The room is in darkness. PAUL FLIDA, BAARD BRATTE *and others of* KING SKULE'S *principal chieftains are standing by the window, looking upwards.*

A CHIEFTAIN. How red it glows!

ANOTHER. It covers half the sky, like a flaming sword.

BAARD BRATTE. Blessed St Olaf, what can such a dreadful sign portend?

OLD WARRIOR. Surely the death of some great chieftain.

PAUL FLIDA. The death of Haakon, my good comrades. He is lying out in the fjord with his fleet. We can expect him tonight. This time, we shall win.

BAARD BRATTE. Don't be too sure. There is little courage in the army now.

OLD WARRIOR. Small wonder. Ever since we fled from Oslo, we have been without a leader. Why has King Skule shut himself away? (*Their eyes turn to the small door.*) Why won't he speak to his men?

1ST CHIEFTAIN. The townspeople don't know whether he is alive or dead.

BAARD BRATTE. I have tried to reason with him. It's no use.

PAUL FLIDA. Our lives are at stake. The King must show himself. (*Goes to the door left and knocks.*) Your Majesty, your people need you! You must rouse yourself!

KING SKULE (*from within*). I am sick, Paul Flida.

PAUL FLIDA. You have not eaten for two days.

KING SKULE. I am sick.

PAUL FLIDA. Almighty God, that cannot be helped! King

Haakon is in the fjord. He may be upon us any moment!

KING SKULE. Kill him, and kill his child.

PAUL FLIDA. You must lead us, my lord.

KING SKULE. No, no. You are surer of victory without me.

PETER (*enters right, dressed for battle*). The people are restive. They are gathering in front of the palace.

BAARD BRATTE. If the King does not speak to them, they will betray him when he needs them most.

PETER. He must speak to them. (*At the door, left.*) Father! The citizens of Nidaros, your loyallest subjects, will abandon your cause unless you give them courage.

KING SKULE. I cannot give what is not mine.

PETER. Then you cannot give away the kingdom; for it is mine as well as yours!

KING SKULE (*after a pause*). I am coming!

PAUL FLIDA. God be praised!

Pause.

KING SKULE (*appears in the doorway. He is pale and haggard, and his hair is heavily streaked with grey*). Don't look at me. I am sick.

PETER (*goes over to him*). Father!

KING SKULE. Give away your kingdom, did you say? Great God, what has possessed me?

PETER. Forgive me, father –

KING SKULE. No, no! I have been asleep. But now I shall be strong –

A LOUD CRY (*outside*). King Skule! King Skule!

KING SKULE. What is that?

BAARD BRATTE (*at the window*). The citizens are gathering. The courtyard is filled with people. You must speak to them!

KING SKULE. Do I look like a King? Can I show myself?

PETER. You must, my noble father!

KING SKULE. So be it. (*Goes to the window and draws back the curtain but lets it go quickly and starts back in terror.*) The sword of fire! It still hangs over me!

PETER. It is an omen. A sword of victory!

KING SKULE. Would it were so! (*Goes to the window, and speaks through it.*) People of Nidaros, what do you want? Here stands your King.

CITIZEN (*outside*). Leave our town! The Birchlegs will burn it and kill us, if they find you here!

KING SKULE. We must stand together. I have been a good King to you. I have asked little from you –

MAN'S VOICE (*from the* CROWD). What about the blood that ran at Laaka?

A WOMAN. Give me back my husband!

A BOY. Give me my father and brother!

ANOTHER WOMAN. Give me my three sons, King Skule!

A MAN. He is not King! The monks did not bring out the shrine!

2ND MAN. He has not been proclaimed at the shrine!

3RD MAN. He is not our lawful King!

KING SKULE (*shrinks behind the curtains*). Not lawful – ! Not King!

BAARD BRATTE. If the townspeople desert us, we cannot hold Nidaros.

KING SKULE. I am nothing without the shrine.

PETER. Then let it be brought forth, now!

PAUL FLIDA (*shakes his head*). Impossible.

PETER. Nothing is impossible, for his sake! Sound the trumpets, summon the assembly, and bring forth the shrine!

SEVERAL MEN (*shrink back*). Sacrilege!

PETER. It is no sacrilege. If the monks support us –

PAUL FLIDA. They fear the Archbishop –

PETER. You call yourselves the King's men, and dare not help him now! My father and my King, the monks *shall* do this! I will beg them, I will entreat them on my knees! Let the trumpets sound! We shall show them who is the lawful King! (*Runs out.*)

KING SKULE (*exultantly*). Did you see him? Did you see my noble son? How his eyes shone! The people will stay with us now! We shall fight and conquer, and end this dreadful war. It is the will of Heaven. (*Points upwards.*) See how God's blazing sword hangs in the stars above our heads! The nights are troubled, women stagger in labour at their prayers, priests rave in the streets proclaiming the Day of Judgement! God is angry. He demands that it be ended. And, by all our holy Saints, it shall!

PAUL FLIDA. What are your orders, sire?

KING SKULE. Burn all the bridges!

PAUL FLIDA (*to a* MAN-AT-ARMS). Bid them burn all the bridges!
The MAN-AT-ARMS *goes out right.*

KING SKULE. Muster my army at the waterside. No man of Haakon's shall set foot in Nidaros!

PAUL FLIDA. Bravely said, my lord!

KING SKULE. Sound the trumpets when the shrine is brought forth. Summon the people.

PAUL FLIDA (*to one of the* MEN). Bid them prepare to sound.
The MAN *goes.*

KING SKULE (*speaks to the* CROWD *beneath from the window*). Hold fast to me, all ye who weep and mourn! Peace and light shall return to our land, as in those first fair days when Haakon was King and the corn flowered twice in every summer! Hold fast to me! Trust and believe in me – I need your trust. I shall watch and fight for you – I shall bleed and fall for you, if God so wills it – but do not abandon me, and do not doubt – ! (*A loud cry as though of terror is heard from among the* CROWD.) What is that?

DISTRAUGHT VOICE. Repent, repent!

BAARD BRATTE (*looks out*). It is a priest possessed by the Devil!

PAUL FLIDA. Rending his cassock and scourging himself.

THE VOICE. Repent, repent! The Day of Judgement is come!

MANY VOICES. Blasphemy! Sacrilege!

KING SKULE. What has happened?

BAARD BRATTE. The crowd is shrinking in terror, as though a wild beast had come amongst them.

PAUL FLIDA. They are fleeing – !

KING SKULE (*utters a cry of joy*). No matter! We are saved! Look, look! The shrine is standing in the centre of the courtyard!

PAUL FLIDA. St Olaf's shrine!

BAARD BRATTE. Yes, by Heaven! There it is!

KING SKULE. The monks are loyal. They have shown their faith –

PAUL FLIDA. Listen! The trumpets!

KING SKULE. Now I shall be lawfully proclaimed.

PETER (*enters right*) Put on your royal robe. The shrine is standing in the courtyard.

KING SKULE. You have saved my kingdom, and yours. We shall reward the pious monks richly for yielding to our entreaties.

PETER. The monks, father? You have nothing to thank the monks for.

KING SKULE. Surely they helped you – ?

PETER. They pronounced the Church's curse on any who dared to touch the holy relic.

KING SKULE. The Archbishop, then! He has yielded at last.

PETER. The Archbishop pronounced a heavier curse than the monks. Excommunication.

KING SKULE. Then I still have loyal subjects! Down there, among the common people, I have friends who dared to risk damnation for my sake.

PETER. Not one of them moved a step towards the church.

KING SKULE. Almighty God, then, has a miracle occurred? Who removed the relic?

PETER. I did, father.

KING SKULE (*cries*). You!

THE MEN (*shrink fearfully*). Sacrilege!

PAUL FLIDA, BAARD BRATTE *and several of the others go out.*

PETER. There was no other way. I begged, I entreated the monks, but to no avail. So I broke open the church door. No one dared follow me. I leaped on to the high altar, seized the handle of the shrine and set my knees against the wall. It seemed as though some mysterious power gave me more than mortal strength. I wrenched, and the shrine broke loose. I dragged it after me down the aisle, while their curses whispered in the rafters like a storm. I dragged it out of the church. The crowd shrank from me as I came down the steps, and fled as I crossed the courtyard. I reached the centre alone, and as I set down the shrine the handle snapped from the casket. Here it is. (*Holds it up.*)

KING SKULE (*quietly, appalled*). Sacrilege!

PETER. For your sake! For the sake of your great ideal. You will bring light and peace – a new and shining dawn for Norway! What does it matter if the night before is stormy? You will wipe out my guilt.

KING SKULE. When your mother brought you to me, I seemed to see a halo about your head. Now God's thunderbolt has withered it.

PETER. Father, father, don't be afraid for my soul. It's your will that I have fulfilled.

KING SKULE. I prayed for you to believe in me, and your faith has become a sin.

PETER (*wildly*). It was for your sake, for you! God will wash it clean!

KING SKULE. Pure and unstained, I promised Ingeborg. And he blasphemes!

PAUL FLIDA (*enters*). The city is in an uproar! This dreadful deed has filled your men with terror. They are fleeing into the churches!

KING SKULE. No, no! Bar the doors!

BAARD BRATTE. The people have risen against you! They are killing our soldiers in the streets!

MAN-AT-ARMS (*enters*). The Birchlegs are sailing up the river!

KING SKULE. Sound the trumpets! Summon my men!

PAUL FLIDA. Impossible. Fear has paralysed them.

KING SKULE (*desperately*). I cannot fail now! My son must not die with a mortal sin on his head!

PETER. Save yourself!

KING SKULE. Yes, we must flee. Any man who would save his life, follow me!

BAARD BRATTE. Which way?

KING SKULE. Over the bridge!

PAUL FLIDA. All the bridges have been burnt, my lord.

KING SKULE. Burnt – ? All the bridges – ?

PAUL FLIDA. All. You should have burnt them in Oslo. Then you could have let them stand in Nidaros.

KING SKULE. We must cross the river. Our salvation is at stake!
He and PETER *run out. The rest follow.*

SCENE TWO

A street. Distant and confused shouting is heard. Cheering CITIZENS
rush across the stage to greet HAAKON.

HAAKON. Who knows where Skule Baardsson is hiding?

SEVERAL. In one of the churches, my lord.

HAAKON. Are you sure?

CITIZENS. Yes, all his men are seeking sanctuary.

HAAKON (*quietly, to* DAGFINN). He must be found. Set guards on all the churches.

DAGFINN. When we find him, is he to be killed?

HAAKON (*softly*). Killed? Dagfinn, I – !

DAGFINN. My lord, you swore a solemn oath in Oslo.

HAAKON. And every man in Norway will demand his death. (*Turns to* GREGORIUS JONSSON, *and speaks so that the others cannot hear.*) Go. You were once his friend. Find him, and tell him to flee the country.

GREGORIUS JONSSON (*joyfully*). God bless you, my lord – !

HAAKON. For my dear wife's sake.

GREGORIUS JONSSON. But if he will not flee? Or cannot – ?

HAAKON. Then in God's name he must die. I cannot break my oath. Go!

GREGORIUS JONSSON. I will do my best. Heaven grant I may succeed! (*Goes out right.*)

HAAKON. Dagfinn, choose trusty men and go down to my ship. You must accompany the Queen and the Prince to St Stephen's Abbey.

DAGFINN. My lord, will she be safe there?

HAAKON. Nowhere safer. Skule's men have locked themselves in the churches, and she has prayed so often to go there. Her mother will be with her.

DAGFINN. Very good, my lord.

HAAKON. Greet Her Majesty most dearly from me; and the Lady Ragnhild also. Tell them that as soon as our enemies have surrendered and received a royal pardon, all the bells in Nidaros shall be rung, as a sign that peace has returned to our land. (*Goes with his men.*)

CITIZENS. Let us hunt out Skule and kill him ourselves!

ALL. Yes, yes! Find him and kill him! (*Exeunt.*)

SCENE THREE

A pine forest in the hills above Nidaros. It is moonlight, but the night is misty, so that the background can be glimpsed only indistinctly, and sometimes hardly at all. Tree-stumps and boulders stand around. KING SKULE, PETER, PAUL FLIDA, BAARD BRATTE *and several others enter through the trees left.*

PETER. Sit down and rest, Father.

KING SKULE. Yes, let me rest, rest. (*Sinks down on a stone.*)

PETER. How is it with you?

KING SKULE. I am sick, sick. I see dead men's shadows.

PETER (*jumps up*). Help him! Bring bread for the King.

BAARD BRATTE. Every man is King here. Our lives are at stake. Stand up, Skule Baardsson, if you are King. You cannot rule the land from there.

PETER. I'll kill you if you mock my father!

BAARD BRATTE. We shall all die, unless we can think of a plan to save ourselves.

SOLDIER. Could we reach St John's Abbey?

PAUL FLIDA. Or St Stephen's? That is nearer.

BAARD BRATTE (*suddenly exclaims*). No. Let us go down to Haakon's ship and seize his child.

PAUL FLIDA. Are you mad?

BAARD BRATTE. No, no! We could do it. There can't be many men on board. They're all in the town, searching the houses and standing guard on the churches. The bridges are all down, so they won't reckon on any of us being this side of the river. We can take them by surprise, and if we get the Prince in our power, we can ransom him for a royal pardon. Who'll come with me?

SEVERAL. I! I will! I!

PETER. I'll join you when I've seen my father in safe hands.

BAARD BRATTE. We must be clear of the river by daybreak. Here, I know a short cut.

CHIEFTAIN. Put out the torches.

ANOTHER. We must make haste.

They go out right.

PETER (*to* PAUL FLIDA). No word of this to my father. By dawn, we shall have the Prince in our hands.

PAUL FLIDA. What will you do if Haakon will not pardon us?

PETER. Kill the child.

PAUL FLIDA. Kill –!

PETER. It cannot be a sin. He stands in my father's way. Whatever happens, the child must die. Our King has a great plan to fulfil. It matters little who is sacrificed.

PAUL FLIDA. It was an evil day for you when you learned you were King Skule's son. (*Listens.*) Hush! Lie flat on the ground. Someone is coming.

They all throw themselves down behind the boulders and tree-stumps. A group of people, some riding and some on foot, is indistinctly glimpsed through the trees. They enter from the left and go out right.

PETER. It is the Queen.

PAUL FLIDA. Yes, yes. Hush. Listen.

PETER (*after a moment*). They're going to St Stephen's Abbey. The Prince is with them!

PAUL FLIDA. And the Queen's women.

PETER. But only four men. Rise, rise, King Skule. Your kingdom is saved!

KING SKULE. My kingdom? It is dark – like the kingdom of the angel who rebelled against God.

A group of MONKS *enters right.*

A MONK. Who is there? Are you King Skule's men?

PAUL FLIDA. King Skule himself.

MONK (*to* SKULE). God be praised that we have found you, my dear lord! We heard you had taken to the hills. We have brought monks' clothing for you and your men. Put them on, and you will gain entry to St Stephen's Abbey. There you can beg Haakon for pardon.

KING SKULE. Yes, give me a cassock. I and my son must seek refuge on consecrated ground. Take us to the abbey –

PETER (*whispers to* PAUL FLIDA). See that my father gets there safely –

PAUL FLIDA. Have you forgotten there are Birchlegs there?

PETER. Only four men. You can easily deal with them, and once you are inside they won't dare to touch you. I'll go and fetch Baard Bratte.

PAUL FLIDA. Think what you are doing!

PETER. It is not in the King's ship, but at St Stephen's Abbey, that we outlaws shall save the kingdom for my father. (*Runs out right.*)

SOLDIER (*whispers to* ANOTHER). Are you going to the abbey with Skule?

2ND SOLDIER. Hush! No. The Birchlegs are there.

MONK. Let us go two by two – every monk with a soldier –

ANOTHER MONK (*seated on a tree-stump behind the others*). I will take King Skule.

KING SKULE. Do you know the way?

MONK. The broad way.

1ST MONK. Hurry! Let us take different paths, and meet outside the abbey gate.

They go out through the trees, right. The mist lifts, and the comet is revealed, red and shining in the hazy air.

KING SKULE. Peter my son – ! (*Starts.*) Ah – there is the burning sword again!

MONK (*sitting behind him on the tree-stump*). And here am I.

KING SKULE. Who are you?

MONK. An old acquaintance.

KING SKULE. I never saw a man so pale.

MONK. You don't recognise me?

KING SKULE. You are the one who is to see me safe to the abbey.

MONK. I am the one who will see you safely to the throne.

KING SKULE. Can you do that?

MONK. I can, if you will it so.

KING SKULE. How?

MONK. By the means I used before. I will lead you up on to a high mountain, and show you all the glory of the world.

KING SKULE. I have seen that before. In dreams, that tempted me.

MONK. It was I who gave you those dreams.

KING SKULE. Who are you?

MONK. A messenger from the oldest pretender in the world.

KING SKULE. The oldest pretender in the world?

MONK. From the first Earl who rebelled against the greatest of Kings, and who founded a kingdom himself that shall last until doomsday.

KING SKULE (*screams*). Bishop Nicholas!

MONK (*rises*). You know me now? We were friends once.

> In the selfsame bark for many a year
> We have steered the same course together.
> I was afraid when we parted. It was night-time and stormy.
> A hawk had fastened its claws in my soul.
> I bade them say masses and ring the bells;
> I paid the monks to pray and sing.
> But still I didn't get in through the gate.

KING SKULE. You've come from – ?

MONK. The kingdom beneath the earth:

> That much-maligned kingdom down below.

KING SKULE. Greet your master from me, and thank him for the friendship he's shown me. You can tell him he's the only King to offer help to Skule the First of Norway.

MONK. Now listen, and I'll tell you why I've been sent.

> This Haakon Haakonsson's no man for us.
> We dislike him. He's always giving us trouble.
> So he must fall and you must reign.
> You alone must wear the crown.

KING SKULE. But how? How?

MONK. At St Stephen's Abbey the royal Prince sleeps.

Once you catch him in the web of death
Your enemies will scatter like dust.
Then you'll be King. Then you will conquer!

KING SKULE. Are you so sure?

MONK. The whole of Norway is crying for peace,
. And a King is no King without an heir;
A son, to inherit his father's throne.
Rise up, King Skule! The deed must be done
Tonight! Either you or he must fall!
Already it's growing light in the north.
Look! Around us the mist is lifting.
The ships are gathering noiselessly;
The earth rings hollow with tramping feet.
.All this is yours if you say the word.
A thousand warriors to march behind you,
And a thousand shining sails to carry you!

KING SKULE. What must I say?

MONK. To stand on the topmost rung of the ladder
You have but to do what your heart commands.
The land and all it contains shall be yours
If your son succeeds you as King of Norway.

KING SKULE (*raises his hand as though in an oath*). My son shall
— ! (*Stops suddenly and cries in terror.*) A church-robber! All
power to him? Ah, now I understand you. You want our
country to be damned! Get away from me, get away from me!
(*Stretches his hands towards heaven.*) O Thou, have mercy upon
me now, when I cry unto Thee for help in my hour of greatest
need! (*Falls to the ground.*)

MONK. Ah, well.
I'm not in a hurry. *Perpetuum mobile* . . . !
My power is assured for generations.
I shall always rule those who fear the light.
They will all be my faithful subjects here.

Comes downstage.

When my good people pursue their ends,
Will-lessly wandering, knowing not whither,

With puckered hearts and grovelling souls,
As weak as willows before the wind,
Agreed on only one thing in the world;
That everything great must be brought low –
The mark of meanness their only banner,
And honour an outcast from their doors –
Then Bishop Nicholas rules in men's hearts!
The faithful Bishop pursuing his calling.

He disappears through the trees into the mist.

KING SKULE (*after a few moments, half-raises himself from the ground and looks around*). Where is he, my dark counsellor? (*Jumps to his feet.*) Guide, guide, where are you? Gone. No matter. Now I know my way, both to St Stephen's Abbey, and beyond. (*Goes out right.*)

SCENE FOUR

St Stephen's Abbey. On the left stands the chapel, with a door opening into the cloister. Its windows are illuminated. Along the opposite side of the cloister stretch several smaller buildings. In the background is the abbey wall, with a heavy gate which is shut. It is a clear, moonlit night. Three BIRCHLEG CHIEFTAINS *are standing at the gate.* MARGARET, THE LADY RAGNHILD *and* DAGFINN THE PEASANT *enter from the chapel.*

RAGNHILD (*half to herself*). No, no, it cannot be! King Skule would never beg for mercy!

MARGARET. Calm yourself, dearest mother.

RAGNHILD. They cannot condemn him to death. He is the King. God will punish you for letting it come to this!

MARGARET. You don't know what you are saying. It is your grief that speaks.

RAGNHILD. Hear me, you Birchlegs! It was Haakon who begged the King for mercy! It was Haakon who pleaded for his life!

MARGARET. She is distraught –

RAGNHILD. King Skule will sit on the throne again. And when

     he does, beware!

MARGARET. Peace, peace!

RAGNHILD (*to* MARGARET). And you can love this usurper! Are you your father's child? May God punish you for your loyalty to this man of blood!

MARGARET. Mother! (*Moves towards her.*)

RAGNHILD. Get away! Keep away from me! I must search the churches and find my husband. Open the door! I must go to Nidaros!

MARGARET. Mother, in God's blessed name – !

There is a loud banging on the abbey gate.

DAGFINN. Who's knocking?

KING SKULE (*outside*). A King.

DAGFINN. Skule Baardsson!

RAGNHILD. King Skule!

MARGARET. My father!

KING SKULE. Open, open!

DAGFINN. There is no place here for outlaws.

KING SKULE. It is a King who knocks, I say! A King without shelter.

MARGARET. Dagfinn, Dagfinn, he is my father!

DAGFINN (*goes to the gate and opens it a fraction*). How many men have you?

KING SKULE. All who stayed loyal in my hour of need.

DAGFINN. How many is that?

KING SKULE. Less than one.

MARGARET. He is alone, Dagfinn!

RAGNHILD. May the wrath of Heaven smite you, if you refuse him entry! This is consecrated ground.

DAGFINN. In God's name, then.

He opens the gate. The BIRCHLEGS *reverently bare their heads.* KING SKULE *enters the cloister.*

MARGARET (*embraces him*). Father! My blessed, unhappy father!

RAGNHILD (*passionately places herself between him and the* BIRCHLEGS). Do not go near him! Do not dare touch him! You pretend to honour him, but you will betray him like Judas!

DAGFINN. He is safe here, on holy ground.

MARGARET. Did no one stay with you?

KING SKULE. The monks and soldiers kept me company on the road. But they stole away from me, one by one. Paul Flida was the last to leave. He came as far as the abbey gate. There he gave me a last embrace, and thanked me for the days when there were great chieftains in Norway.

DAGFINN (*to the* BIRCHLEGS). My lords, go in and guard the Prince. I must ride to Nidaros, and tell the King that Skule Baardsson is here.

MARGARET. Oh, Dagfinn, Dagfinn, can you do this?

DAGFINN. I would be a poor servant of my King and my country if I did not. (*To the* BIRCHLEGS.) Close the gate behind me, guard the child, and do not open to anyone until the King comes. (*Softly to* SKULE.) Farewell, Skule Baardsson – and God grant you a good end.

He goes out through the gate. The BIRCHLEGS *close it behind him, and go into the chapel.*

RAGNHILD. Let Haakon come. I won't let them take you. I shall hold you in my arms, and keep them from you.

MARGARET. Oh, how pale you look – and how aged! You're as cold as death!

KING SKULE. I am not cold. But I am tired, tired.

MARGARET. Then come in, and rest –

KING SKULE. Yes, yes. It will soon be time for me to rest.

SIGRID (*from the chapel*). You have come at last, my brother!

KING SKULE. Sigrid!

SIGRID. I promised you we would meet when you needed me in your soul's extremity.

KING SKULE. Where is your child, Margaret?

MARGARET. He is sleeping in the sacristy.

KING SKULE. Then all our house is gathered here tonight.

SIGRID. Yes. We are together after the long years of straying.

KING SKULE. Now we lack only Haakon Haakonsson.

MARGARET (*clings tightly to him*). Father!

RAGNHILD (*also clings to him*). My husband!

KING SKULE (*looks at them both, moved*). Ragnhild, Margaret! Have you loved me so much? I sought fulfilment in the world outside, and never realised I had a home where I might find it. Oh, Ragnhild, my wife, I have sinned so greatly against you, yet you come to me warm and loving in my hour of need, you tremble and fear for the life of a man who has never cast a glint of sunshine on your road.

RAGNHILD. You – sinned? Oh, Skule, do not speak so. Do you think I would ever dare blame you for that? I have never been worthy of you, my noble husband. You have done no wrong to me.

KING SKULE. Have you believed so steadfastly in me, Ragnhild?

RAGNHILD. From the first day I saw you.

KING SKULE. Oh, you gentle and loving women – it is still good to live! When Haakon comes I will beg for pardon. I will implore him for – !

SIGRID (*fearfully*). Skule, my brother! Beware, if you stray from your path tonight!

A noise without. A moment later, there is a banging on the gate.

MARGARET. Who is that?

RAGNHILD. Who is knocking at the gate?

VOICES (*without*). Citizens of Nidaros! Open up! We know Skule Baardsson is there!

KING SKULE. Yes, he is here! What do you want with him?

SHOUTS (*from without*). Come out, come out! Evil man, you must die!

MARGARET. You dare to threaten him!

A VOICE. King Haakon has condemned him to death!

ANOTHER. It is every man's duty to kill him!

MARGARET. I am the Queen! I command you to leave this place!

A VOICE. It is Skule's daughter who speaks, and not the Queen.

ANOTHER. You cannot save him now. The King has condemned him!

RAGNHILD. Go into the chapel, Skule! In God's blessed name, do not let these murderers come near you.

KING SKULE. Yes, into the chapel. My wife, my daughter! At last

I have found peace and light. It must not be taken from me so soon! (*Turns to hasten into the chapel.*)

PETER (*outside*). My father, my King! Victory is in our hands!

KING SKULE (*with a cry*). Peter! (*Sinks down on the chapel steps.*)

CITIZENS (*outside*). Look, look! The blasphemer! He is climbing over the roof!

OTHERS. Stone him! Stone him!

PETER *appears on a roof to the right, and jumps down into the cloister.* SKULE *looks at him in horror.*

PETER (*passionately*). Where is the Prince?

MARGARET. The Prince?

KING SKULE (*jumps to his feet*). What do you want with him?

PETER. Baard Bratte and his men are on their way. I told them this was where they would find the Prince.

MARGARET. Oh, God!

KING SKULE. You told them!

PETER (*to* MARGARET). Where is the Prince, woman?

MARGARET (*standing against the chapel door*). Asleep in the sacristy.

PETER. I wouldn't care if he was asleep on the altar! I have stolen a shrine from a church, and I am not afraid to steal a prince!

RAGNHILD (*cries to* SKULE). Is this the son you love?

KING SKULE. He was as pure as the lamb of God when his mother brought him to me. His faith in me has damned him.

PETER (*not listening to him*). The child must be brought out! Kill him, kill him in his mother's arms! Those were King Skule's words, and a saint could obey them with a clear conscience, for the sake of his great ideal.

CITIZENS (*beating on the gate*). Open up! Come out, blasphemer, or we will burn down the abbey!

KING SKULE (*as though suddenly resolved*). My great ideal! Yes, that is what has poisoned your soul! Pure and unstained I promised to hand you back to her; your belief in me has driven you on from crime to crime, from sin to mortal sin. But I can still save you. I can save us all. (*Calls.*) Wait, citizens, wait! I am coming!

MARGARET (*clasps his hand in terror*). Father, what are you going to do?

RAGNHILD (*cries, clinging to him*). Skule!

SIGRID (*tears them from him and cries, joyfully and radiantly*). Let him, go, women, let him go! His soul has found wings at last.

KING SKULE (*in a strong, firm voice to* PETER). Peter, listen to me. You saw in me the chosen one of Heaven. The one who would accomplish a mighty deed for Norway. Open your eyes, blind boy, and look at me! These rags of kingship in which I have decked myself are borrowed and stolen. Now I put them off, one by one.

PETER (*in anguish*). My great and noble father, do not speak thus!

KING SKULE. The idea was Haakon's, not mine. He alone was endowed by God to fulfil it. You have believed in a lie. Turn from me now, and save your soul.

PETER (*brokenly*). The idea – Haakon's!

KING SKULE. I yearned to be the greatest man in the land. Oh, God, God! See, I humble myself before Thee, and stand in Thy sight the meanest of all.

PETER. O Lord, take me from this earth! Punish me for all my sins, but take me from this earth, for I am homeless here now. (*Sinks down on the chapel steps.*)

KING SKULE. I had a friend who died for me in Oslo. He said: 'A man can die for another's life-work, but if he is to live, he must live for his own.' I have no life-work of my own to live for, and I cannot live for Haakon's. But I can die for it.

MARGARET. No, no! Never!

KING SKULE (*takes her hand and looks at her gently*). Do you love your husband, Margaret?

MARGARET. More than anything in the world.

KING SKULE. You could bear to hear him sentence me to death. But could you bear it if he carried out that sentence?

MARGARET. God of Heaven, grant me strength!

KING SKULE. Could you, Margaret!

MARGARET (*quietly shuddering*). No, no. We would have to part. I could never bear to see him again.

KING SKULE. You would shut out the light from his life, and from yours. Don't be afraid, Margaret. You will not have to do it.

RAGNHILD. Flee the country, Skule! I will follow you, no matter where!

KING SKULE (*shakes his head*). With a shadow dividing us and mocking us? I have found you tonight for the first time. No shadow must come between us now, my loyal and gentle wife. We must not meet again, on this earth.

SIGRID. My royal brother! I see you do not need me. You know which way you have to go.

KING SKULE. There are men who were created to live, and men who were created to die. I always longed to go where God's finger did not point for me; and so my way has always been dark. But now I see it clearly. Margaret, look! Look upwards! See how it pales and fades, the flaming sword that has been drawn above me! Yes! God has spoken, and I have understood Him, and His wrath is stilled. My sanctuary is not here. I shall not beg for mercy from an earthly King. I shall enter the great church whose roof is the stars, and beg for mercy and forgiveness from the King of Kings.

MARGARET. Father!

SIGRID. Do not prevent him! Do not oppose the will of God! A dawn is breaking for Norway and for his restless soul. Have not we women hidden long enough in our rooms, listening to all the terror without, the blood-letting that has drained our country dry? Have we not lain pale and petrified in the churches, not daring to look out, as the disciples of Christ lay in Jerusalem on that sad Friday when He walked to Golgotha? (*To* SKULE.) Use your wings, and woe to those who would bind you now!

RAGNHILD. Go hence in peace, my husband! Go where no mocking shadow will stand between us when we meet again! (*She hurries into the chapel.*)

MARGARET. Father – goodbye! Goodbye! (*She follows* RAGNHILD.)

SIGRID (*opens the chapel door and calls in*). Come forth, come forth, women! Join your voices in prayer! Let your song rise up to

God and tell Him that Skule Baardsson is returning home repentant from his journey of disobedience on earth.

KING SKULE. Sigrid, my loyal sister, greet King Haakon from me. Tell him that even in my last hour I do not know whether he is royally born – but that this I know assuredly. He is the one whom God has chosen.

SIGRID. I shall give him that greeting.

KING SKULE. And there is one more greeting you must give. There sits a woman sorrowing in the north. Tell her that her son has gone ahead. He went with me, because his soul was in danger.

SIGRID. I will tell her.

KING SKULE. Tell her he did not sin with his heart. When she meets him again, she will find him pure and unstained.

SIGRID. I will tell her. (*Points to the gate.*) Listen! They are breaking the lock!

KING SKULE (*points to the chapel*). Listen. They are singing to God of salvation and peace.

SIGRID. Listen, listen! All the bells in Nidaros are ringing – !

KING SKULE (*smiles sadly*). They are ringing a King to his grave.

SIGRID. No. They are ringing you to your true coronation. Farewell, my brother! Let the purple cloak of blood flow over your shoulders. It will wash away all sins. Go in, go in to the great church, and receive the crown of life!

She hurries into the chapel. During the remainder of the scene, the singing and the sound of the bells continue.

VOICES (*outside the gate*). We have broken the lock! Do not force us to violate the sanctuary!

KING SKULE. I am coming!

CITIZENS. The blasphemer must come too!

KING SKULE. Yes, the blasphemer shall come too. (*Goes over to* PETER). My son, are you ready?

PETER. Yes, father. I am ready.

KING SKULE (*looks upwards*). O God, I am a poor man, I have only my life to give. But take it, and grant that Haakon's great ideal may be fulfilled. (*To* PETER.) Come now. Give me your hand.

PETER. Here is my hand, father.

KING SKULE. And don't be afraid.

PETER. No, father. I am not afraid, when I am with you.

KING SKULE. We never trod so safe a road together. (*He opens the gate. The* CITIZENS *are standing outside in great numbers, their weapons raised.*) Here we are. We come freely – but do not wound him in the face.

They go out, hand in hand. The gate swings shut.

A VOICE. Aim not, spare not! Strike them where you can!

A brief clash of arms; then heavy falls are heard. For a moment, there is silence. Then the royal trumpet sounds.

A VOICE. The King!

ALL CITIZENS. Hail, King Haakon! All your enemies are dead.

GREGORIUS JONSSON (*stops for a moment by the two bodies*). Then I have come too late. (*Goes into the cloister.*)

DAGFINN. It would have been an evil day for Norway if you had come before. (*Cries.*) Enter, King Haakon!

HAAKON (*stops*). This body lies in my way.

DAGFINN. If Haakon Haakonsson is to go forward, he must go over Skule Baardsson's body.

HAAKON (*looks down at* SKULE'S *body*). All men judged him wrongly. He was a riddle that no man solved.

DAGFINN. A riddle?

HAAKON (*grips him by the arm and says softly*). Skule Baardsson was God's unwanted child on earth. That was his riddle.

He steps over the body. The WOMEN'S *song rises louder from the chapel. All the bells in Nidaros are ringing.*

Note on the Translation

I have followed the text of the second (1870) edition, in the few instances wherein it differs from the original edition of 1863. In 1867 Georg Brandes, in an article in *Dansk Maanedsskrift*, while praising the play, criticised Ibsen's tendency to put generalised aphorisms into the mouths of his characters, and when *The Pretenders* came to be republished by Gyldendal of Copenhagen Ibsen amended several of these, to the obvious advantage of the dialogue.

Norwegian linguistic structure being what it is, the original text is full of combination words based on *kong* (king): *kongsbarn* (prince), *kongssæde* (throne), *kongsret* (royal right), *kongsværk* (a kingly deed). The word "king" thus echoes throughout the play in a way that cannot fully be reproduced in English. A word that recurs with particular frequency is *kongstanke* (kingly thought); I have translated this variously as "great plan," "great idea" and "great ideal"; no single English phrase quite suffices.

The Norwegian title, *Kongsemnerne*, means simply "The Claimants to the Crown", (literally "the material of which kings are made"), and lacks the secondary meaning of the English word "pretenders." But the English title loses nothing by this extra significance; indeed, this is one of the few instances where the translated title is if anything slightly better than the original.

The names of the characters should be pronounced as follows: Hawkon; Skoolë; Daagfinn; Eevar Boddë; Yoonsson; Fleeda; Ingheborg; Yatgheir; Board Brattë.

I gladly express my thanks to Mr Val May for innumerable suggestions. As already explained in the introduction, the credit for the adaption is largely his.